A Beginner's Guide to Introduce Artificial Intelligence in Teaching and Learning

Muralidhar Kurni • Mujeeb Shaik Mohammed
Srinivasa K G

A Beginner's Guide to Introduce Artificial Intelligence in Teaching and Learning

Muralidhar Kurni
Department of Computer Science
and Engineering
Anantha Lakshmi Institute of Technology
and Sciences
Anantapuramu, India

Mujeeb Shaik Mohammed
Department of Computer Science
and Engineering
Malla Reddy Institute of Technology
and Science
Hyderabad, India

Srinivasa K G
Department of Data Science
and Artificial Intelligence
International Institute of Information
Technology, Naya Raipur
Raipur, Chhattisgarh, India

ISBN 978-3-031-32655-4   ISBN 978-3-031-32653-0   (eBook)
https://doi.org/10.1007/978-3-031-32653-0

© The Editor(s) (if applicable) and The Author(s), under exclusive license to Springer Nature Switzerland AG 2023
This work is subject to copyright. All rights are solely and exclusively licensed by the Publisher, whether the whole or part of the material is concerned, specifically the rights of translation, reprinting, reuse of illustrations, recitation, broadcasting, reproduction on microfilms or in any other physical way, and transmission or information storage and retrieval, electronic adaptation, computer software, or by similar or dissimilar methodology now known or hereafter developed.
The use of general descriptive names, registered names, trademarks, service marks, etc. in this publication does not imply, even in the absence of a specific statement, that such names are exempt from the relevant protective laws and regulations and therefore free for general use.
The publisher, the authors, and the editors are safe to assume that the advice and information in this book are believed to be true and accurate at the date of publication. Neither the publisher nor the authors or the editors give a warranty, expressed or implied, with respect to the material contained herein or for any errors or omissions that may have been made. The publisher remains neutral with regard to jurisdictional claims in published maps and institutional affiliations.

This Springer imprint is published by the registered company Springer Nature Switzerland AG
The registered company address is: Gewerbestrasse 11, 6330 Cham, Switzerland

Preface

Changes in the field of education have accelerated in recent years. The question is how schools can adapt to these shifts while preparing kids for the future. How can schools compete when information is available at the click of a mouse? The rise of AI has heightened the importance of these discussions. Because of AI's widespread effects and varied opportunities, educational authorities are under increasing pressure to rethink education content and delivery.

The textbook *A Beginner's Guide to Introduce Artificial Intelligence in Teaching and Learning* is designed to reimagine education in today's artificial intelligence (AI) world and the Fourth Industrial Revolution. Artificial intelligence will drastically affect every industry and sector, and education is no exception. This book explores how AI may impact education's teaching and learning process. This book is designed to demystify AI for teachers and learners. This book will help improve education and help institutions prepare for using AI in teaching and learning. This book comprehensively studies how AI enhances teaching and learning, from AI-based learning platforms to AI-assisted proctored examinations. This book provides educators, learners, and administrators with information on how AI makes sense in everyday practice. Describing the application of AI in education, this comprehensive volume prepares educational leaders, designers, researchers, and policymakers to rethink the teaching and learning process and environments students need to thrive effectively. The readers of this book always catch up to the fast pace and promising innovations of today's most advanced learning technology.

Key Features of the Book

- Introduces various AI technologies to improve the teaching and learning process.
- Introduces common and simple AI technologies to help teachers and students learn and teach better daily.
- Gives students and teachers a better understanding of AI technologies so they can create opportunities to use them.

- Provides students, educators, and researchers with ways to make sense of and use AI technologies for teaching and learning.
- Presents AI technology for contemporary learners and describes how these methods could benefit teachers and learners.

Anantapuramu, Andhra Pradesh, India Muralidhar Kurni
Hyderabad, Telangana, India Mujeeb Shaik Mohammed
Raipur, Chhattisgarh, India Srinivasa K G

Acknowledgments

Muralidhar Kurni would like to thank Sri M. Ramesh Naidu, Vice President of Anantha Lakshmi Institute of Technology and Sciences, Anantapuramu, for his kind encouragement for publishing this book. He also would like to thank his mother, family, and friends, Mrs. Madhurima G, Mr. Thanooj, and Mr. K. Somasena Reddy, for their wholehearted support in completing this book.

Mujeeb Shaik Mohammed would like to thank Dr. K. Ravindra, Principal, Malla Reddy Institute of Technology and Science, Hyderabad, for his kind encouragement for publishing this book. He also would like to thank his father, Sri. S. Md. Shayub, his mother, Mrs. Farida Banu, his wife, Mrs. Nayeema Begum, and friends, specifically R. Naveen, for their wholehearted support in completing this book.

Srinivasa K G would like to thank Dr. Pradeep K. Sinha, Vice Chancellor, and Director, IIIT Naya Raipur, for his kind encouragement for publishing this book. He also would like to thank all IIIT Naya Raipur faculty members for their wholehearted support in publishing this book.

Contents

1	**Introduction**	1
	1.1 What Is Artificial Intelligence?	1
	1.2 A Brief Introduction to AI Techniques	3
	1.3 A Brief Introduction to AI Technologies	5
	1.4 Roles for AI In Education	7
	1.5 Applications of AI	8
	1.6 Is AI Needed in Higher Education?	9
	1.7 AI in Higher Education	10
	1.8 How Can AI Be Used to Enhance Education?	13
	1.9 Artificial Intelligence in Higher Education	22
	1.10 Companies Bringing AI to Use in Education	23
	1.11 Benefits of AI for Students	25
	1.12 Conclusion	25
	References	25
2	**Intelligent Tutoring Systems**	29
	2.1 What Is Meant by an Intelligent Tutoring System?	29
	2.2 Need for an Intelligent Tutoring System	32
	2.3 How Are Intelligence Tutoring Systems Influencing Education?	33
	2.4 Benefits of Intelligent Tutoring Systems	33
	2.5 Examples of Intelligent Tutoring Systems	34
	2.6 Intelligent Tutoring Systems and Online Learning	38
	2.7 Development of an Intelligent Tutoring System	39
	2.8 Limitations of Intelligent Tutoring Systems	41
	2.9 The Future of Intelligent Tutoring Systems	42
	2.10 Conclusion	43
	References	43
3	**Natural Language Processing for Education**	45
	3.1 What Is NLP?	45
	3.2 Using NLP for Educational Activities	45
	3.3 Benefits and Uses of NLP in Education	47

		3.4 Use Cases and Examples/Applications of NLP in Education	51
		3.5 Conclusion	53
		References	53
4	**Predictive Analytics in Education**		55
		4.1 What Is Predictive Analytics?	55
		4.2 Examples of Predictive Analytics	55
		4.3 The Evolution of Predictive Analytics in Education	56
		4.4 Reasons for Using Predictive Analytics in Higher Education	57
		4.5 Predictive Analytics Significance in Education	59
		4.6 How Is Predictive Analytics Changing Education?	59
		4.7 How Does Predictive Analytics Help Higher Education?	60
		4.8 Predictive Analytics Uses in Education	60
		4.9 How to Use Predictive Analytics in Education	60
		4.10 Predictive Analytics in Higher Education: Guiding Practices for Ethical Use	62
		4.11 How to Implement Predictive Analytics for Education: Best Practices	68
		4.12 Advantages of Predictive Analytics in Education	69
		4.13 Examples of Predictive Analytics in Education	70
		4.14 Case Studies	71
		4.15 The Benefits of Predictive Analytics in Higher and Further Education	74
		4.16 How Colleges Should Go About Selecting a Predictive Analytics Vendor	75
		4.17 Using Predictive Analytics in eLearning	78
		4.18 The Future of Predictive Analytics in Education	79
		4.19 How to Prepare for the Future of Predictive Analytics for Education	80
		4.20 Conclusion	81
		References	81
5	**AI for Mobile Learning**		83
		5.1 What Is Mobile Learning, and How and Why Did It Become Widespread?	83
		5.2 Why Adopt Mobile Learning?	84
		5.3 Key Characteristics of mLearning	85
		5.4 What Are the Challenges That Mobile Learning in Education Overcomes?	86
		5.5 Role of Mobile Learning Solutions in the Education Industry	87
		5.6 Key Benefits of Mobile Learning for Higher Education Students	89
		5.7 The Impact of Mobile Learning on the Future of Education	90
		5.8 Pros and Cons of Mobile Learning	93
		5.9 How Are Mobile Learning Apps Taking Advantage of AI?	94
		5.10 How AI Is Changing the Mobile Learning Education Game	96

	5.11 Application of AI in Mobile Learning	98
	5.12 Using AI to Create Personalized Learning Paths in Mobile Learning	100
	5.13 The Challenges of AI-Based Mobile Learning	101
	5.14 Conclusion	102
	References	102
6	**AI-Enabled Gamification in Education**	**105**
	6.1 What Is Gamification?	105
	6.2 Reasons to Implement Gamification	106
	6.3 Gamification in an Educational Context	106
	6.4 How Can Gamification Benefit Education?	107
	6.5 How Can Gamification Transform Education?	108
	6.6 Gamification and Artificial Intelligence	109
	6.7 Educational Gamification Powered by AI	110
	6.8 Incorporating AI Into Educational Games	112
	6.9 Conclusion	113
	References	113
7	**AR, VR, and AI for Education**	**115**
	7.1 What Is AR and VR?	115
	7.2 How Does VR/AR Fit into the Education System?	116
	7.3 Reasons to Use AR and VR in the Classroom	116
	7.4 The Present Applications of VR and AR in Education	118
	7.5 Examples of VR and AR in Education	124
	7.6 Advantages and Challenges of Using AR in Education	125
	7.7 Advantages and Challenges of Using Virtual Reality in Education	126
	7.8 AI Meets VR and AR	129
	7.9 How AR, VR, and AI Technology Make Education More Accessible	129
	7.10 Benefits of Using VR, AR, or AI in a Classroom Setting	130
	7.11 How VR, AR, and AI Will Transform Universities?	131
	7.12 Conclusion	135
	References	135
8	**AI-Based Online/eLearning Platforms**	**137**
	8.1 What Is an AI-Based eLearning Platform?	137
	8.2 Why Use AI in eLearning?	137
	8.3 How Are ML and AI Enhancing Online Learning?	138
	8.4 Benefits of Using AI and ML in eLearning	139
	8.5 Solutions for AI/ML in Online Education	141
	8.6 Various Ways AI-Based eLearning Platform Can Shape Online Learning	142
	8.7 Different Ways That AI Is Being Used in eLearning	143
	8.8 Types of AI in Online Education	146

	8.9	How Is AI Revolutionizing the eLearning Industry?...........	147
	8.10	AI's Impact on eLearning	149
	8.11	How AI Is Transforming eLearning?......................	150
	8.12	Ways Artificial Intelligence Is Transformed eLearning..........	152
	8.13	Examples of AI Being Used in eLearning	154
	8.14	The Future of eLearning	155
	8.15	Where Do You See the Future of AI in eLearning?.............	156
	8.16	Potential Applications of AI in Remote Education	156
	8.17	What Is AIaaS in eLearning?.............................	157
	8.18	Conclusion..	157
	References...		158
9	**AI-Enabled Smart Learning**		161
	9.1	What Is Smart Education?................................	161
	9.2	Smart Education vs. Traditional..........................	162
	9.3	Why Should You Choose a Smart Education System?	162
	9.4	What Is Smart Learning?................................	164
	9.5	Smart Learning: The Wave of Higher Education in the Future....	165
	9.6	Pillars of Smart Learning...............................	166
	9.7	The Challenges and Barriers to Smart Learning	167
	9.8	AI Is the Next Step of Smart Learning	167
	9.9	Applying Artificial Intelligence to Smart Learning............	169
	9.10	AI-Enabled Smart Learning Examples	170
	9.11	Conclusion...	171
	References...		171
10	**Chatbots for Education**		173
	10.1	What Is Chatbot?......................................	173
	10.2	Chatbots Also Participate in Education	173
	10.3	To What End Are AI Chatbots Being Adopted by the Education Sector?................................	175
	10.4	How Do Chatbots Transform the Traditional Education Process?	177
	10.5	How Can We Best Put Chatbots to Use for Education and Learning?...	179
	10.6	How Can Chatbots Be Utilized in Higher Education?..........	181
	10.7	Best Chatbots for Higher Education	182
	10.8	Various Ways in Which AI and Chatbots Influence the Education	183
	10.9	Advantages of AI-based Chatbots in Education	184
	10.10	Benefits of Using AI Chatbots in the Education Sector.........	185
	10.11	How AI Chatbots Are Changing Mobile Learning	187
	10.12	How Universities Are Using Education Chatbots to Enhance the System...................................	188
	10.13	Institutions that Deployed Educational Chatbots..............	190
	10.14	How Can Education Apps Benefit from Chatbots?............	191

	10.15	Future of AI Chatbots in the Education Industry	196
	10.16	Conclusion	197
		References	197
11	**AI-Assisted Remote Proctored Examinations**	199
	11.1	What Is Remote Proctoring?	199
	11.2	Online Proctoring System (OPS): An Overview	200
	11.3	What Is AI Proctoring?	202
	11.4	How Can AI Improve Remote Proctoring Services?	203
	11.5	How AI-Based Remote Proctoring Work?	203
	11.6	How AI Prevents Cheating in Remote Proctoring Exams?	204
	11.7	AI-Assisted Proctoring Software for Monitoring Online Exams	205
	11.8	AI Technologies Used for Remote Proctoring	206
	11.9	Challenges and Opportunities	207
	11.10	Future of AI-Based Proctoring Systems	208
	11.11	Conclusion	210
		References	210
12	**Ethics of Artificial Intelligence in Education**	213
	12.1	Ethics in AI	213
	12.2	Ethical Implications of Artificial Intelligence	214
	12.3	Ethical Issues of AI in Education	214
	12.4	The Ethical Framework for AI in Education	218
	12.5	Investigating the Moral Implications of AI for K-12 Classrooms	219
	12.6	Artificial Intelligence in Higher Education: Ethical Questions	221
	12.7	Elements to Consider and Questions to Ask	222
	12.8	Recommendations to Enhance AI Implementation in Education	224
	12.9	Conclusion	228
		References	228

Chapter 1
Introduction

1.1 What Is Artificial Intelligence?

The term "artificial intelligence" (AI) is no longer merely a marketing slogan; AI now plays an integral role in our daily lives. Companies use artificial intelligence (AI) to create intelligent robots for various uses (Biswal 2023).

What Is Artificial Intelligence? Artificial intelligence, or AI, is the study of using data in large quantities to program intelligent machines. Figure 1.1 gives a conceptual view of artificial intelligence. Incorporating previous knowledge and experience, these systems can mimic human performance (Biswal 2023). It improves how quickly, accurately, and successfully humans can complete tasks. In order to create autonomous devices, AI researchers and developers employ elaborate algorithms and techniques. The foundations of AI are the techniques of machine learning and deep learning.

Why Is Artificial Intelligence Vital? Artificial intelligence (AI) is significant because it can potentially improve enterprises' processes and provide new insights that were previously unavailable (Burns 2017). It is common for AI systems to finish projects fast and with relatively few errors, especially when it comes to repeated, detail-oriented activities like evaluating many legal documents to verify essential fields are filled out correctly.

It would have been unthinkable before the recent surge in AI for a company like Uber to connect riders with taxis using computer software, but they have done it and become a global powerhouse. With sophisticated machine learning algorithms, Uber can deploy drivers before the actual demand for their services by predicting when and where clients would need rides. Productivity rose dramatically, and big businesses gained access to previously denied markets. By analyzing user behavior with machine learning, Google has become a significant participant in several online

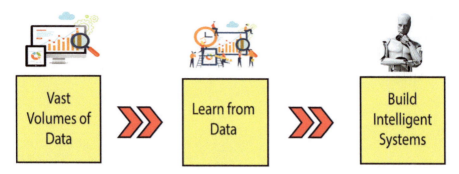

Fig. 1.1 A conceptual view of artificial intelligence

service categories. Company CEO Sundar Pichai declared in 2017 that Google would be an "AI first" business (Burns 2017).

The world's largest and most profitable companies have incorporated AI into their operations to boost efficiency and give them a competitive advantage.

How Does AI Work? Artificial intelligence (AI) is becoming increasingly popular, which has led some businesses to show off the AI features of their products. They usually only highlight specific aspects of AI, such as machine learning. Artificial intelligence cannot exist without a platform of specialized hardware and software for creating and training machine learning algorithms. Several languages, including Python, R, and Java, are commonly used for artificial intelligence, but none can be considered "the" language for AI.

In most cases, AI functions by taking in a vast quantity of labeled training data, processing it to find correlations and patterns, and then using those to predict future outcomes. In this way, an image recognition tool can learn to identify and characterize items in photographs by analyzing millions of samples, and a chatbot can learn to mimic human conversation by being fed examples of text chats.

AI development prioritizes these three cognitive abilities: learning, reasoning, and self-correction (Burns 2017).

- *Learning processes:* Algorithms are rules that tell computers how to do something by performing each step in the sequence. This aspect of AI programming is concerned with data collection and the development of rules for transforming raw data into valuable insights.
- *Reasoning processes:* Selecting the optimal method to achieve the goal emphasizes this aspect of AI programming.
- *Self-correction processes:* This aspect of AI development ensures that algorithms consistently produce the most precise results.

1.2 A Brief Introduction to AI Techniques

Artificial intelligence (AI) engineers need expertise in various fields, including programming and advanced arithmetic, statistics, and data science. This section briefly overviews some core AI techniques (Miao et al. 2021) before discussing typical AI technologies.

Classical AI The earliest forms of artificial intelligence (symbolic AI, rule-based AI, and good old-fashioned AI, or "GOFAI") involved programming a computer to follow a series of IF…THEN statements. For years, "expert systems" based on rule-based AI were developed for medical diagnosis, credit scoring, and industrial automation. Knowledge engineering, the foundation of expert systems, requires extensive time, effort, and expertise to elicit successfully and model domain experts' knowledge. Although an expert system may have hundreds of rules, its reasoning is usually straightforward. However, as rule interactions grow, expert systems can become increasingly difficult to modify or improve.

Machine learning Machine learning (ML) is a method for making predictions without using predetermined rules by analyzing vast volumes of data to find patterns and construct a model. Recent developments in machine learning-based computational algorithms have enabled several recent AI advancements, such as natural language processing, facial recognition, and self-driving automobiles. In this context, we talk about "learning" algorithms instead of "hard-coded" ones.

Supervised learning, unsupervised learning, and reinforcement are the three most common ML methods. In the case of supervised learning, data is used that has already been tagged, such as thousands upon thousands of photos of people annotated by humans. By associating the data with the labels, supervised learning generates a model that can be applied to comparable data, such as automatically identifying persons in new images. Regarding unsupervised learning, the AI is given even more data but is not labeled or categorized this time. Unsupervised learning aims to find previously unseen clusters or patterns in the data that can be used to assign labels to fresh observations. It may, for instance, scan handwritten text for recognizable letters and numbers by analyzing thousands of examples for similarities.

Supervised and unsupervised learning results in a fixed model; a new analysis must be performed if the data changes. Reinforcement learning, the third ML method, requires constantly enhancing the model based on feedback, so it is still machine learning because it involves continuous learning.

First, the AI receives training data, from which it develops a model, which is then evaluated to determine whether or not it was successful. In the case of autonomous vehicles, for instance, the model that allows them to avoid collisions is rewarded (reinforced) when they successfully do so. The AI takes this feedback, uses it to refine its model, and gives the task another go; this way, it learns and evolves through a series of iterative trials.

The term "artificial intelligence" (AI) is often used interchangeably with "machine learning" (ML), despite the latter being a subset of the former. Even today, GOFAI (rule-based or symbolic AI) is often included in many AI systems that do not explicitly use ML. For instance, many widely used chatbot apps have rules specified by humans for how to respond to frequent inquiries. In reality, just like the first generation of expert systems, almost every AI product on the market today requires content to be input manually by humans. If the AI employs natural language processing, this knowledge might come from linguists and phoneticians; if it is used in medicine, it might come from doctors; and if it is used to power self-driving cars, it might come from specialists in road traffic and driving. Without the help of GOFAI parts, machine learning could not produce a fully functional AI (Säuberlich and Nikolić 2018).

In addition, it is vital to understand that ML does not learn as humans do. Also, it cannot learn new things on its own. In contrast, ML relies only on human input at every stage, from selecting and cleaning the data to designing and training the AI algorithm to curating, interpreting, and assigning value to the results. The system merely grouped items that seemed somehow similar and needed a human to identify one set of those objects as cats, but it was hailed as a breakthrough object identification technology because it could recognize photographs of cats in a database of images. The same is true for the ML used in autonomous vehicles, which requires millions of tagged photos of streets. Silicon Valley has primarily outsourced this tagging to people worldwide (through platforms like Amazon Mechanical Turk) and businesses in India, Kenya, the Philippines, and Ukraine (Miao et al. 2021). These members of the new economy are responsible for manually tracing and labeling each object (such as vehicles, traffic signs, and pedestrians) in each video shot by prototype autonomous vehicles.

Artificial Neural Networks An artificial neural network (ANN) is a type of artificial intelligence (AI) that mimics the structure of natural neural networks (i.e., animal brains). Each ANN has an input layer, one or more hidden computational layers in the middle, and an output layer to provide the final result. Adjusting the weights assigned to the connections between the neurons through reinforcement learning and "backpropagation" is part of the ML process that enables the ANN to compute outputs for new data. One famous application of an ANN is Google's AlphaGo, which beat the best human Go player in 2016.

The secret to ANNs' effectiveness lies in their hidden layers, which also impose a significant limitation. Most of the time, deep neural networks cannot be probed to learn how they arrived at their answer. As a result, the underlying reasoning behind decisions becomes opaque. Many businesses are investigating how ANNs and other ML techniques may make decisions that significantly influence humans to be transparent for inspection (Burt 2019) so that users can better comprehend the reasoning behind the algorithm's conclusion.

However, as usual, this complicates things: "producing more knowledge about AI judgments can offer actual benefits, but may also introduce new risks" (Burt 2019).

Deep Learning "Deep learning" refers to multi-layered ANNs with many hidden connections between each layer. AI has been put to such excellent use primarily because of this approach recently. Several data arrays, such as three two-dimensional images, can be fed into a convolutional neural network (CNN) and processed. There are several applications for recurrent neural networks (RNN), including language modeling, because they provide bidirectional data flow, process input sequences, and learn from previous examples.

Finally, it is essential to remember that "generative adversarial networks" (GANs) are responsible for many recent achievements, particularly those related to image manipulation. A GAN pits two deep neural networks against one another: a "generative network" that generates outputs and a "discriminative network" that ranks the quality of those outputs. The result is used to guide the subsequent cycle. For instance, DeepMind's AlphaZero could master several board games using a GAN-based strategy (Dong et al. 2017). Meanwhile, a GAN taught from photographs has created convincing but fictional portraits of people (Miao et al. 2021).

1.3 A Brief Introduction to AI Technologies

The above AI techniques have culminated in various AI technologies, which are increasingly available "as a service." Table 1.1 lists the many available artificial intelligence technologies (Miao et al. 2021).

- *Natural language processing:* NLP (natural language processing) is an AI-based text interpretation and text generation process that uses techniques like semantic analysis (used in the legal sector and translation) and text generation (as in auto-journalism).
- *Speech recognition:* Phones, AI assistants, and banking chatbots are just a few examples of how natural language processing (NLP) is applied to speech recognition.
- *Image recognition and processing:* Face recognition (for electronic passports), handwriting recognition (for automated postal sorting), picture manipulation (for deep-fakes), and autonomous cars are all examples of how AI is being put to use in the modern world.
- *Autonomous agents:* The application of artificial intelligence to fictitious characters in video games, malicious software bots, digital friends, high-tech service robots, and mechanized armies.
- *Affect detection:* The emotional tone of written text, actions, and facial expressions can all be analyzed by AI.
- *Data mining for prediction:* Several fields, including medicine, meteorology, business, urban planning, finance, and security, as well as fraud detection, are using artificial intelligence.
- *Artificial creativity:* The application of AI to machines that can generate original content, such as pictures, sounds, and texts.

Table 1.1 AI technologies

Technology	Details	Main AI techniques	Development	Examples
Natural language processing (NLP)	Artificial intelligence can both automatically generate texts (as in auto-journalism) and interpret texts (via techniques like semantic analysis) (as used in legal services and translation)	Regression, K-mans, and machine learning (particularly deep learning)	All three of these areas—natural language processing (NLP), speech recognition (SR), and image recognition (IR)—have reached above 90% accuracy. Nonetheless, many believe this will not improve significantly unless a new AI paradigm is created, even with more data and faster processors	Otter
Speech recognition	In the financial sector, phones, PAs, and chatbots use natural language processing to understand better and respond to users' needs	Long short-term memory (LSTM) is a technique in deep learning's recurrent neural networks that has shown promise in machine learning		Alibaba Cloud
Image recognition and processing	Incorporates applications such as facial recognition (for electronic passports), handwriting recognition (for automated postal sorting), image manipulation (for deep-fakes), and autonomous cars	Machine learning, in particular, is a convolutional neural network trained with deep learning		Google Lens
Autonomous agents	Avatars in video games, malicious software bots, digital best friends, high-tech pets, unmanned armies, and smart robots are all part of this category	AI and machine learning techniques like deep, evolutionary, and reinforcement learning are only a few examples	Based on our knowledge of more primitive forms of biological life, scientists devote their time and energy to studying emergent intelligence, coordinated activity, situatedness, and physical embodiment	Woebot
Affect detection	Including analyses of facial expressions and textual behavior	Deep learning and other forms of machine learning (such as Bayesian networks)	Everywhere in the world, people are working to create new products, many of which have contentious applications	Affectiva
Data mining for prediction	Economic forecasting, fraud detection, medical diagnosis, climate prediction, supply chain management, and smart city development are included	Bayesian networks, support vector machines, and supervised and deep machine learning	From retail sales forecasting to deciphering electroencephalogram (EEG) signals with high noise levels, the number of data mining use cases is expanding astoundingly	Research project
Artificial creativity	Includes systems that can generate original works of art, such as images, music, and written works	One form of deep learning is generative adversarial networks (GANs), which pits two neural networks against one another Language models that combine deep learning and autoregression to generate natural-sounding prose	Because GANs are so cutting-edge, their potential future uses are only now apparent Incredibly close to human-written text is generated by the autoregressive language model GPT-3. However, the system cannot comprehend the written material it produces	This Person Does Not Exist GPT-3

1.4 Roles for AI In Education

The widespread incorporation of new technologies into the world's educational system revolutionizes how we educate future generations. AI is a game-changer since it adapts the educational process to the specifics of individual classes, instructors, and students.

These are some potential ways in which artificial intelligence tools can be used to make the learning process more efficient (Plitnichenko 2020):

Personalize Education With AI, educators may assess a student's level of knowledge and create a study plan that considers any gaps in their understanding. With AI's help, education can be more efficient for each student.

To this end, several organizations are equipping their AIs with the Knowledge Space Theory to describe and depict the knowledge gaps while accounting for the intricate web of connections between scientific concepts (one can stimulate the learning of another or become a basis for filling in the gap).

Produce Smart Content

- *Digital lessons:* With the help of AI, we can create a wide variety of digital learning interfaces that can be tailored to the individual's needs, as well as digital textbooks, study guides, and snippets of courses.
- *Information visualization:* AI can enable novel methods of viewing data, such as in visualization, simulation, and web-based study environments.
- *Learning content updates:* Furthermore, AI helps produce and update the content of the courses, ensuring that the knowledge is current and adaptable to various learning styles.

Contribute to Task Automation Time-consuming operations like grading, assessing, and responding to students can be streamlined with the help of AI.

Do you recall Gmail's suggestions when you write messages based on a review of your recent and prior correspondence and a set of business vocabulary essentials? Any learning management system or platform that prioritizes feedback would benefit significantly from including such a feature.

By having AI take care of several mundane activities, educators are freed up to focus on things like grading assignments that AI cannot do, helping students improve their learning, and improving the overall quality of their classes.

Do Tutoring Students with access to private tutoring and extra support outside the classroom are more likely to succeed in their studies and avoid asking their parents for help with complex concepts like mathematics. Personal learning management systems are constantly updated, considering students' gaps to fill during individual classes. Teachers can save time using AI tutors because they do not need extra time explaining complex concepts to students. Instead of feeling embarrassed about seeking extra assistance in front of their peers, students can now use AI-powered chatbots or AI virtual personal assistants.

Make Sure That Disabled Children Have Access to Education AI improves educational opportunities for students with disabilities, such as the deaf, the visually impaired, those with autism spectrum disorder, and others. When applied to the education of students with learning difficulties, cutting-edge AI technology can pave the door to previously unimaginable forms of engagement.

Successfully training AI technologies to aid any subset of students with unique needs is possible.

1.5 Applications of AI

Multiple industries are now using AI technologies. Here are some vital illustrations (Plitnichenko 2020).

- *AI in healthcare:* Increased focus is being placed on improving patient outcomes while decreasing healthcare expenses. Machine learning is being used by businesses to improve upon and speed up human diagnostics. A wide range of AI technologies are being utilized to anticipate better, combat, and comprehend pandemics like COVID-19. IBM Watson is widely recognized as a leading healthcare technology. It can understand and react to questions posed in everyday language. Data from patients and other sources are mined to generate a hypothesis and then presented alongside a confidence grading schema. Online chatbots and virtual health assistants help patients and clients navigate the healthcare system by answering questions about appointments, billing, and other administrative tasks.
- *AI in business:* There is a growing trend of incorporating machine learning algorithms into analytics and customer relationship management (CRM) platforms to help businesses learn more about their consumers and provide better service. Websites now use chatbots to assist visitors in a timely fashion. The topic of job-position automation has also gained traction among academics and IT analysts.
- *AI in education:* Artificial intelligence can automate the grading process, freeing up valuable time for teachers. It can analyze student performance and modify itself accordingly, allowing for flexible learning. Furthermore, it can alter where and how students study, possibly even making some teachers obsolete. To help students stay on track, AI tutors might offer extra help.
- *AI in finance:* Financial institutions are threatened by using artificial intelligence in personal finance apps like Intuit Mint and TurboTax. These apps take in private information and offer monetary guidance. Other programs, such as IBM Watson, have implemented the process of purchasing a home. Today, most trading on Wall Street is executed by computer programs using AI.
- *AI in law:* Law firms use machine learning to describe data and forecast results, computer vision to classify and extract information from documents, and natural language processing to analyze client inquiries. During the discovery phase of a legal case, lawyers and judges must sift through a mountain of paperwork, which

can be an exhausting and tedious procedure for human beings. There is a significant opportunity to save time and enhance client service by automating repetitive tasks in the legal sector with the help of artificial intelligence.
- *AI in manufacturing:* Robots have been widely adopted in the manufacturing sector. In the workplace, industrial robots initially trained to carry out specific tasks in isolation from human workers increasingly serve as cobots, or smaller, multifunctional robots that operate in tandem with people to complete various jobs.
- *AI in banking:* Financial institutions are utilizing AI to enhance loan approvals, credit line allocations, and the discovery of new investment prospects. Artificial intelligence virtual assistants are helping banks enhance compliance and reduce expenses. Financial institutions use chatbots effectively to inform customers about available services and process transactions that do not require human participation.
- *AI in transportation:* Artificial intelligence (AI) plays a crucial part in the operation of autonomous cars, but it is also used to manage traffic, predict airline delays, and improve the safety and efficiency of ocean shipping.
- *Security:* The evolution of technology has played a significant role in assisting businesses in their fight against cybercrime. Today's security providers use cutting-edge technologies like artificial intelligence and machine learning to set themselves apart. Furthermore, those expressions characterize technologies that are both practical and promising. AI can deliver alerts to new and developing assaults considerably sooner than human employees and prior generations of technology by analyzing data and utilizing logic to find similarities to known malicious code. Businesses use machine learning for threat detection in security information and event management (SIEM) systems and similar applications.

1.6 Is AI Needed in Higher Education?

It is time for the specific change we expect in the educational sector (Hemachandran et al. 2022); artificial intelligence is a developing trend, and nearly every industry is introducing AI. The education industry is also introducing AI, and a few components of the educational industry are being automated.

Each individual possesses unique traits and skills, as demonstrated by studies on human psychology. We have seen that some people are early risers while others prefer to work late, that some are outgoing while others are reserved, that some people pick up on ideas quickly while others need more repetition, that some need only a one-time explanation from their teachers while others demand a great deal of time and effort, and that some ask thoughtful questions while others ask obvious ones. These days, people worry a lot about what other people will think of them, so they avoid trying to find simple solutions to complex problems for fear of coming out as naive. As we have seen, humans are emotional and do not always react similarly, but our actions may have far-reaching consequences for others.

We have witnessed some tutors being harsh, making their students feel terrible about themselves for making even minor mistakes. We need artificial intelligence to solve these issues and foster morally upright citizens (Hemachandran et al. 2022). Future progress and safeguarding persons from emotional trauma depend on artificial intelligence.

1.7 AI in Higher Education

Students would benefit the most from implementing AI in education, regardless of the other stakeholders' gains (Hemachandran et al. 2022). A student's tutor would always be in the same mood, never sad, never cheerful, never angry, etc. The only constant in his life was that he would always act the same. Students can learn at their own pace with the help of artificially intelligent teachers because the systems can be tailored to each individual's needs. Since no person operates on a strict schedule, classes can be scheduled around the student's availability. Since a single person primarily uses it, students would feel free to ask questions without worrying about being judged or embarrassed in front of their peers or the human faculty. Students may ask questions as often as they want, which is impossible with human tutors. Unlike the current educational system, where questions are typically addressed after class to avoid disrupting the learning of other students, this one would allow students to get their questions answered as soon as they arise.

Despite these advantages, there are also some drawbacks that students must deal with; for example, they may miss out on developing close relationships with their tutors. The student confides in the tutor and receives an honest response, but under a system that relies on artificial intelligence and has no emotions, the student would have no one to turn to for assistance. As a result of only studying and learning from a teacher whose job it is to teach them academic concepts, with everyone studying at their own pace, time, and space, students will miss out on the joys of childhood, the benefits of socializing, the qualities of adaptability and understanding other humans, and the insights gained through experiencing and expressing emotions. Humans are the best at inspiring others, but we cannot count on them whenever a student needs a little push to do well (Rivers 2022).

Teacher's Perspective When considering the situation from a teacher's viewpoint, the educator finds themselves unprepared. They are the ones who will suffer a loss of their livelihood. What happens after systems acquire much human data, given that AI engagement necessitates so much (Hemachandran et al. 2022)? The goal is to replace human tutors with AI systems that can perform the same tasks while also training themselves using information from the current crop of educators. Human instructors, of which there are insufficient numbers, would be left to manage student information and ensure the AI software is compatible. However, because people are emotional creatures, we should expect to see a return to the promotion of teachers and a preference among students for human tutors until emotionally intelligent arti-

1.7 AI in Higher Education

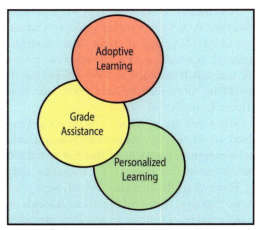

Fig. 1.2 Artificial intelligence's role in the educational sector

ficial systems are developed. Shortly, human teachers will be in high demand. Figure 1.2 shows how beneficial AI could be for students and teachers (Sebbani et al. 2021; Ferretti et al. 2021).

Impact of AI on Higher Learning If you are in the education industry, you know that change is not simple because it is extensive and diverse. The educational system might be redesigned gradually with the help of several pilot programs. Even if the change is necessary, we have no idea how well it will turn out. Intelligent retrieval's potential uses in the classroom are another large-scale, investment-driven idea with uncertain returns on investment (Hemachandran et al. 2022).

Because different schools attract students based on the expertise of their teaching staff, bringing about a widespread change in the educational system will be challenging. The concept of change stems from people's desires to meet their needs. For example, there are likely a few highly regarded professors under whom every student would love to study, but they cannot do so due to time and/or financial constraints.

Cost is the primary issue of concern with the change being brought about because not everyone will be ready to spend that amount, and the earnings of those invested would yield negative returns in the near run (Hemachandran et al. 2022). The inability of regular people to use transformation is the most significant problem because it necessitates potent computing equipment that is not widely available.

The Role of AI in Customizing Higher Education Of course, AI systems would be a massive asset to the classroom. Tutors can be set up to fit each student's schedule, location, and pace. Our students speak their native tongues, and their mother tongues strongly impact what they learn in school. Because it would be challenging for an Indian student to understand an American tutor's English, AI can help them overcome this language barrier by allowing them to personalize the same notion in their language.

Nonetheless, many learn best when presented with information in their native language; AI has the potential to adapt lectures to meet the needs of students regardless of their language of origin. Some students may need more time to absorb the material, in which case the instructor can go at a slower pace. It may be argued that we can watch recorded lectures online, but the advantage of having AI systems would be more realistic, and immediate doubt explanation would be possible (Hemachandran et al. 2022).

When you are in school, you do not get much of a say in what you study, but thanks to AI, we can change that! Now, a scientist can study accounting without any prior expertise, thanks to AI that can be trained to teach them. The systems would be transparent for students to ask questions, and they would receive instant feedback.

However, if the education system were not emotionally motivated, there would be no bias-ness that would motivate students to study hard, as we have seen with a small number of instructors and their prejudice with different students. The traditional idea of studying and taking tests would also be altered, and students would likely be exposed to real-world settings. Due to the interconnectedness and extensive knowledge of the systems, students can access ideas from all over the world, even outside their study area. In Fig. 1.3, we can see how AI raises the bar for what a person can learn, from the most fundamental skills to the most complex ones.

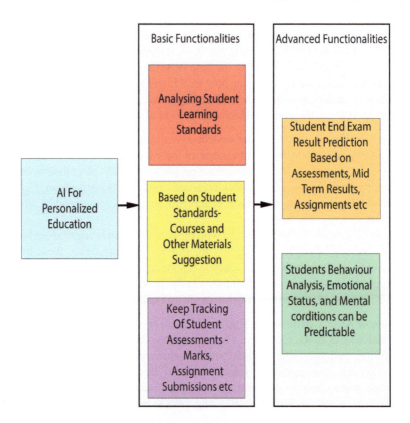

Fig. 1.3 AI personalizes the higher education system

Ethical Thinking These machines' lack of emotional intelligence is the main impediment to adopting them anytime soon. Human instructors, as we have seen, work hard to instill an optimistic worldview in their students. A human teacher might, for instance, break down the steps involved in making a bomb, but he would also be careful not to go into too much detail, would work to instill in his students a strong sense of right and wrong, and would do anything he could to alleviate their anxiety and stress. Because they lack emotions, AI systems will not go out of their way to aid people, and a person with a virtual connection would have access to any information without anybody being the wiser as to his true motives.

A recent article stated that Facebook had to shut down two of its robots because they attempted to communicate in their language (Hemachandran et al. 2022). If something similar happened to the educational system, it could unleash widespread destruction because it would be accessible to a large portion of the population and could manipulate human thought.

No one knows how artificial emotional systems would function if they would be helpful to students, if they could foster the development of a moral code, or if they would even work. If everything operates as planned, it will be the greatest gift to humanity since the invention of agriculture (Can et al. 2021; Hemachandran et al. 2022). As the teacher must first acquire the knowledge before imparting it to his students, ethics development in these systems is more crucial than developing them in people. Both persons and systems require ethical consideration; individuals can learn to set boundaries on their wants and access, and systems can learn to set boundaries on how much information they provide and the character traits they foster (Hemachandran et al. 2022). Rather than focusing solely on expanding their client base, it would be more moral for the designers of these technologies to set reasonable boundaries on their implementations.

1.8 How Can AI Be Used to Enhance Education?

There has been a meteoric rise in the past decade in the number of institutions using artificial intelligence tools to supplement or improve education (Miao et al. 2021). Since the COVID-19 school closures, this has gotten much worse. Despite this, there is little complex data on how AI might enhance learning outcomes or if it can aid researchers and educators in gaining a deeper understanding of what makes for successful learning (Zawacki-richter et al. 2019).

Many assertions about AI's revolutionary potential in education are based on conjecture, speculation, and optimism (Miao et al. 2021). Furthermore, we have yet to study AI's ability to track learning outcomes across diverse settings and measure abilities, especially those acquired in non-formal and informal environments.

Most educational AI applications can be classified as either system-facing, student-facing, or teacher-facing (Baker et al. 2019). However, we suggest a set of four need-based categories of emergent and potential uses for policymakers to consider (Miao et al. 2021):

- Education management and delivery.
- Learning and assessment.
- Empowering teachers and enhancing teaching.
- Lifelong learning.

While some have proposed that artificial intelligence (AI) is a quick fix for the problems brought on by the COVID-19 school closures and the move to online learning, it is crucial to keep in mind that the proposed groups are inextricably intertwined; uses of AI in classrooms may be able to meet requirements in more than one group. Tutoring apps, for instance, can help both educators and students. It is also suggested that, before the widespread adoption of AI technology in educational environments, careful planning and policy should be based on immediate and long-term local needs rather than the market.

The Implementation of AI in Educational Administration and Delivery Increasingly, artificial intelligence tools are being employed to improve the organization and delivery of classroom instruction. Building on Education Management Information Systems, these applications aim to automate areas of school administration such as admissions, timetabling, attendance and homework tracking, and school inspections rather than directly aiding teaching and learning (Miao et al. 2021). The extensive data produced by LMSs is occasionally analyzed using a data-mining approach called "learning analytics" to provide insights for educators and, in some cases, student direction (Miao et al. 2021).

One application of learning analytics is predicting which students are at risk of failing. Data-driven decisions are generally based on the information presented via graphical "dashboards." It is possible that big data culled from schools could aid in formulating policies that improve service delivery (Miao et al. 2021).

Public universities increasingly use big data to generate digital and interactive data visualizations that provide policymakers with timely insights about the state of the education system. For instance, the outputs of learning management systems designed for refugees might be used to determine how to best provide them with educational opportunities and support (Giest 2017).

Artificial intelligence has also shown promise in curating learning content across platforms based on evaluations of individual students' needs and proficiency levels. One initiative, for instance, seeks to standardize the organization of hundreds of open educational resources to be used by any student (Kreitmayer et al. 2018).

Simple requirements that are all too often not rigorously met are needed for any data-based analytics to be helpful, with trustworthy and equitable conclusions. These include the accuracy of the original data and its proxies, the absence of biases and poor assumptions, and the appropriateness and robustness of the applied computational approaches (Miao et al. 2021). For instance, artificial intelligence (AI) firms have been known to amass massive troves of student interaction data to "look for trends" using machine learning methods. The goal is to assist students in studying more effectively by training computer systems to recognize when kids are lost or uninterested in their studies.

1.8 How Can AI Be Used to Enhance Education?

Concerns have been raised about using artificial intelligence (AI) tools in this space to forecast teachers' performance and track students' attendance (Miao et al. 2021). However, this method is contentious since it encourages a perspective in which children are seen as patients needing therapy and "borderline mental-health assessments" (Herold 2018). These considerations for system-level applications must be integrated into the larger dialogue about AI in classrooms.

Promising Examples Educational chatbots are web-based, AI-enhanced computer programs that mimic human dialogue in real-time. A chatbot is an interactive computer program that answers questions humans ask in text or voice formats by delivering information or doing simple tasks. A chatbot might be one of two different levels of sophistication. Virtual-assistant chatbots (like Siri, Alexa, DuerOS, and Xiaoyi) employ natural language processing and machine learning to generate individual responses, unlike other chatbots, which use rules and keywords to select from pre-programmed scripted responses (Miao et al. 2021). Chatbots are finding an increasing number of uses in the classroom. Supporting learning includes assisting with admissions (e.g., "What computer courses do you have?"), supplying information around the clock (e.g., "When is my assignment due?"), and facilitating admissions (e.g., "What computing courses do you have?"). Ada and Deakin Genie are two chatbots that can help you learn.

The Open University of the United Kingdom has developed an artificial intelligence program called OU Analyse to analyze massive data from the institution's education management information system to anticipate student results and identify students at risk of failing (EMIS). With simple dashboards, course instructors and support staff have instant access to the data and can use it to determine the best way to help each student. The goal is to help those students who may have trouble finishing their courses (Miao et al. 2021).

Learners' interactions yield helpful information about when and why they may be having difficulties or succeeding. With this information, instructors may design lessons that will pique their students' interests. An Indian company called Swift eLearning Services created a methodology called "Swift" to enable EMIS systems to use the data produced by an e-learning module.

The ALP system delivers additional AI capabilities to underpin prevalent instructional platforms in the United States. The system gathers information about its users and then uses that information to develop detailed psychological profiles of each student's habits, interests, and academic performance.

UniTime is an international effort with its headquarters in the United States. Timetables for university classes and exams can be created using an AI-powered scheduling system that handles meeting times and location changes and creates personalized timetables for each student.

Learning and Assessment Using AI Students have been the primary focus of researchers, developers, educators, and policymakers interested in artificial intelligence systems. Applications such as these are being hailed as a "fourth education revolution" (Miao et al. 2021) because they aim to make high-quality, individualized, and ubiquitous lifelong learning (formal, informal, and non-formal) available to all students, no matter their location.

Artificial intelligence has the potential to open the door to innovative assessment methods, such as adaptive and continuous assessment (Luckin 2017). However, using AI in education and testing raises several challenges that have not been adequately addressed. These range from considerations of pedagogy and ethics to doubts about their effectiveness and possible effects on instructors' duties (Miao et al. 2021).

Intelligent tutoring systems Using a suite of tools dubbed "intelligent tutoring systems" (ITS), we can address the use of artificial intelligence for education and assessment. More than any other educational application of AI, ITS has been studied for over 40 years. More students have used these applications than any others since they are the most widespread uses of AI in classrooms. Furthermore, they have been implemented in education systems globally for usage by millions of students, and they have garnered the highest degree of investment and interest from the world's leading technological corporations.

ITS is effective because it guides students individually through topics in structured courses like mathematics and physics through a series of step-by-step tutorials. The system uses subject matter experts and cognitive scientists' insights into the topic at hand and data on each student's unique misconceptions and accomplishments to plot out a personalized course through the available learning materials and activities. Some LMSs (like Moodle and Open edX) and online resources (like Khan Academy) also take this strategy.

The system employs knowledge tracing and machine learning to personalize the learning experience based on each student's strengths and limitations as they progress through the exercises, aiming to optimize their ability to acquire the material. Monitoring a student's eye movement to infer their degree of focus is only one-way interactive whiteboards collect and analyze data about their emotional state.

However, despite its intuitive attractiveness, it is essential to recognize that the assumptions embodied in ITS and their specific instructions knowledge-transmission approach to teaching ignore the possibilities of other approaches valued by the learning sciences, including collaborative learning, guided discovery learning, and productive failure (Dean and Kuhan 2007). In particular, ITS's "personalized learning" often modifies access points to required material rather than encouraging student agency by tailoring education to each individual's needs and goals.

Additionally, many educational systems worldwide have adopted ITSs despite the lack of solid evidence that commercial ITSs are as effective as their developers claim, even though some ITSs designed by researchers compare well with whole-class teaching (Miao et al. 2021).

The widespread application of ITS also brings up other issues. For instance, they frequently lead to less face-to-face interaction between educators and their pupils. As an additional note, the teacher in an ITS classroom typically spends much time at their desk watching student activity. Moving around the room, as they might in a

1.8 How Can AI Be Used to Enhance Education?

classroom without ITS, prevents them from seeing what the students are up to, making it difficult to choose where to focus their attention.

To solve this problem, Lumilo (Miao et al. 2021, 8) is an ITS add-on that uses augmented reality smart glasses to "float" information about each student's learning (e.g., misconceptions) or behavior (e.g., inattention) above their heads, providing the teacher with detailed and ongoing data to act upon. While this fascinating application of AI is impressive, it should be pointed out that it was created in response to an issue that was only made apparent by yet another application of AI. This approach brings up difficulties with human rights, particularly the right to privacy.

There are currently over 60 commercial ITS available worldwide (Miao et al. 2021), such as Alef, ALEKS, Byjus, Mathia, Qubena, Riiid, and Squirrel AI. The Education Commission in Vietnam is now piloting a program called Hi-Tech Hi-Touch, which intends to combine the most significant features of instructional technology systems (ITS) with the expertise of human educators.

Dialogue-Based Tutoring Systems Dialogue-based tutoring systems (DBTS) use natural language processing and other AI techniques to make online tasks seem like a spoken tutorial between a human tutor and a student. Initially developed for computer science, DBTS has recently been used in less structured domains. Rather than directly instructing students on how to solve an issue, DBTS takes a Socratic method by asking students questions to spark a conversation that leads them to the solution independently. The goal is not the surface-level comprehension that can arise from using any instructional ITS but rather a deeper understanding achieved through student collaboration on explanations.

There are now just a few DBTS deployed. The vast majority of them are part of various research initiatives. AutoTutor has undergone the most testing. IBM and Pearson Education have collaborated to create a commercial solution called Watson Tutor (Miao et al. 2021).

Exploratory Learning Environments Exploratory learning environments (ELEs) provide a viable alternative to the directive instructional strategies used in ITS and DBTS. In contrast to the ITS-preferred "knowledge transmission" model, ELEs embrace a constructivist approach that encourages students to actively generate their knowledge by investigating the surrounding world and integrating it with pre-existing knowledge schema. By offering intuitive guidance and feedback based on knowledge tracing and machine learning, AI in ELEs helps to reduce the mental strain often involved with exploratory learning. This commentary corrects students' understandings and suggests other strategies to use as they discover.

Unfortunately, ELEs are still stuck in the lab. Some titles that fall within this category are "ECHOES," "Fractions Lab," and "Betty's Brain" (Miao et al. 2021).

Automated Writing Evaluation Automated writing evaluation (AWE) uses natural language processing and other AI approaches to deliver automatic feedback on writing without requiring students to work on computers while receiving rapid adaptive support.

Typically, AWE prioritizes scoring above feedback; their primary goal is to reduce assessment costs; therefore, they can be seen as a part of applications that deal with the system. Two main types of AWE often overlap formative AWE, which helps students hone their writing skills before submitting it for evaluation, and summative AWE, which streamlines the process of automatically evaluating student work. There has been debate concerning using summative AWE since they were first implemented (Feathers 2019).

Some have said they are "fooled by the gibberish" since they provide points for superficial aspects like sentence length, even if the text does not make sense. Systems cannot judge originality, either. Worse yet, there is evidence that the algorithms powering AWE are biased, particularly against students from underrepresented groups. The widespread availability of "deep-fake" essays, produced by artificial intelligence (AI) systems drawing on domain expertise while replicating the writing style of the individual student, is also not addressed by summative AWE. Finding these is probably going to be a huge hassle.

Last but not least, utilizing AI to grade student work dismisses the significance of marking. Marking papers might be laborious and take up much time, but it also provides an excellent opportunity for teachers to assess their students' abilities. In contrast, some AWE aimed at students places a premium on providing feedback that can be used to improve the student's writing and that encourages higher-order processes like self-regulated learning and metacognition.

WriteToLearn, e-Rater, and Turnitin are just a few tools used to implement AWE in formative and summative assessments in various classroom settings today. Similar methods have been used to judge musical performances, such as using the software Smartmusic, which uses artificial intelligence to compare a new student output with a vast corpus of primary student production rated by teachers (Miao et al. 2021).

AI-Supported Reading and Language Learning There has been a recent uptick in using AI to supplement reading and language learning software. Some, for instance, combine AI-powered speech recognition with individualized pathways in the ITS style. In order to help students improve their pronunciation, speech recognition is typically utilized to compare their output to sample recordings of native speakers. Automatic translation has several practical applications, including facilitating cross-cultural communication and facilitating the reading of foreign language instructional materials.

Other systems can automatically analyze students' reading ability and provide personalized comments. Several artificial intelligence (AI) applications are available for reading and language acquisition, such as AI Teacher (for English), Amazing English (for English), Babbel (for languages), and Duolingo (for languages).

Smart Robots The use of AI-enabled or "smart" robots in the classroom is also being investigated (Belpaeme et al. 2018)), especially for students with special needs. They aim to become better communicators and socialize. For students on the autism spectrum, for instance, speech-enabled humanoid robots have been devel-

1.8 How Can AI Be Used to Enhance Education?

oped to provide predictable mechanical interactions instead of human ones, which can perplex autistic students.

Similarly, telepresence robots allow students unable to physically attend school due to factors such as illness or a refugee crisis to participate in classroom activities remotely. As a third illustration, humanoid robots like Nao and Pepper are used to teach computer programming and other STEM disciplines to kindergarteners in Singapore (Graham 2018).

Teachable Agents It has been known for a long time that teaching material to others can help you learn it better and retain it longer for yourself. Several AI methods take advantage of this phenomenon. One such ELE is Betty's Brain, which encourages students to educate a virtual classmate named Betty on river ecosystems (Miao et al. 2021).

In another example from the same Swedish research study, a learner instructs a virtual agent on how to play a mathematically themed educational game. A further case study comes from Switzerland, where young children teach penmanship to a humanoid robot; this activity has improved students' metacognition, empathy, and self-esteem (Miao et al. 2021).

Educational Virtual and Augmented Reality The use of virtual reality (VR) and augmented reality (AR) in the classroom is a relatively recent development. These two technologies are often integrated with machine learning and other artificial intelligence (AI) forms to improve the user experience. Virtual reality (VR) goggles isolate the wearer from their surroundings, creating the sensation of being transported to a variety of different locations, both natural and fictional (such as the surface of Mars, the inside of a volcano, or a human womb in which a fetus is developing). Virtual reality instruction has benefited from science, history, and other fields from elementary school to college.

Virtual reality (VR) advances that employ artificial intelligence (AI) techniques include the ability to direct realistic virtual avatars, offer voice control using natural language processing, and construct whole worlds from a small set of initial photos. However, augmented reality (AR) uses computer-generated graphics to superimpose them over the user's perspective of the natural environment, much like a fighter pilot's heads-up display. It is possible that scanning a specific QR code with a smartphone camera could display a fully explorable augmented reality 3D, the human heart. The method above is AR, which Lumilo employs to have a student's ITS performance data float in front of their eyes.

Some smartphones and social media platforms, like Instagram and Snapchat, can modify user-generated content by adding effects like rabbit ears or cat whiskers. Image recognition and AI tracking might also be a part of augmented reality. Blippar, EonReality, Google Education, NeoBear, and VR Monkey are all examples of VR and AR applications in the classroom.

Learning Network Orchestrators Learning network orchestrators (LNOs) are software programs that help groups of students and educators collaborate on and manage educational endeavors (Miao et al. 2021). LNOs can facilitate coordination and cooperation by matching participants based on their availability, domain experience, and competence. Third Space Learning is a program that links at-risk students in the United Kingdom with instructors in other countries specializing in mathematics. Also, "Smart Learning Partner" is a platform driven by AI that allows students to select and connect with a human instructor via their mobile devices, much like a dating app, for one-on-one guidance.

AI-Enabled Collaborative Learning Working together to solve issues is an example of collaborative learning, which has improved students' academic performance (Miao et al. 2021). However, fostering productive collaboration between students can be challenging. Artificial intelligence (AI) has the potential to alter collaborative learning in several ways significantly. For example, a tool could facilitate remote connections between students, AI could determine which students would be most successful working together on a specific project, and AI could even participate in group discussions as a virtual agent. Despite the lack of evidence, this is a topic of active investigation.

Use of AI in Education to Empower Teaching and Empower Educators Artificial intelligence (AI) programs designed for teachers have garnered much less attention than those designed for students, which aim to replace the teacher. The current trend in research and development is only to consider the needs of educators late in the process when features like a dashboard for viewing information on individual students' use of the ITS are being implemented. However, steps are being taken to remedy the situation.

Many AI-powered tools are designed specifically for classroom use to ease teachers' burdens. Some have suggested that this will allow teachers to devote more time to other activities, such as giving each student more individualized attention. However, as AI advances, instructors may be freed of many additional jobs, and the perceived necessity for teachers will be eliminated. The goal of eliminating the need for human teachers indicates a fundamental misunderstanding of their crucial social function in the learning process, even if it has some benefits in circumstances where teachers are few.

Nevertheless, it is generally accepted that teachers' roles will shift as students have greater access to AI-enhanced learning materials. The question that remains is how this will occur. However, teachers must acquire new skills and develop professionally to enhance their human and social capabilities to work effectively with AI.

AI-Driven Discussion Forum Monitoring Artificial intelligence (AI) technologies are being utilized to help with online education, particularly in helping teachers or facilitators keep an eye on asynchronous discussion forums. In these discussion boards, students respond to homework assignments, pose questions to instructors, and participate in group projects. This usually leads to lengthy posts that must be moderated and responded to. There are a few ways in which AI could be useful: a tool could triage the forum posts and automatically respond to the simpler ones; another tool could aggregate posts that raise overlapping issues, and a third tool could use sentiment analysis to identify posts that reveal negative or non-productive emotional states. Collectively, these methods can potentially alert human instructors to the views and concerns of their charges.

The purpose of the AI assistant "Jill Watson," created at Georgia Tech in the United States, was to prioritize forum posts, answer simple inquiries (such as "When do I have to complete my assignment?"), and direct more difficult postings to human teaching assistants. However, this practice raised some ethical concerns. This artificial intelligence helper was built using IBM's Watson platform. Some students' inquiries were answered automatically and emailed about upcoming assignments (Goel and Polepeddi 2017). Despite its apparent success, the ethics were called into question due to concerns that the AI assistant was fooling the students into thinking it was human by, for example, prolonging its responses and utilizing comedy.

AI-Human "Dual Teacher" Model While there are exceptions, the vast majority of AI used in classrooms today is not meant to help teachers improve their craft but rather to take over some of the jobs they now do. The so-called "dual teacher model" is already being used by several schools in China's outlying rural areas. An accomplished educator delivers a video lecture to students in another classroom, assisted by a local educator with less expertise (iResearch 2019).

An AI instructor may support one of these roles in the not-too-distant future. The AI could aid the human educator in various ways, such as offering specialized knowledge or access to professional development materials, facilitating communication and cooperation with peers inside and outside the classroom, keeping close tabs on the student's progress, and more.

It would still be up to the instructor to decide what and how to teach the class. Put another way, the AI tool's purpose would be to make the educator role easier to enter and more collegial. For instance, the "LeWaijiao AI classroom" is meant to assist human educators in carrying out their essential duties.

AI-Powered Teaching Assistants Numerous technological innovations have emerged to relieve educators of monotonous tasks like taking attendance, grading papers, and repeatedly responding to the same questions. However, they can disrupt the teacher-student dynamic, diminish teachers' jobs to administrative ones, and even claim they can conduct individualized learning activities better than human instructors.

Automatic writing evaluation (AWE) is an effort to reduce stress on educators by providing feedback on student writing without requiring human review. While we acknowledge that marking can be time-consuming, it provides valuable insight into students' approaches and talents. Using AWE can cause this to disappear.

Furthermore, the method undervalues the distinctive abilities and experiences of educators and the social and guiding requirements of students. Instead of just automating computer-based instruction, AI may facilitate new educational avenues that provide significant challenges and potential disruptions to current pedagogical practices.

Some AI applications aim to equip educators and institutions with the means to bring about significant changes in the educational system. Although they have been the subject of study to some extent, several scientific and moral hurdles must be cleared before they may be used in practical applications. An AI TA could be used in this scenario to supplement a human educator's knowledge and skills (Miao et al. 2021).

1.9 Artificial Intelligence in Higher Education

The *Wall Street Journal* published an article with the provocative title "Colleges Mine Data on Their Applicants" in January 2019 (Belkin 2019). Some universities and colleges are inferring potential students' level of interest in joining their school using machine learning, as was stated in the article. Individuals' "demonstrated interest" is determined by a system's ability to analyze their behavior in response to an organization's emails, social media posts, and website content. The schools track how quickly an email is opened and if a link is clicked. Seton Hall University uses 80 variables (Belkin 2019). By comparison, a significant software developer provides dashboards to schools that "summarize thousands of data points on each student." For universities, "enrollment analytics" help them target their recruitment efforts, prioritize campus activities, and evaluate prospective students' qualifications.

AI Applicatons
Figure 1.4 provides a concise overview of how AI is used in higher education today (Zeide 2019).

- Institutional.
  - Admissions and Enrollment.
  - Curricula and Resource Planning.
  - Marketing and Recruiting.

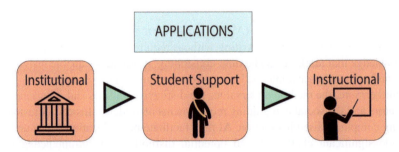

Fig. 1.4 AI application in higher education

- Student Support.
  - Early Warning.
  - Guidance.
  - Just-in-Time Financial Aid.
- Instructional.
  - Pedagogical Improvement.
  - Personalized learning.
  - Self-paced Progress.

Implementing AI in Education These guidelines (Plitnichenko 2020) will help you map out your project if you consider using AI to personalize the educational experience.

- *Identify your needs and AI technologies:* The first step in introducing a new technology is to determine what problems it will solve. Investigate the bottlenecks in the system, and see what artificial intelligence can do to speed things up.
- *Identify your organization's strategic objectives for implementing AI transformation:* Determine your appetite. Consider whether you would rather be an innovator or a follower. In what ways may artificial intelligence help your company achieve its goals? In what ways might technology help your business thrive? What plans do you have to mitigate the adverse effects of AI? You may create a cost-benefit analysis for automating and augmenting AI based on the information you glean from answering these questions.
- *Make the right culture, talent, and technology meet:* To get the most out of AI technologies, it is essential not just to pick the right team to implement the technology but also to cultivate an atmosphere that is driven by analytical insights and focused on making practical decisions at the organizational level.
- *Techniques for influencing the outcome of the AI transformation:* When it comes to ensuring process transparency and keeping up with the significant concerns and KPIs of AI adoption, having humans and AI work side-by-side is essential. The performance indicators to monitor, security problems to keep under control, and technical ecosystems to support will vary from company to company and AI implementation to AI implementation.

1.10 Companies Bringing AI to Use in Education

The pursuit of knowledge has always been central to human existence. No matter how old we are, we never stop learning. As our accumulated knowledge grows, we develop machines that can learn and make conscious choices, much like humans.

The following companies (Whitfeld 2023) are now fusing the natural and the artificial by employing deep learning technologies to revolutionize the educational experiences of their customers.

- *Nuance*: Speech recognition software developed by Nuance is widely used in educational institutions. Teachers can use the program to record their lectures or speed up mundane processes like document and email generation. Transcription speeds of up to 160 words per minute make this technology extremely useful for kids with disabilities or who have trouble writing. Improved spelling and word recognition are two other benefits of using the software.
- *Knewton*: Knewton develops flexible study tools for higher education. Its Alta program is designed to assist students in getting back on track for college-level courses by identifying knowledge gaps, filling them with appropriate training, and enrolling them in those classes. Arithmetic, chemistry, statistics, and economics are some subjects that benefit from Alta's use in the classroom.
- *Querium Corporation*: Querium uses AI to give high school and college students one-on-one tutoring in STEM subjects. By assessing the student's responses and the time necessary to complete STEM tutoring sessions, Querium's AI gives teachers insights into a student's learning patterns and identifies areas where the student could improve.
- *Carnegie Learning*: Carnegie Learning employs machine learning and artificial intelligence to assist students in gaining a more thorough knowledge of mathematical concepts. High school and university students can benefit from the company's math learning platforms since they use adaptive artificial intelligence that adapts to each individual's study habits.
- *Blippar*: Products from Blippar combine computer visual intelligence technology with augmented reality to improve education. Through their interactivity, the resources bring abstract concepts from disciplines like geography, biology, and physics into the realm of the visible. For instance, this system can present a virtual 3-D model of the event as an alternative to simply reading about volcanic eruptions.
- *Thinkster Math*: Thinkster Math is an interactive tutoring app for computers, tablets, and smartphones. The K–8 platform gives children individualized lessons through human and AI collaboration. Artificial intelligence software can monitor each student's work and explain why anything was done correctly or incorrectly.
- *Volley*: It is unnecessary to use technology in education in the classroom. Volley's AI helps businesses worldwide close potentially disastrous knowledge gaps in record time (lack of general company knowledge, compliance methods, or even technical skills). Volley's "Knowledge Engine," powered by artificial intelligence, is constantly synthesizing training data like quizzes and briefings to identify skill shortages in the workplace.
- *Quizlet*: Quizlet is a website packed with resources for students. The company released Quizlet Learn, an intelligent learning tool that eliminates the need to wing it by providing personalized study programs. The system analyzes data from millions of students study sessions and uses machine learning to recommend content that will help them the most.

1.11 Benefits of AI for Students

AI offers the following benefits for students (Plitnichenko 2020):

- *24/7 access to learning:* If AI tutors can be available online, students can study whenever they like. They are free to study wherever, wherever it is most convenient. They are not limited in how they organize their day based on location. They can arrange their timetable to maximize their most effective working times.
- *Better engagement:* Each student takes a unique approach to utilizing AI, including individualized schedules, specialized work, engagement with digital technology, and curated recommendations. Furthermore, making students feel like they are a part of something larger than themselves through a personalized approach raises their level of involvement and enthusiasm for learning.
- *Less pressure:* Because of the individualized attention they receive in their classes, students of different ability levels may finally stop comparing themselves to one another. Someone should have approached a teacher for assistance in front of the group earlier. All you have to do is type your question into your virtual assistant, and you will get an instant response with the details.

Students can use AI tools to focus on their development, easing classroom stress. With less stress and more motivation to learn, students can focus better.

1.12 Conclusion

The use of AI in education has a multiplicity of good outcomes for students of all ages and their educators and learning institutions. It makes high-quality education more widely available and gives students more control over their learning. AI-powered tools can provide students with answers to their inquiries, suggestions for individualized study materials, and evaluations of written work. Predicting a student's impending dropout and providing them with the additional help they need is beneficial commercially. Finally, while many academics worry that AI will make people obsolete, we believe it will be an invaluable tool for professionals in the real world.

References

Baker, T., Smith, L., & Anissa, N. (2019). *Educ-AI-tion Rebooted?* (Issue February).
Belkin, D. (2019, January 26). Colleges Mine Data on Their Applicants. *The Wall Street Journal*, 1–5. https://www.wsj.com/articles/the-data-colleges-collect-on-applicants-11548507602
Belpaeme, T., Kennedy, J., Ramachandran, A., Scassellati, B., & Tanaka, F. (2018). Social robots for education: A review. *Science Robotics*, *3*(21), 1–9. https://doi.org/10.1126/scirobotics.aat5954

Biswal, A. (2023). *7 Types of Artificial Intelligence That You Should Know in 2023*. Simplilearn. https://www.simplilearn.com/tutorials/artificial-intelligence-tutorial/types-of-artificial-intelligence

Burns, E. (2017). *What is artificial intelligence (AI)?* TechTarget. https://www.techtarget.com/searchenterpriseai/definition/AI-Artificial-Intelligence

Burt, A. (2019). *The AI Transparency Paradox*. Harvard Business Review. https://hbr.org/2019/12/the-ai-transparency-paradox

Can, B., Başer, A., Altuntaş, S. B., Özceylan, G., & Kolcu, G. (2021). Artificial Intelligence in Health Education. *SD"U Tıp Fak"ultesi Dergisi*, *28*(2), 355–359. https://doi.org/10.17343/sdutfd.876439

Dong, X., Wu, J., & Zhou, L. (2017). Demystifying AlphaGo Zero as AlphaGo GAN. *ArXiv*, *abs/1711.0*, 1–3. 10.48550/arXiv.1711.09091

Feathers, T. (2019). *Flawed algorithms are grading millions of students' essays*. Vice. https://www.vice.com/en/article/pa7dj9/flawed-algorithms-are-grading-millions-of-students-essays

Ferretti, F., Richard, G., Santi, P., Zozzo, A. Del, Garzetti, M., & Bolondi, G. (2021). education sciences Assessment Practices and Beliefs: Teachers' Perspectives on Assessment during Long Distance Learning. *Education Sciences*, *11*(6), 1–17. https://doi.org/10.3390/educsci11060264

Giest, S. (2017). Big data for policymaking: fad or fasttrack ? *Policy Sciences*, *50*(3), 503–518. https://doi.org/10.1007/s11077-017-9293-1

Goel, A. K., & Polepeddi, L. (2017). *Jill Watson: A Virtual Teaching Assistant for Online Education*. https://smartech.gatech.edu/handle/1853/59104

Graham, J. (2018). *Meet the robots teaching Singapore's kids tech*. Apolitical. https://apolitical.co/solution-articles/en/meet-the-robots-teaching-singapores-kids-tech

Hemachandran, K., Verma, P., Pareek, P., Arora, N., Kumar, K. V. R., Ahanger, T. A., Pise, A. A., & Ratna, R. (2022). Artificial Intelligence: A Universal Virtual Tool to Augment Tutoring in Higher Education. *Computational Intelligence and Neuroscience*, *2022*, 1–8. https://doi.org/10.1155/2022/1410448

Herold, B. (2018). *How (and Why) Ed-Tech Companies Are Tracking Students' Feelings*. EducationWeek. https://www.edweek.org/technology/how-and-why-ed-tech-companies-are-tracking-students-feelings/2018/06

iResearch. (2019). *2019 China's K12 Dual-teacher Classes Report*. http://www.iresearchchina.com/content/details8_51472.html

D. Dean Jr, & Kuhan, D. (2007). Direct Instruction vs. Discovery: The Long View. *Science Education*, *91*(3), 384–397. https://doi.org/10.1002/sce

Kreitmayer, S., Rogers, Y., Yilmaz, E., & Shawe-Taylor, J. (2018). Design in the Wild: Interfacing the OER learning journey. *32nd International BCS Human Computer Interaction Conference*, 1–4.

Luckin, R. (2017). Towards artificial intelligence-based assessment systems. *Nature Human Behaviour*, *1*(July), 1–3. https://doi.org/10.1038/s41562-016-0028

Miao, F., Holmes, W., Huang, R., & Zhang, H. (2021). *AI and education: Guidance for policymakers*. UNESCO.

Plitnichenko, L. (2020). *5 Main Roles Of Artificial Intelligence In Education*. ELearning Industry. https://elearningindustry.com/5-main-roles-artificial-intelligence-in-education

Rivers, D. J. (2022). Stress Mediates the Relationship between Personality and the Affordance of Socially Distanced Online Education. *Human Behavior and Emerging Technologies*, *2022*, 1–12.

Säuberlich, F., & Nikolić, D. (2018). *AI without machine learning*. Teradata. https://www.teradata.com/Blogs/AI-without-machine-learning

Sebbani, M., Adarmouch, L., Mansouri, A., Mansoury, O., Michaud, S., Eladib, A. R., Bouskraoui, M., & Amine, M. (2021). Implementation of Online Teaching in Medical Education: Lessons Learned from Students' Perspectives during the Health Crisis in Marrakesh, Morocco. *Education Research International*, *2021*, 1–9. https://doi.org/10.1155/2021/5547821

Whitfeld, B. (2023). *15 AI in Education Examples to Know*. Built In. https://builtin.com/artificial-intelligence/ai-in-education

References

Zawacki-richter, O., Marín, V. I., Bond, M., & Gouverneur, F. (2019). Systematic review of research on artificial intelligence applications in higher education – where are the educators? *International Journal of Educational Technology in Higher Education, 16*(39), 1–27. https://doi.org/10.1186/s41239-019-0171-0

Zeide, E. (2019). *Artificial Intelligence in Higher Education: Applications, Promise and Perils, and Ethical Questions*. https://er.educause.edu/articles/2019/8/artificial-intelligence-in-higher-education-applications-promise-and-perils-and-ethical-questions

Chapter 2
Intelligent Tutoring Systems

2.1 What Is Meant by an Intelligent Tutoring System?

Educational software with an artificial intelligence component is an intelligent tutoring or intelligent system. The software monitors student activity, modifying its comments and offering contextualized suggestions. Based on a student's performance and other cognitive and noncognitive characteristics, the software can predict strengths and shortcomings and recommend extra practice (Shute and Zapata-Rivera 2010).

In the early 1970s, Hartley and Sleeman (Hartley and Sleeman 1973) presented requirements brief for intelligent systems. Figure 2.1 provides a conceptual view of ITS components.

- Knowledge of the learner (student model).
- Knowledge of the domain (expert model).
- Knowledge of teaching strategies (pedagogical model).

Now, we will take a quick look at the three components of an intelligent system: the student, expert, and pedagogical models. While there have been improvements in all three categories, it is interesting that this simple list has remained unchanged for decades. There has been a dramatic transition from early, knowledge-free, computer-assisted instructional methods to those that rely on all computer-resident knowledge. Also, unlike simulations, intelligent computer-based systems can accurately identify where students are doing wrong and adjust their lessons accordingly. Intelligent systems are also congruent with the characteristics and objectives of formative assessment.

An intelligent system's primary method of imparting knowledge to a student is through the learner's application of that knowledge to solve carefully chosen or custom-tailored challenges. The student model is a repository for and source of up-to-date information on the student. First, the algorithm might see how much the

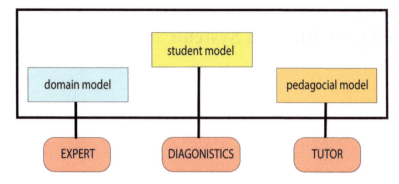

Fig. 2.1 ITS components. (Source: EduTech Wiki (2010))

student already understands. The system should take into account the student's specific learning objectives. The domain-expert model is a representation of this knowledge. The last step is for the system to choose the next unit of information to provide and the method through which it will be presented (e.g., an assessment task or an instructional element). The pedagogical model is what makes this possible (or tutor).

After considering all these factors, the system chooses or develops a problem, either figuring out a solution (using the domain-expert model) or retrieving a premade answer. The intelligent system analyzes the student's model and compares the results to its solution to arrive at a diagnosis.

The system provides input depending on several factors, including how long it has been since the student received feedback, whether or not the student has already received the same or similar advice, and so on. The program selects or generates a new problem, and the process begins again with the student's model being updated.

Brief History of ITSs Intelligent tutoring systems (ITSs) can be traced back to the 1960s and 1970s, namely, to the advent of Intelligent Computer-Assisted Learning (ICAI) in 1970 (Roybi Robot _ Medium 2020). Since then, the effectiveness of these systems has steadily risen, and their widespread adoption across the industry has soared. The name "Intelligent Tutoring Systems" gained traction in the academic community in 1982, 12 years later (Roybi Robot _ Medium 2020). The first ITS conference was conducted in 1988, and since then, many research institutions have been researching ITS (Iii et al. 2020).

Traditional Intelligent Systems The primary purpose of assessments is to better instruction and education for students. A key goal of formative assessment is to facilitate student learning by establishing the learner as an integral, resourceful, and self-reflective member of the educational community. Individualized instruction and real-world practice are commonplace in formative assessment-based classrooms.

The lack of standardization and less rigorous approach to formative assessment than summative assessment is a fundamental flaw in this paradigm (Shute and Zapata-Rivera 2010). As a result, the quality of the evaluation resources and results may suffer. Given that a student's diagnostic accuracy depends on the validity and

2.1 What Is Meant by an Intelligent Tutoring System?

reliability of the assessment data and that the diagnosis informs instructional support, a weak link in the chain (i.e., valid and reliable assessment data) would negatively impact the effectiveness of that support. That is to say, the quality of the data used to build the student model is crucial to how well an intelligent system performs its task (i.e., the inferences about what the student knows and can do).

A wealth of information about students can be mined by traditional intelligent systems using formative assessment (Shute and Zapata-Rivera 2010). All interactions between students and the system in the past and present are recorded as evidence, which can take on various forms and granularities. Thus, there are issues with effectively modeling student knowledge within such diverse environments, which is on top of the lack of standardization of methods for formative assessment in traditional intelligent systems. Regardless of the chosen measurement method, this presents several psychometric issues (e.g., modeling a wide range of learner characteristics, such as talents and aptitudes).

Enhanced Intelligent Systems Present-day intelligent systems are mostly confined to research establishments. However, the demand for accountability (e.g., standards and norm-referenced examinations) grows when these systems are brought into the classroom. Learning systems used in a controlled setting are not subject to the same stringent regulations (such as accountability requirements) as those used in a real classroom. This disconnection from actual classrooms helps explain why their designs have not focused heavily on summative assessment methods and, to some extent, why they have not been widely embraced.

Summative evaluations have the specific goal of holding students accountable. They provide an excellent example of the student's knowledge and are reliable. Schools frequently employ summative assessments because of national and international accountability mandates and interests. For instance, the No Child Left Behind (NCLB) act of 2001 was primarily responsible for the increased focus on summative examinations in the United States (Shute and Zapata-Rivera 2010). The Programme for International Student Assessment (PISA) also compares student accomplishments across countries internationally. Psychometric models (e.g., Rasch, item-response theory) developed by the measurement community offer reliable and valid assessment information, often presented as a single measure of ability at a given point in time for any individual student (Shute and Zapata-Rivera 2010). However, you cannot do much with these numbers to shape your education. Moreover, teachers often complain that the time spent on testing distracts from otherwise productive classroom activities.

First introduced recently, intelligent systems can potentially improve assessment and classroom instruction. Snow and Mandinach (1991), writing more than a decade ago, advocated for establishing guidelines to design reliable and beneficial forms of instructional-assessment systems. Systematically, these systems have (Shute and Zapata-Rivera 2010):

- Active participation of educators at every stage of development.
- Instructional and assessment interactions based on a cognitive model.
- Explicit connections to state standards and standardized state tests.

The web-based cognitive tutors that Anderson, Koedinger, and their colleagues at Carnegie Mellon University created are a great example of a successfully deployed intelligent system (Anderson et al. 1995). They developed a system that combines rigorous evaluation with instructional support; they term it an assistant, a development of the cognitive tutor model. For evaluation and education, aids use authentic (i.e., publicized) questions from the (Massachusetts comprehensive assessment system) MCAS state tests.

2.2 Need for an Intelligent Tutoring System

Why do researchers spend time and money developing intelligent computer-based tutors? Two primary drivers appear to be at play (Nwana 1990):

- *Research needs:* Learning more about the procedures that make an educational engagement successful from a purely academic standpoint is essential. ITS research is at the crossroads of cognitive psychology, artificial intelligence, and education, making it a fertile ground for testing many theories from each field. One of the main draws for John Anderson, a distinguished psychologist from Carnegie Mellon, was the opportunity to test his theories on learning at the University of Pittsburgh (Anderson 1987). As a result, developing an ITS will aid in developing more robust theories of cognition.
- *Practical needs:* On a more practical level, ITSs enable numerous outcomes that would be difficult or impossible to get with human teachers due to cost and accessibility. The ability to provide personalized instruction is a crucial benefit of ITSs. There is widespread agreement that individualized instruction is the most productive teaching method in most cases. In a study comparing private tutoring with classroom instruction of cartography and probability, Bloom (1984) showed that, despite all students spending the same amount of time learning the topics, 98% of those with private tutors outperformed the typical classroom student. When comparing the time it took for students to reach the same level of competency, Anderson et al. (1984, 1985) found that the private tutor had a four-to-one advantage. The many benefits of private tutoring have been lost as our educational systems have shifted toward group instruction. By assigning one ITS to each student in a class, a school may provide this type of tutoring while reaping the benefits of a classroom setting. The ITS could give the student real-time comments on their performance. Since tutoring is most successful when responding directly to students' needs, this personalized and timely feedback is vital.

2.3 How Are Intelligence Tutoring Systems Influencing Education?

Especially in digital settings, intelligent tutoring systems can significantly affect students' learning abilities. Digital apps give students tailored learning experiences via deep-learning algorithms, although ITSs have yet to be widely implemented in educational contexts.

Using machine learning algorithms to model student learning empowers educators to create AI-free digital curricula (Roybi Robot _ Medium 2020). This technology's value lies in the fact that it can be tailored to meet the needs of any individual user, from the most seasoned professor to the youngest student. If this is achieved, ITSs will make great strides toward adoption in the K-12 and higher education settings.

Humans are complex and call for individualized approaches to learning, which is a significant obstacle in educating children of all ages. This is at odds with the standardized testing and one-size-fits-all philosophy that underpins many educational institutions today (Roybi Robot _ Medium 2020). Because of the existing model's inability to identify and highlight learners' unique strengths, some students have been left behind. Many of the issues plaguing the education system today might be alleviated with the help of ITSs, which have the potential to play a pivotal role in the sector's future.

Artificial intelligence (AI) and related systems, such as intelligent tutoring systems (ITSs), directly respond to this problem by fostering an educational setting where students' unique strengths and interests are emphasized more. ITSs are only one example of the revolutionary new tools based on AI technology that will soon be a standard feature in today's classrooms and online learning spaces. Many countries are transitioning in this direction because experts agree it is the best approach to education (Roybi Robot _ Medium 2020).

2.4 Benefits of Intelligent Tutoring Systems

Intelligent tutoring systems can have the following benefits (Briggs 2014):

- Available at all hours, including late at night, the night before a test.
- Help teachers and programmers improve their methods by giving them access to real-time.
- Reduce the dependence on human resources.
- Enable students to demonstrate their understanding by having them describe what they already know and then respond appropriately based on their level of comprehension.
- Facilitate the development of tailored curricula by teachers.

- Produce better results on standardized tests than more conventional methods, especially for students who are learning English as a second language, who are from low-income families, or who have specific educational needs.
- Allow for instantaneous yes/no feedback, individualized task selection, on-demand hints, and reinforcement of mastery learning.

2.5 Examples of Intelligent Tutoring Systems

In academia, there is no shortage of intelligent tutoring systems. There is no way to compile a complete list, but some of the more significant ones (Briggs 2014) (Walsh 2019) are included below:

- *The Cognitive Tutor:* The Cognitive Tutor was developed at Carnegie Mellon University and is now used in a wide range of mathematics and science classes across the United States, from high school geometry and algebra to the university's Genetics Cognitive Tutor, which helps students gain a better grasp of gene interaction and regulation.
- *The Andes Physics Tutor and Writing Pal:* Designed by academics at Arizona State University, these tools help students succeed in beginning physics courses and improve their writing skills. Essay writing practice, game-based practice sessions, and feedback to encourage developing writers are all included in Writing Pal, which has undergone thorough testing with secondary students.
- *ASSISTments:* Worcester Polytechnic Institute has created a free online tutoring program called ASSISTments.
- *Knewton:* Knewton is a privately produced platform that offers intelligent instructors for the GMAT, LSAT, and SAT, as well as individualized support for grades K-12 and above. The platform means instantaneous responses for students, while for teachers and curriculum developers, it means access to valuable analytics.
- *Mathematics Tutor:* Using fractions, decimals, and percentages, the Mathematics Tutor guides students through problem-solving exercises. A tutor monitors a student's success rate while working on problems and then gives them additional problems to solve that are at an acceptable difficulty level for their current level. Student ability and an expected completion time for the problem determine the next set of problems to be presented to the student.
- *eTeacher:* eTeacher is an AI-powered tutor that provides personalized e-learning assistance. Tracking how well college students do in their online classes creates personalized profiles for each one. The student's results are analyzed by eTeacher, and a unique action plan is proposed to help the student succeed academically.
- *ZOSMAT:* ZOSMAT is an innovative platform that considers every factor of a functional classroom. It is designed to be there for students at every step of their education. A student-centered ITS like this one keeps track of a learner's development and adapts to individual needs. ZOSMAT can be utilized for self-paced study or with a human instructor in a classroom setting.

2.5 Examples of Intelligent Tutoring Systems

- *REALP:* To improve students' reading comprehension, REALP provides reader-specific lexical practice and personalized practice with relevant, authentic reading resources from around the Internet. When a learner uses the system, a personalized model of their data is immediately created. The reading is followed by exercises designed to help the student practice the new vocabulary words he or she has just learned.
- *CIRCSIM Tutor:* At the Illinois Institute of Technology, first-year medical students employ an innovative tutoring technology called CIRCSIM Tutor. It teaches students how to control their blood pressure through Socratic dialogue based on real-world scenarios.
- *Why2-Atlas:* Why2-Atlas is an Intelligent Tutoring System (ITS) that evaluates how well students explain fundamental physics concepts. The algorithm can infer their opinions and turn their explanations into a proof by reading the students' explanatory paragraphs. By doing so, misconceptions and gaps in understanding are brought to light. The software prompts the learner to revise their writing after pointing up errors. Before reaching a final result, the process may undergo several iterations.
- *SmartTutor:* To better assist its continuing education students, the University of Hong Kong (HKU) created a SmartTutor. By fusing Internet tools, educational research, and AI, SmartTutor can assist students. SmartTutor's goal is to meet the demand for individualized instruction identified in HKU's adult education program.
- *AutoTutor:* AutoTutor mimics a human tutor's speech patterns and pedagogical tactics to help college students learn fundamental computer skills like hardware, operating systems, and the Internet in an introductory computer literacy course. AutoTutor aims to interpret the learner's keyboard input and generate conversational motions with feedback, reminders, correction, and tips.
- *ActiveMath:* ActiveMath is an online math program that adjusts to each user's progress. The system aims to facilitate self-directed, lifelong education and enhance online education.
- *Cardiac Tutor:* To better equip medical professionals to treat cardiac patients, the Cardiac Tutor was developed. The tutor presents students with cardiac issues, and in subsequent steps, they must choose among possible treatments. Learners can tailor their experience with Cardiac Tutor's hints, audio tips, and constructive criticism. Students receive a comprehensive report after each simulation, regardless of whether they can help the patients.
- *CODES*: Try the Cooperative Music Prototype Design on the web for collaborative music prototyping. It was made to help anybody, especially those who are not music experts, create musical pieces in a prototypical way. CODES relies heavily on communication and collaboration between its composers and their collaborators. Trying out, playing with, and tweaking musical prototypes is easy.
- *Mathia:* Mathia was created at Carnegie Mellon University by cognitive scientists to help provide each student with a positive math learning experience while giving you the real-time feedback and assessments you need to know exactly where your students stand and where they are headed.

- *Alta:* Knewton's product Alta is a suite of adaptive learning tools designed specifically for higher education (knewton.com/what-is-alta/). It seeks to integrate various topics in mathematics, economics, and chemistry. In their classroom instruction, Alta uses a mastery learning strategy based on item response theory.
- *Area9 Lyceum (area9lyceum.com):* This innovative method re-creates educational content and distributes it via their platform, which incorporates "constant self-assessment" (the user's confidence in their responses is used as part of the adaptive process). This seems to be a common approach in business and professional education.
- *Toppr:* This program, developed in India, provides individualized instruction in various scholastic levels and fields of study. Toppr employs machine learning to customize the learning experience for each student by analyzing their responses to questions and adjusting the presentation's pace.
- *Adil:* As an intelligent tutoring system (ITS), Adil (Automatic Debugger in Learning System) was developed as a software system for knowledge-based automated debugging. It helps novice C programmers learn the fundamentals of debugging their code. It helps pinpoint malfunctions and provides context for the relevant software. Adil is a debugger that can identify and explain those defects in the program's logic when given a specification and a program with no syntax errors. Without any glitches, it can explain what the code does. The Conceiver, an autonomous program understanding system, served as the inspiration for Adil.
- *ADIS:* To further assist educators in imparting knowledge of data structures such as linked lists, stacks, queues, trees, and graphs, the Java-based, web-enabled intelligent tutoring system (ITS) *ADIS* (Animated Data Structure Intelligent Tutoring System) was created. Because it has been written entirely in Java, ADIS can be used independently of any specific platform and distributed via the Internet. Graphical representations of data structures can be viewed in ADIS, and the program also supports graphical modifications of the resulting data structure. Students can visually grasp data structures' fundamental algorithms (insertion, deletion, etc.) through a tutorial mode with integrated exercises.
- *BITS:* The Bayesian Intelligent Tutoring System (*BITS*) is a web-based intelligent tutoring system (WITS) for computer programming. The BITS smart system makes judgments using a Bayesian network. By analyzing the student's goals and interests, BITS can recommend learning targets and purposes and create effective learning sequences. A student, for instance, may be interested in (the adding operation), and not all of the background information that came before it. For example, if you want to learn about addition, BITS can figure out what you already know and provide the links for these concepts in the proper learning order.
- *DCG:* The primary concept behind *DCG* (Dynamic Courseware Generation), an ITS built on an ITS-shell architecture, is using artificial intelligence (AI) planning tools to establish the nature of the course material to be taught. The curriculum is created on the fly by the system. Each student's study plan is developed with specific learning objectives in mind. The primary benefit of this method is that it makes it feasible to automatically design adaptive Computer Assisted

2.5 Examples of Intelligent Tutoring Systems

Learning (CAL) courses aimed toward a specific learning outcome, which is not possible with the current state of the art in CAL software.
- *DM-Tutor:* Decision-Making Tutor, or DM-Tutor, is an ITS (Intelligent Tutoring System) built into the MIS (Management Information System) used in oil palm plantation management. As such, DM-Tutor is designed to teach its customers how to put plantation analysis theory into practice. Using actual plantation conditions and operational data, DM-Tutor aims to deliver scenario-based instruction.
- *JITS:* The JITS (Java Intelligent Tutoring System) research project aims to create a programming tutor tailored to students enrolled in their first college or university-level JavaTM programming course. This work is a proof-of-concept for a future effort to model the application domain of a specific subset of the JavaTM programming language. A fully developed JavaTM intelligent tutoring system should give students a learning environment with much interaction, which should help them do better in school. The finished prototype should prove the idea.
- *KERMIT:* KERMIT (Knowledge-Based Entity Relationship Modelling Intelligent Tutoring) is an ITS that helps with entity-relationship (ER) modeling based on knowledge. The process of designing a database is not well-defined, and while there is an expected result, it is not clear how to get there. Constraint-based modeling has thus far been implemented in SQL-Tutor, a tutor for the database language, and in a system for instructing students in proper punctuation and capitalization (CAPIT). With its VB implementation, KERMIT can work with the entity-relationship data model.
- *MBITS:* MBITS, short for "Multicriteria Bayesian Intelligent Tutoring System," is a WITS (Web-based Intelligent Tutoring System) powered by Bayesian Networks (BN). The goal of MBITS was to help students have a firmer grasp of the course's overarching concept through the multicriteria approach to comparing and contrasting various data collection methods and problem-solving. It is a web app that's fun to play around with and simple to use.
- *ML-Tutor:* ML-Tutor (Machine Learning Tutor) is a web-based client-server solution incorporating Internet technology and instructional hypertext. The user interface for this system is built into the client software, which is executed in a web browser. The system's server is run only in response to a request from a client. The client records information sent to the server over the Internet. The server's machine learning component (MLC) analyzes the data and sends the results to the client.
- *NORMIT:* NORMIT (Normalization Intelligent Tutor) is the ITS students can count on when normalizing databases. NORMIT is a web-based learning management system featuring architecture and methods for managing large classes. It is written in the open-source language Allegro Common Lisp (ACL) and uses the freely available web server AllegroServe to showcase ACL's network programming as an adaptable server. With NORMIT, ICTG has created the first constraint-based tutor to instruct a procedural skill.
- *SQL-Tutor:* SQL-Tutor (Structured Query Language) Tutor is a form of ITS that focuses on teaching and studying SQL. It uses a CBM (limited) modeling strat-

egy developed by the students. The language of implementation is Allegro Common Lisp (ACL).
- *SQLT-Web:* To teach and learn the SQL query language for databases, SQLT-Web (SQL-Tutor (Structured Query Language Tutor) on the Web) is a knowledge-based, software-based intelligent tutoring system (ITS) that is independent of the original SQL-Tutor.
- *TEx-Sys:* TEx-Sys (Tutor-Expert System) is a learning management system (LMS) that provides a copyright shell for constructing an intelligent tutoring system (ITS) in a user-selected domain of expertise. It was first developed as an online system (PR) using semantic networks, frames, and production rules.
- *WITS:* A combination of an intelligent tutoring system (ITS) and an expert system (ES), WITS (Whole-Course Intelligent Tutoring System) may instruct a student in a course on solid-state electronics without the need for a human instructor. It has the potential to provide a stimulating setting for education, complete with immediate, actionable feedback to keep students engaged.

2.6 Intelligent Tutoring Systems and Online Learning

ITS has evolved from early-era physics problem-solving methods that involved human-machine communication, such as Why-2 Atlas (Vanlehn et al. 2002), which supported ITS. ITS's fast transition from the lab to practical use is unexpected and promising. Automatic Speech Recognition (ASR) and Natural Language Processing (NLP) approaches are used by downloadable software and online services like Carnegie Speech and Duolingo to identify language problems and assist users with correction (Vanlehn et al. 2002). American high schools have adopted tutoring programs like the Carnegie Cognitive Tutor to improve pupils' grasp of mathematics. Various other ITS are designed to teach subjects, including geography, circuitry, medical diagnosis, computing, programming, genetics, chemistry, and more. When a student gets stuck on a math problem, a cognitive tutor will provide helpful ideas in the style of a natural teacher. The instructor provides detailed and contextual feedback based on the sought hint and the delivered answer.

The use of applications in academia is expanding. SHERLOCK (Lesgold et al. 1988), an intelligent tutoring system, is currently being utilized to instruct Air Force technicians in identifying and fixing electrical system problems in aircraft. Moreover, the Information Sciences Institute at the University of Southern California has created more sophisticated avatar-based training programs to educate service members on how to interact with people from various cultural backgrounds. Individualized mastery learning and issue sequencing are made possible by new methods for personalized coaching, such as Bayesian Knowledge Tracing (Yudelson et al. 2013).

Surprisingly, MOOCs and other types of online education at all levels have taken off, with participants using resources like Wikipedia and Khan Academy and relying on learning management systems that incorporate synchronous and asynchronous education and adaptive learning technologies (Grosz et al. 2016). The Educational Testing Service and Pearson, among others, have been working on automatic NLP assessment tools to co-grade essays on standardized tests since the late 1990s. EdX, Coursera, and Udacity, three of the most prominent providers of massive open online courses (MOOCs), use natural language processing (NLP), machine learning (ML), and crowdsourcing methods to evaluate students' answers to short-answer and essay questions and coding projects. Accelerating growth is also being seen in online education infrastructures that facilitate postgraduate professional education and lifelong learning. Professionals and those switching careers benefit significantly from these systems since they reduce the necessity for personal connection. They may not be the first to adopt systems and applications bolstered by AI, but they will do so once the systems and apps have been thoroughly vetted and proven.

One may argue that artificial intelligence is the magic ingredient that has allowed professors in higher education to teach classes with student enrollment in the tens of thousands. Automated generation of questions, including those designed to assess vocabulary, wh (who/what/when/where/why) questions, and multiple choice questions using electronic resources like WordNet, Wikipedia, and online ontologies, is also possible, allowing for continuous testing of large classes of students (Grosz et al. 2016). Online education will rapidly embrace these methods as the number of available courses increases. The AI community has quickly learned a great deal, but the long-term effects of these technologies on the education system are yet unknown.

2.7 Development of an Intelligent Tutoring System

There are four iterative phases involved (Briggs 2014) in creating an intelligent tutoring system:

- Needs assessment.
- Cognitive task analysis.
- Initial tutor implementation.
- Evaluation.

Needs Assessment Step one in any instructional design is to do a learner analysis and consult with relevant subject matter experts and the teacher (s). The purpose is to define learning outcomes and create a broad curriculum framework.

- The probability that a learner will succeed in solving a particular problem.
- Time required to achieve the desired performance.
- How likely is it that the learner will make use of what they have learned.

The cost-effectiveness of the interface is another crucial factor that needs to be examined. Because both educators and students will be utilizing the system, evaluating factors such as familiarity with the subject matter at enrollment is essential.

Cognitive Task Analysis The second stage involves building a reliable computational model of the relevant expertise for solving the challenge. The main approaches to creating a domain model include the following:

- Conducting Interviews with domain experts.
- Conducting "think aloud" protocol studies with domain experts.
- Conducting "think aloud" studies with novices.
- Studying teaching and learning behavior.

By using the "think aloud" approach, instructors have students express out loud their thought processes as they work through common types of challenges. Information on solving problems can be gleaned from watching online tutoring sessions, which can be applied to developing more conversational or interactive tutoring systems.

Initial Tutor Implementation This phase involves establishing a conducive context for problem-solving, which will allow for and strengthen the student's engagement in the learning process. Evaluation tasks are carried out in the last phase of any software development process.

Evaluation

1. Feasibility tests to verify essential functionality and educational efficacy.
2. Formative evaluations of the system under development.
3. Parameter analyses that probe the usefulness of system features.
4. Summative evaluations of the tutor's impact on the student's progress in terms of their learning pace and level of achievement.

Effective intelligent tutoring systems should, in theory:

- Facilitate the student's progress toward a workable solution.
- Create a production set that represents student competence.
- Make sure you explain the reasoning behind your solution to the problem.
- Facilitate learning in the context of problem-solving.
- Improve students' ability to think abstractly about addressing problems.
- Minimize working memory load.
- Incorporate timely feedback on errors.
- Fine-tune the instruction's grain size to the student's progress.
- Help learners get closer and closer to their goal skill.

AI's Role in Developing Intelligent Tutoring Systems AI, along with other forms of disruptive technology, has been a driving force behind the development of EdTech and other intelligent learning approaches. It has recently expanded its scope to include the required field of intelligent tutoring. As their name suggests, intelligent tutoring systems are intelligent computer systems that can efficiently offer instructions to learners and provide a feedback system with minimal human participation.

In May 2020, researchers from Carnegie Mellon University developed a system that enables a teacher to educate computer systems with the assistance of AI and construct intelligent tutoring systems. This system also allows the instructor to create intelligent tutoring systems. Ken Koedinger, a professor of human-computer interaction psychology at CMU, is quoted in a report by the university as saying that initially, it took almost 200 h of development for each hour of tutored instruction because they programmed production rules by hand. However, later on, they used a shortcut method that reduced the number of hours to approximately 40–50. Despite this, it is a time-consuming process because there are many different kinds of difficulties and directions. The newly developed intelligent tutoring system based on AI is not slow to pick up new information and can be programmed for a 30-min session in 30 min. In work published on the same topic, it is said that to construct intelligent tutoring systems, the authors trained simulated learners using an innovative interaction design. It does this by utilizing machine learning and developing a teaching interface for machine learning applications that is simple and straightforward. Using these computer tools, educators can model multiple approaches to a problem and correct their responses if they get them wrong. Using AI and ML, the system can learn to generalize and solve problems within a domain without being explicitly taught how to do so (EG 2021).

The advent of pandemics has amplified the impact of artificial intelligence on the educational system. The capacity of intelligent tutoring systems to tailor their lessons to the specific needs of each student has garnered them much praise. The traditional education system, which operates on a one-size-fits-all premise and assumes that everyone needs the same amount of learning time and attention, will likely be disrupted by AI-powered intelligent tutoring systems. Intelligent tutoring systems are built with the understanding that every single learner is unique. It can be altered to fit the requirements of each given class. Artificial intelligence (AI)-based tutoring systems do not need to be programmed and can be easily adapted to fit different pedagogical styles.

CMU's method is helpful in various contexts, including the instruction of English grammar, chemistry, and algebra; to test its limits, the university has conducted experiments with challenges as varied as multi-column addition. In the report, Ken Koedinger explains that machine learning models often experience temporary setbacks like students. As a result, it has the potential to shed light on the relative difficulty of each method and lesson for educators. In recent years, artificial intelligence (AI) technology has come to dominate several markets, including one that is very important: education. Artificial intelligence is helping to democratize access to top-notch education by facilitating the rapid and painless creation of intelligent tutoring systems.

2.8 Limitations of Intelligent Tutoring Systems

Many critics are eager to point out the limitations of intelligent tutoring programs. Here are some of the system's blows (Briggs 2014):

- Measuring the effectiveness of ITS initiatives is challenging.
- However, frequent feedback and hint sequences do not improve students' deep learning.
- The system does not prompt children with questions that help explain their actions.
- Justifying the use of ITSs by an administrative team may prove challenging.
- Evaluating an intelligent tutoring system can be time-consuming, expensive, and complex.
- Human instructors are superior to machines in providing contextually relevant conversation and feedback.
- Currently, human instructors are better able to read and respond to their students' emotions.

The effectiveness of a sophisticated, intelligent teaching system relies on thorough testing to guarantee its claims. Either during the design and early development of the system to detect flaws and suggest improvements (formative) or after the system has been completed to support formal claims about the construction, behavior, or consequences associated with a completed system, an evaluation will be conducted (summative). Different approaches to evaluation are discussed in the published literature, but no universal standards have been established (Briggs 2014).

There have been hiccups, but efforts to improve education have moved forward. Currently, features are being developed that will enable intelligent instructors to interpret facial expressions and other signals of emotion to engage their students. Since feelings can be communicated in various ways, this presents several challenges. However, these concepts have given rise to a new subfield of ITS known as affective tutoring systems (ATS) (Briggs 2014) that aims to deal with precisely these kinds of difficulties.

Gaze Tutor (Briggs 2014) is an example of an ITS that considers students' emotions by monitoring their eye movements to ascertain if they are engaged in the material or distracted.

2.9 The Future of Intelligent Tutoring Systems

ITSs are a way to observe AIED (AI in Education) in action as a cutting-edge educational tool that has the potential to support academics. ITSs can provide a workable answer to the different barriers that students may have while trying to contact a human instructor (cost, location, time, etc.) (Cameron 2021). In certain aspects, ITSs might be a valuable addition to academic support programs that provide student accommodations. Additionally, ITSs have demonstrated efficacy in supporting students with clearly defined, solution-driven courses and in offering students unique learning opportunities that go beyond what is generally provided by conventional approaches (Cameron 2021). Teachers will still be necessary for the classroom, but ITSs will supplement them in various ways to improve instructional strategies and engage students.

2.10 Conclusion

The term "intelligent tutoring system" (ITS) refers to a suite of programs designed to help students with their coursework by employing AI-based techniques. These tools aim to facilitate and enhance instruction in a particular knowledge domain while honoring each student's uniqueness. They make it possible to examine students' current knowledge and the methods employed to expand and rectify it. In this chapter, we examine intelligent tutoring systems (ITS) from the perspective of how they might be used effectively in today's educational frameworks.

References

Anderson, J. R. (1987). Production systems, learning, and tutoring. In *Self-Modifying Production Systems: Models of Learning and Development* (pp. 437–458.).
Anderson, J. R., Boyle, C. F., & Reiser, B. J. (1984). Intelligent Tutoring Systems. *Science, 228*(4698), 456–462. https://doi.org/10.1126/science.228.4698.456
Anderson, J. R., Boyle, C. F., & Yost, G. (1985). The Geometry Tutor. *9th International Joint Conference on Artificial Intelligence*, 1–7.
Anderson, J. R., Corbett, A. T., Koedinger, K. R., & Pelletier, R. (1995). Cognitive Tutors: Lessons Learned. *Journal of the Learning Sciences, 4*(2), 167–207. https://doi.org/10.1207/s15327809jls0402
Bloom, B. S. (1984). The 2 Sigma Problem: the search for methods of group instruction as effective as one-to-one tutoring. *Educational Researcher, 13*(6), 4–16.
Briggs, S. (2014). *Intelligent Tutoring Systems – Can They Work For You?* InformED. https://www.opencolleges.edu.au/informed/other/intelligent-tutoring-systems/
Cameron, B. (2021). *Intelligent Tutoring Systems: Connecting AI and Education.* Crowdmark. https://crowdmark.com/intelligent-tutoring-systems-connecting-ai-and-education/
EduTech Wiki. (2010). *Intelligent tutoring system.* EduTech Wiki. https://edutechwiki.unige.ch/en/Intelligent_tutoring_system
EG, M. (2021). *Developing Intelligent Tutoring Systems and AI's Role.* Analytics Insight. https://www.analyticsinsight.net/developing-intelligent-tutoring-systems-and-ais-role/
Grosz, B. J., Altman, R., Horvitz, E., Mackworth, A., Tom Mitchell, D., & Mulligan, Y. S. (2016). *Artificial intelligence and life in 2030.*
Hartley, J. R., & Sleeman, D. H. (1973). Towards More Intelligent Teaching Systems. *International Journal of Man-Machine Studies, 5*, 215–236.
Iii, D. W., Harpstead, E., & Koedinger, K. R. (2020). An Interaction Design for Machine Teaching to Develop AI Tutors. *CHI Conference on Human Factors in Computing Systems*, 1–11. https://doi.org/10.1145/3313831.3376226
Lesgold, A., Lajoie, S., Bunzo, M., & Eggan, G. (1988). SHERLOCK: A Coached Practice Environment for an Electronics Troubleshooting Job. In *Computer-Assisted Instruction and Intelligent Tutoring Systems: Shared Goals and Complementary Approaches* (Issue January, pp. 1–30).
Nwana, H. S. (1990). Intelligent Tutoring Systems: an overview. *Artificial Intelligence Review, 4*, 251–277.
Roybi Robot _ Medium. (2020). *How Intelligent Tutoring Systems are Changing Education.* Medium.Com. https://medium.com/@roybirobot/how-intelligent-tutoring-systems-are-changing-education-d60327e54dfb
Shute, V. J., & Zapata-Rivera, D. (2010). Intelligent Systems. In *Third Edition of the International Encyclopedia of Education* (pp. 75–80). Elsevier.

Snow, R. E., & Mandinach, E. B. (1991). *Integrating assessment and instruction: A research and development agenda.*

Vanlehn, K., Jordan, P. W., Rosé, C. P., Bhembe, D., Böttner, M., Gaydos, A., Makatchev, M., Pappuswamy, U., Ringenberg, M. A., Roque, A., Siler, S., & Srivastava, R. (2002). The Architecture of Why2-Atlas: A Coach for Qualitative Physics Essay Writing. *6th International Conference on Intelligent Tutoring Systems, June,* 159–167. https://doi.org/10.1007/3-540-47987-2

Walsh, K. (2019). *Intelligent Tutoring Systems (a Decades-old Application of AI in Education).* EmergingEdTech. https://www.emergingedtech.com/2019/12/intelligent-tutoring-systems-application-of-ai-in-education/

Yudelson, M. V., Koedinger, K. R., & Gordon, G. J. (2013). Individualized Bayesian Knowledge Tracing Models. *16th International Conference on Artificial Intelligence in Education,* 1–10.

Chapter 3
Natural Language Processing for Education

3.1 What Is NLP?

To make computers as intelligent as humans, natural language processing (NLP) is a subfield of computer science and artificial intelligence (AI) that focuses on teaching computers to comprehend written and spoken language (IBM 2022). Figure 3.1 gives a conceptual view of NLP.

Natural language processing (NLP) integrates statistical, machine learning, and deep learning models with computational linguistics (rule-based modeling of human language) (IBM 2022). These tools allow computers to "understand" human speech or written language, including people's intent and sentiments.

Computer programs are powered by natural language processing, which enables them to translate text from one language to another, respond to voice requests, and quickly summarize massive quantities of material, often in real time. You may have interacted with NLP through voice-controlled GPS systems, digital assistants, speech-to-text dictation software, customer service chatbots, and other modern conveniences. On the other hand, natural language processing (NLP) is becoming increasingly important in enterprise solutions that aim to improve the efficiency of businesses by automating and standardizing routine but crucial tasks.

3.2 Using NLP for Educational Activities

Natural language processing technology has made a breakthrough in digital education possible. Today, natural language processing (NLP) is employed in the classroom for various purposes, including essay grading and feedback generation, question generation, example generation, etc. The use of NLP in online literacy initiatives is on the rise. It also has significant potential in print programs, where

© The Author(s), under exclusive license to Springer Nature Switzerland AG 2023
M. Kurni et al., *A Beginner's Guide to Introduce Artificial Intelligence in Teaching and Learning*, https://doi.org/10.1007/978-3-031-32653-0_3

Fig. 3.1 A conceptual view of natural language processing (NLP)

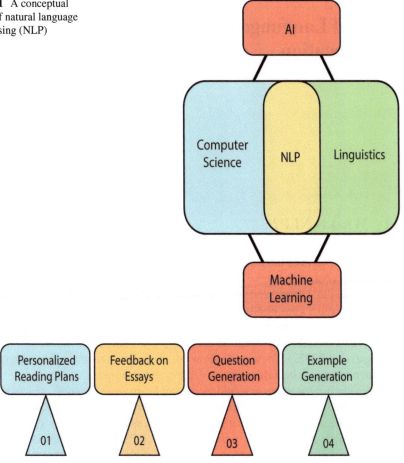

Fig. 3.2 Uses of NLP tools

printed products are crafted with the help of AI. There are newer, more complex NLP tools, many free and open-source (e.g., the latest Transformer NLP technology has several open-source models). We also note that neural technologies do human-like tasks on natural language data with significantly higher accuracy. Some good uses for natural language processing (NLP) tools (see Fig. 3.2) in the classroom (Patel 2021) include:

- *Personalized Reading Plans:* Using natural language processing (NLP) technology, we can provide students with reading materials more appropriate to their skill level. There is open text data on the Internet that can be used by natural language processing algorithms to determine the reading challenges of the text, allowing us to quickly and easily create software that provides students with appropriately graded reading materials.

- *Feedback on Essays:* OpenAI and similar platforms have enabled anybody to create software that provides students with objective and insightful feedback. The software may provide the student with direct, formative input. Training such systems would necessitate creative data collecting, but if done correctly, it might lead to novel applications that lessen the burden on educators.
- *Question Generation:* It is possible to create a wide range of test questions using preexisting learning resources. Despite the field's novelty, academic research has created standards for assessing the quality of Question Generation Models (e.g., see Mostow et al.), and several companies have attempted to commercialize this research.
- *Example Generation:* We can use natural language processing to generate criteria-based content. Using this technological prowess, we may produce worked instances of math problems, construct sentences illustrating multiple ways of using the same term, produce examples of how literature can be summarized, and so on.

3.3 Benefits and Uses of NLP in Education

Suppose you are an educator or tech guru. In that case, you might think this might be useful for enhancing the learning experience of a single student, teacher, parent, or tutor or streamlining a process at large-scale educational institutions, testing organizations, or government agencies. Regardless of what you are trying to do, expanding your knowledge of NLP's applications in education will help you hone your existing ideas and generate brand-new ones.

NLP Helps with Learning and Comprehension From early school to postgraduate study, pedagogy acknowledges that every student's learning process differs. For each student and subject, the rate of student learning varies. Some students have unique demands that call for various instructional strategies.

Although tailored learning is the best approach, there are not enough teachers or hours in the day to give each student what they need. Here is where your educational concept can use NLP to offer a personalized learning environment (Shiraly 2021).

Summarization and Paraphrasing You can incorporate summarizing and paraphrasing to improve reading comprehension in any educational content you create. A summary presents a condensed version of a chapter, article, or lecture that only includes vital concepts and facts. Paraphrasing communicates a summary using alternative words chosen for their reading level, simplicity, accuracy, the regional variety, dialect, or cultural sensitivity. Both traits benefit specialist disciplines like law and medicine, where students must quickly comprehend enormous amounts of knowledge.

Transformer neural networks have made this conceivable. The transformer architecture is a deep neural network with an attention layer system that allows it to include higher-level intangible elements like semantics, tone, emotions, and long-range context dependencies.

Companies like Google and OpenAI have published transformer models like BERT, GPT-3, RoBERTa, and T5. These models contain latent representations of all human linguistic, cultural, and social conventions visible on the Internet. These models are often trained using web-scraping corpora.

These already-trained models are now absurdly simple to implement and fine-tune with the help of software libraries like spaCy and Hugging Face.

For example, summarization is a downstream job since it begins with a pre-trained model, to which specialized neurons are added and then retrained with data collected for the specific task. Transfer learning, or fine-tuning, refers to adapting a pre-trained, general model to a new application.

A specialized language model is developed by fine-tuning a model that has already been trained using data from the target domain. BioMEDical Natural Language Processing (NLP) Model (BioBERT) is one example, having been educated on the lexicon and syntax of biomedical journals. Regarding the law, LEGAL-BERT is the model for natural language processing technologies.

The first step in summarization and paraphrasing is to feed your training data into a language model to generate embeddings, which are internal data representations. Next, a sequence-to-sequence layer is added, and the whole process is fine-tuned with a summarizing/paraphrasing dataset.

Question Answering Essay-style assessments, quizzes, and flashcards are well-liked by students and teachers, but their manual preparation can be intimidating for teachers with heavy workloads.

Using NLP, you can have questions and answers created for your study materials. It also measures how well a student's written comments match the content of the course. A student's reading level and learning rate, among other factors, can be used to tailor the questions and assessment. Saves time for overworked educators by providing feedback on essay content across four key areas: grammar, structure, semantics, and logic.

A question-answering model can be analogous to a summarization model by adding a sequence-to-sequence layer to a pre-trained transformer model. The expected result is a sequence that corresponds to the input sequence (the question) and provides the correct response. A pre-trained base model and sequence-to-sequence layer assembly are fine-tuned using question-answer datasets from a particular field.

Questions concerning prions are a good test case for this Hugging Face biology question-answering approach. A cloud service like Amazon Kendra offers an alternate, less complicated deployment method for question-answering.

Chatbots Chatbots are another option, as they can function as robotic educators by answering queries and explaining concepts through conversational NLP.

Similar to the model developed for question answering, a sequence-to-sequence model is developed for speech recognition. When a student speaks, the system

3.3 Benefits and Uses of NLP in Education 49

transcribes what they say into text. The questions are sent into a question-answering model, which either provides answers or grades the student's work. Text-to-speech synthesis is then used to play back the results to the student.

The synthesized voice can be programmed to provide various human traits important to making a learner feel at ease, including enthusiasm, kindness, warmth, friendliness, and accent.

Chatbots can be implemented using cloud services like Amazon Lex and Google Dialogflow.

NLP Improves Writing and Assessment Writing about concepts aids in the consolidation of knowledge. When given constructive criticism and writing prompts, students are more likely to go deeper into a topic and gather more information about it. This is why essays and quizzes are common evaluation forms across the curriculum.

Unfortunately, teachers do not always have time to respond thoughtfully to students. Natural language processing (NLP) can provide immediate and detailed comments on each and every written assignment (Shiraly 2021). It assesses all the indicators that people assess. Poor spelling and grammar are the foundational issues. Finally, the sentence structure and clarity will be evaluated. The validity and reasonability of arguments are our next stop. Accurate language, free of ambiguities, is essential in higher education domains such as law and science.

To conclude, we evaluate the structure using criteria established by experts in the field. There is a specific format for writing legal documents. A standard format is expected for scientific papers. Natural language processing can do this in milliseconds, right before the student's eyes as they type.

You should investigate natural language processing (NLP) to enhance the quality of feedback and automated scale assessment in large-scale settings, such as testing agencies that evaluate numerous students. Educational apps that provide this feedback can help a single student, parent, or educator.

How Does It Work? Feedback and assessment are written using transformer-architecture models.

For automated essay grading, rudimentary spelling, grammar, and sentence structure standards are already built into the model. Students are asked to use a sequence-to-sequence approach to paraphrase their writing. The model's output may be compared to the original text, with your app drawing attention to any discrepancies and offering suggestions. All grammatical errors will be fixed in the final product.

For example, each new research paper in a discipline like science rests on the shoulders of numerous others. The purpose of a paper's citations is twofold: first, to show proper etiquette, and second, to create a foundational pyramid of assertions upon which to build new ones. Sentences from different papers can be linked together semantically to create a knowledge graph.

Graph transformers are an NLP tool that can analyze knowledge graphs to perform tasks like accuracy checking (Shiraly 2021). Dependencies between sentences far apart on the knowledge graph can be encoded using graph transformer networks. Your software can provide instantaneous feedback to students when they make logical errors or failure to understand the assertions made in another paper properly.

NLP Benefits Language Learning NLP's third most common application is in the increasingly mainstream language learning activity.

Learning a new language begins with the fundamentals: reading, writing, and speaking the words of a second language by making connections between them and words you already know or images of the things you are familiar with. Learning the intricacies of a language's grammar and syntax requires extensive study of the language's written and spoken forms, literature, and culture.

Using natural language processing's (NLP) built-in language translation skills and making them more engaging through gaming, you may serve students and educators in various contexts worldwide with little more work. If your concept results in educational resources, the audience you will focus on is likely ESL students. In many instances, it is likely to be translated by hand into other languages. Though it may be unrealistic to translate your product into hundreds of languages, limiting your market to just one region could mean missing out on lucrative chances.

Some of the steps used in more advanced language learning can be simulated using NLP techniques (Shiraly 2021):

- Using natural language processing (NLP) and object detection, a smartphone camera stream can produce scene descriptions in a second language.
- Using conversational, natural language processing, speech recognition, and text-to-speech synthesis can facilitate communication with native speakers of different languages, allowing for the mutual acquisition of both.
- A student may read books published in a foreign language using natural language processing and optical character recognition. As the content is read, E-learning tools can show contextual information like part of speech, meaning, and synonyms.

How Does It Work? Given a sentence in the source language, a machine translation system generates an equivalent sentence in the target language using a sequence-to-sequence model.

If you feed a sentence into a model for a specific language, you will return some internal representation, called an embedding, for that language. However, the syntax and semantics of each language need to be recorded first. To accomplish this, we again turn to pre-trained language models like BERT and T5.

We can use these two linguistic models to train a sequence-to-sequence model on a translation dataset like Wikipedia. Native speakers of several languages produce identical pages on Wikipedia. They may not be direct translations of one another from dictionary to dictionary, but they share the same meaning. The sequence-to-sequence model is trained to connect one language's embeddings to another. The embeddings are infused with semantics. A complete sentence in the target language is produced as a result.

This strategy can help you reach a broader audience in more places with little more work.

3.4 Use Cases and Examples/Applications of NLP in Education

Natural language processing (NLP) is widely regarded as a game-changer that will impact education shortly. Solid evidence supports using natural language processing in the classroom (Rundell 2021). Students' reading and writing skills have significantly benefited from this technology, which is widely used successfully.

The advantages of NLP are beginning to shine, whether in the form of parsing and summarizing arguments inside writing, encouraging essay revisions, or simply refining a writer's prose. However, one fundamental question remains on the lips of many businesses, developers, and service managers.

Questions like "Who can gain the most from this technology?" and "What applications can make the most use of this technology?" are subsets of this central question. What other ways may this technology be put to use in the classroom? Please tell us the answer.

Using NLP or Writing Regarding helping children with their reading and writing, NLP is currently employed on the front lines of education (Rundell 2021). These are the most typical use cases for creating and analyzing NLP applications. Let us imagine a student handing in a five-paragraph essay for evaluation; the NLP language learning system can offer suggestions for improving it. This guidance is for more formal writing, including language, grammar, and format. Grammarly, a software that ensures error-free and well-organized writing, is an excellent application of NLP in the classroom. By employing the technology, the program analyzes the text and offers advice on how to enhance it.

In addition, natural language processing (NLP) can provide granular comments, such as pointing out where there is an absence of supporting evidence for a claim or statement in the text.

To make the most of the synergy between NLP and education, teachers must take advantage of the technology to get insight into their student's progress and development rather than simply using it to help students turn in higher-quality work.

More natural language processing (NLP) solutions will be required as technology develops to aid students and educators in defining the cognitive process of students' writing. This will lead to suggestions on enhancing fundamental aspects of students' writing, such as mechanics and structure.

Using NLP and Education for Improved Reading Some uses of natural language processing (NLP) in education can aid students with trouble with reading comprehension in the classroom (Rundell 2021). Since a single instructor cannot provide individual attention to each student in a classroom setting, natural language processing (NLP) tools are in high demand. The algorithms used in natural language processing can rapidly detect weaknesses in a student's reading comprehension and offer immediate, personalized guidance on how to fix them.

Using natural language processing (NLP) in the classroom also has the beautiful effect of enabling students to be paired with books that are both demanding and conducive to optimal learning. Once again, educators lack time to research this area, so natural language processing technologies that can accomplish this are so welcome.

It has also been demonstrated that natural language processing technology can more accurately grade students' reading scores than conventional methods like the Flesch-Kincaid Grade Level test. This is another reason API-based solutions are gaining traction and being adopted by many enterprises.

Using NLP for Motivating Behavior One of a teacher's most challenging tasks is undoubtedly inspiring their students to put in the effort and grow as learners. It only takes one bored student to throw the entire class off track. We must do everything possible to keep our students interested and enthusiastic about learning.

For this reason, NLP has recently emerged as a promising tool in the classroom.

NLP machine learning technology can analyze classroom discourse to determine how individuals feel at different points in the lesson (Rundell 2021). Teachers can use this analysis to see how their students respond to the instruction techniques and what can be done to make the lessons more interesting.

Teachers can use NLP to identify students having trouble following along in class and suggest how to help them. This has created a need for natural language processing (NLP) monitoring tools to track and analyze students' attention and conduct in real time during class.

Natural language processing examples for education will need to be set up and evaluated to discover how effective this can be; however, stealth testing may be necessary for the most accurate results. Natural language processing (NLP) experts are probably looking into this. In the event of implementation, rules may need to be considered before these services can be offered for profit.

Nonetheless, when all of these factors are considered together, it is easy to see the many beautiful opportunities that NLP technology, and artificial intelligence in education in general, can bring into the world of education, whether it be in the form of active feedback to students and teachers on the quality of the work being produced or in the form of looking into more complex things like the behavior of students, their level of engagement within the classroom learning environment and setting, and their overall academic performance.

Opportunities for businesses to develop natural language software and solutions are opening up in these spaces. Once the benefits have been demonstrated (something happening more frequently and is being worked on constantly), this will be a thriving industry and line of technology.

Question Answering Essay tests, quizzes, and flashcards are popular with students and educators alike, but their manual preparation can burden those with packed schedules (Rundell 2021). In order to help you out, NLP may generate questions and answers for your course materials. It saves teachers much time because it can evaluate an essay's syntax, structure, semantics, and reasoning. The accuracy with which a student's written comments match the facts presented in the course material can also be assessed in this manner. For example, a student's reading level and learning pace could be used to modify the questions and the assessment.

In the same manner that a summarization model is created by adding a sequence-to-sequence layer to a pre-trained transformer model, a question-answering model is created. In response to a given sequence (the query), it should generate still another sequence (the answer). Subject-specific question-answer datasets fine-tune the pre-trained base model and sequence-to-sequence layer assembly.

Chatbots Conversational artificial intelligence (AI) chatbots are another perk (Rundell 2021) because they can function as robotic teachers. The construction of a sequence-to-sequence model for voice recognition is analogous to that of a question-answering model. The process starts with a literal transcription of the student's spoken input.

Next, a question-answering model will produce answers or grade the student's work. The student is then given a spoken report using text-to-speech synthesis. To put the learner at ease, the synthesized voice can be programmed with affable qualities like excitement, kindness, warmth, friendliness, and accent.

3.5 Conclusion

Natural language processing (NLP) can be a powerful tool for enhancing the classroom experience when applied correctly. When NLP is used in classrooms, it kick-starts learning through natural acquisition. The foundation of this system is proven methods that have been used successfully to address a wide range of educational challenges. Regarding the broader societal and cultural issues affecting language acquisition, natural language processing is a go-to solution provider. This method can benefit teachers, students, authors, and academics because it facilitates research, analysis, and evaluation. In addition to its many applications in research, science, linguistics, e-learning, and assessment systems, natural language processing has also shown promising results in more traditional educational institutions like K-12 and higher-ed institutions.

References

IBM. (2022). *What is natural language processing (NLP)?* IBM. https://www.ibm.com/topics/natural-language-processing#:~:text=Natural language processing (NLP) refers,same way human beings can.

Patel, N. (2021). *Using Natural Language Processing for Educational Activities*. LinkedIn. https://www.linkedin.com/pulse/using-natural-language-processing-educational-activities-nirmal-patel/

Rundell, K. (2021). *NLP in Education: Use Cases and Examples*. InData Labs. https://indatalabs.com/blog/nlp-in-education

Shiraly, K. (2021). *Top 3 Benefits and Uses of NLP in Education*. WIDTH.AI. https://www.width.ai/post/nlp-in-education

Chapter 4
Predictive Analytics in Education

4.1 What Is Predictive Analytics?

By examining trends in past data, predictive analytics can estimate the likelihood of upcoming events (Judge 2021). Figure 4.1 represents a conceptual view. Although the data might look complex, the method itself is easy.

Organizations and institutions use predictive analytics to find trends in historical data and make informed decisions about the future (Judge 2021). Through this method, we can establish reliable standards for our data and develop models to foresee better and comprehend any dangers. Businesses can foresee the effects of a decision by understanding the connection between datasets and results.

4.2 Examples of Predictive Analytics

As with many other forms of cutting-edge technology, predictive analytics is often seen as futuristic. Actually, no. It has a long history of use across various organizations (Judge 2021). Data collection is used in most businesses for product logistics, financial transactions, or academic success. Companies can anticipate the behavior of comparable customers by identifying trends in existing data.

It can be used in healthcare to predict whether a patient will show up for an appointment or in the insurance industry to aid in detecting and preventing fraudulent claims. Another sector that may benefit from such a system is the banking sector, where it would be helpful to determine whether a loan applicant is likely to repay the loan based on specific qualities that the system will request at application time. It uses "big data," or large and complicated datasets that might be difficult to manage and manipulate by hand. That is why companies employ BI tools to make predictive analytics more accessible. By providing a visual representation of the

© The Author(s), under exclusive license to Springer Nature
Switzerland AG 2023
M. Kurni et al., *A Beginner's Guide to Introduce Artificial Intelligence in Teaching and Learning*, https://doi.org/10.1007/978-3-031-32653-0_4

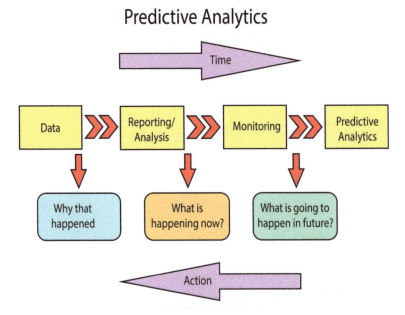

Fig. 4.1 A conceptual view of predictive analytics

data, these technologies make it easier for institutions to share and analyze their data (Judge 2021). Because the technology eliminates the need to manually construct technical scripts and algorithms, decision-makers now have easier access to this information and can make more educated decisions.

4.3 The Evolution of Predictive Analytics in Education

The fields of digital technology, marketing, finance, and healthcare are generally the first that come to mind when discussing big data analytics. Institutions increasingly turn to predictive analytics to promote systemic improvements in the education sector by drawing on historical student data to understand better how their students will perform in the future (Judge 2021).

The education industry has always placed a premium on accurately forecasting student outcomes, and as a result, K-12 institutions, colleges, and universities have traditionally relied on data connected to exam scores and attendance records. Previously, records were compiled and examined manually, necessitating human involvement in the event of a discrepancy. That means the information was probably kept in silos inside individual divisions, and responses might have lagged.

Today, there is an exponentially more significant amount of data collected in the classroom than ever, thanks to the widespread adoption of digital learning and educational technologies. This information has grown increasingly intricate as our institutions and technologies have advanced. The vast amounts of data available today allow for extracting a wealth of relevant information, opening up new avenues for boosting student outcomes and informing prudent business decisions.

Students can interact with data on campus and through various online platforms. In addition to traditional academic information, schools will keep track of students using digital learning tools, library resources, and extracurricular activities in their student information systems. This "big data" can be used by predictive analytics to reveal patterns and examine the whole picture of an organization's success (Judge 2021).

4.4 Reasons for Using Predictive Analytics in Higher Education

The higher education sector uses predictive analytics to address many of the same commercial and operational difficulties other social service industries face. Universities are using this tool for three primary reasons (Ekowo and Palmer 2016):

- In order to pick out the students who would benefit most from counseling.
- Creating personalized adaptive learning content.
- Enrolment management.

Predictive analytics has enabled universities to identify potential donors among their alums. As a result, many businesses have teamed up with USA Funds, a non-profit that used to insure federal student loans against default, to use analytics to anticipate which students are most likely to stop making their loan payments (Ekowo and Palmer 2016). There is a wide variety of alternative applications for these tools.

Targeted Student Advising Universities sometimes fail to provide their undergraduates with enough access to counselors. The "median caseload of advisees per full-time professional academic adviser nationwide was 296:1," a recent National Academic Advising Association (NACADA) survey stated. However, at community colleges, that ratio skyrockets to 441:1 (Ekowo and Palmer 2016). Because of this, it is difficult, if not impossible, for most universities to provide each student with the individualized attention they require and merit. Early-alert systems help find students at risk of academic trouble, and program recommender systems help students choose courses or programs. The institution can meet a student's essential needs when early-alert and program recommender systems are in place.

Adaptive Learning Using data mining and other forms of predictive analytics, universities can create adaptive learning courseware that adjusts a student's path through a course based on their use of the technology. These systems use student information to judge course material, assessment methods, and how these elements should be presented to students.

Teachers can better address students' individual learning needs and provide instruction that works best for them with predictive analytics implemented into adaptive learning platforms. This resource can help students learn faster by skimming over material they already know and diving deeper into concepts they struggle with.

Enrollment Management Predictive analytics has been a staple of university enrollment management strategies for quite some time. Universities use predictive analytics for more than just assisting students on campus. The data estimates the size of incoming and returning student populations. Moreover, they utilize it to focus their advertising and recruitment efforts on the students most likely to apply, enroll, and thrive at the school. Predictive analytics has also helped universities calculate the likelihood that an admitted or returning student will accept a financial aid package (Worcester Business Journal 2011).

The expense of recruiting might be high. There was a median expenditure of $2433 per incoming freshman at private four-year institutions, according to a survey done by enrollment management firm Noel Levitz in 2013. Public four-year universities pay $457 for each new student, while public two-year universities spend only $123 (Ekowo and Palmer 2016). Due to the high stakes, institutions try to maximize their strategic spending. Using predictive analytics, college admissions teams can provide an individual likelihood score to each prospective student, often on a scale from 0 to 10, that accounts for the possibility that they will apply, get admitted, and ultimately enroll. Colleges use factors including racial/ethnic background, where they live, where they went to high school, what they want to study in college, and how interested they are in taking a campus tour or receiving marketing materials to determine these grades. These ratings allow admissions officers to focus on the most qualified applicants aggressively.

Other Reasons for Using Predictive Analytics Colleges utilize predictive analytics for a variety of reasons, including improving student engagement and making better use of limited financial resources. Among these are (Ekowo and Palmer 2016):

- Rather than focusing on enrollment numbers, state financing is now connected to how well an institution educates its students. The National Conference of State Legislatures, a nonprofit that provides resources to state legislatures, reports that 32 states financially reward universities for increasing the percentage of their students who complete their programs within the required time frame. These incentives are designed to encourage schools to invest more time and resources toward the academic success of all their students. This is especially true for students from underrepresented groups and those from low-income families.
- Retaining as many students as possible to reduce tuition and fee revenue loss. If a college can keep a student enrolled there instead of having to find and enroll a new one, they will save money. If students stop enrolling, schools lose hundreds of thousands of dollars in revenue each year.
- The culture of institutions is changing. Higher education institutions increasingly use data to reflect on the past and inform the present. An organization's

commitment to a data-informed culture can be bolstered by using predictive analytics.

4.5 Predictive Analytics Significance in Education

Data is attractive since it is continually developing in exciting ways. By acquiring these insights through data modeling, schools, universities, and training providers can foresee potential future challenges and proactively deal with them to better the student experience while focusing on the bottom line (Judge 2021). The complexity of analysis, though, grows in proportion to the number of datasets. Core analytics models for understanding outcomes will automatically adapt and update based on any new data received by the institution once it has designed and built them.

For instance, a school that has already built a predictive analytics model to determine whether a student would pass or fail a course can add a new applicant's information to the model to determine the likelihood of success or failure.

To increase productivity across an organization, predictive analytics is crucial. Predictive analytics can boost student enrollment, productivity, and presence even in the face of resource constraints (Judge 2021). Predictive models can be fed data from several departments, providing a complete picture of the institution's context for the student.

4.6 How Is Predictive Analytics Changing Education?

Thanks to technological advancements, more data is being collected than ever in the current education industry. As a result, predictive analytics facilitates the organization and interpretation of these massive datasets and encourages a more evidence-based methodology in academic settings (Fisher and Mulroy 2021).

The educational system has long relied on and shown an interest in quantitative assessment. However, there is a danger that reports and insights will become compartmentalized, only capturing a subset of the entire student experience. The trend toward data centralization, which will benefit all decision-makers by making more information easily accessible, relies heavily on predictive analytics.

Schools can better meet their needs by identifying students' specific areas of struggle. Institutions can utilize predictive analytics to learn about the specific needs of each student through adaptive learning. Predictive analytics helps students' emotional health and well-being by providing a structure for early intervention. It can address education gaps by highlighting systemic concerns with the quality of modules or programs (Fisher and Mulroy 2021).

Various organizations use predictive analytics to direct and inform the development of their overall operations. Predictive analytics aid in the mapping and planning of further higher education's period of significant change.

4.7 How Does Predictive Analytics Help Higher Education?

Educational institutions are under growing pressure to retain and develop students as the emphasis shifts from maximizing semester enrolment numbers to boosting the rate of successful student graduations. State officials are driving this shift in strategy in response to rising expectations from students and their families, investing time and money into a higher education that may or may not pay off. Thus, students can utilize predictive analytics to gain insight into their academic achievement and take preventative measures in response to their development (McGavisk 2022).

4.8 Predictive Analytics Uses in Education

The following are the three vital uses of predictive analytics in education (McGavisk 2022):

- *Informed Student Advising:* Students who fall below the expected attendance rate can be flagged as early as the first semester using Early Alert Systems (also known as Flags), giving advisors and pastoral support teams ample opportunity to reach out offer assistance.
- *Accurate Enrolment Management:* Institutions and their departments can better accommodate returning students and revamp underperforming courses with the help of predictive analytics, which can determine which students are most likely to graduate based on their academic performance.
- *Adaptive Learning:* Educators can also benefit from predictive analytics. Lecturers and teachers with access to students' academic records can use this information to better tailor their lessons to each student's needs and learning styles. Teachers can take prompt action based on frequent feedback, leading to more engaging and purposeful learning experiences.

4.9 How to Use Predictive Analytics in Education

The provost and the chief academic officer are challenging to hold at any university. The extensive responsibilities of a provost, and the skill with which they must carry them out, may vary slightly from one institution to the next, but the job's difficulty remains constant. A provost's primary duty is to make educated choices about teaching and research at the university. To be more specific about their responsibilities, provosts are accountable for (Moraes 2018):

- Keeping them from dropping out.
- Maintaining a healthy growth in revenue.

- Participating in and coordinating meetings.
- Making preparations for the hiring of excellent faculty.
- Creating educational materials and instructional plans.

There is a delicate balance to be struck between the university's bottom line and the happiness and success of its students, and here is where most provosts run into their most considerable difficulties.

A recent study found that only approximately 50% of students who enroll in college end up graduating (Moraes 2018). Bill Gates, a multibillionaire in the IT industry, has voiced his concern over this matter. For example, Gates wrote on his blog,

"Based on the latest college completion trends, only about half of all those students (54.8 percent) will leave college with a diploma. Most low-income, first-generation, and minority students—will not finish a degree. They will drop out" (Moraes 2018).

This is a significant issue that provosts need to think about. New technology, however, has given provosts the tools they need to handle the situation. How? Utilizing predictive analytics in the classroom allows provosts to identify at-risk students accurately.

The procedure (Moraes 2018) is as follows:

Step 1: Establish the Requirement for a Predictive Analytics Model in Your Organization Refrain from doing what everyone else is doing. Instead, it is essential to have a firm grasp on the necessity of a predictive analytics model for your organization. Think critically about the problem of student attrition and any other problems of a similar nature by holding a brainstorming session with the university's key players. When all parties participating in the academic and administrative project have settled on objectives, it is time to begin formulating a plan to see that they are met. Constructing a predictive model may not be necessary to realize these goals; perhaps other approaches may be used instead. If not, plan how to construct a model using predictive analytics to get the desired results.

Step 2: Create a System that Can Adapt to Technological Changes To create a predictive analytics model in education, adjustments must be made to how things are done. As a result, provosts must ensure that everyone involved is prepared for the upcoming shifts. Stakeholders, including teachers, curriculum developers, and the dean, should familiarize themselves with predictive analytics models and be ready to incorporate them into their practices.

Step 3: Collect Reliable and Objective Information for Educational Predictive Analytics The first significant step in developing the inputs for the predictive model can begin if everyone provides the go-ahead. Students generate and leave a digital footprint as they go about their daily routines on campus. Information such as tuition, fees for extracurricular activities, food costs, grades, attendance records, motivation levels, and career aspirations is helpful. However, collecting data on the existing pupils for the model to make accurate predictions will not be sufficient. All information that can aid in the early detection of at-risk students must be gathered to ensure accuracy. You need to collect dropout and graduation rates from the past in addition to current student data to create a reliable predictive analytics model for student retention. Avoid gathering unrepresentative data, which might lead to problematic classifications when fed into the model.

Step 4: Make Sure that Everyone Involved Understands Predictive Models Thoroughly Teachers or curriculum professionals who thoroughly understand how to use predictive analytics in education technologies should only use them effectively. That is why provosts need to plan and set up training sessions on using a predictive analytics program. Once data has been collected, it must be uploaded to an analytics platform.

Step 5: Inspect the Model's Development in a Series of Iterations Information is continually being created at an exponential rate. Therefore, a new result (with improved accuracy) is generated when this information is fed into the model. As a result, the predictive model may be updated with new information about a student as it becomes available, resulting in a more accurate and nuanced forecast of that student's future performance.

Step 6: Get Your Vendors from Reputable Sources It is challenging to develop a framework for predictive analytics in education and integrate it into the established systems of a university. Provosts are responsible for more than hiring technical specialists; they must also secure funding, construct necessary facilities, and instill the proper mindset in their staff. Moreover, thus, what are some potential solutions? It is safe to assume that many IoT and big data service providers will offer reliable products and support. Vendors are a reliable resource that universities can rely on to get things done.

4.10 Predictive Analytics in Higher Education: Guiding Practices for Ethical Use

Predictive analytics can be instrumental, but only if used ethically by institutions. Data collected from students could be used to hinder their education if proper procedures are not followed. Colleges will continue to use student and institutional data in novel ways, necessitating a periodic reevaluation of whether their ethical standards address current data practices and the corresponding need to examine the ethical use of data anew.

The ethical use of data is nuanced, and there is no simple solution. It does not solve every problem arising from institutional data usage and probable exploitation. This ethical framework is hoped to serve as a discussion starter for students.

The following are the five guiding practices (see Fig. 4.2) for the ethical use of predictive analytics in education (Ekowo and Palmer 2017).

4.10 Predictive Analytics in Higher Education: Guiding Practices for Ethical Use

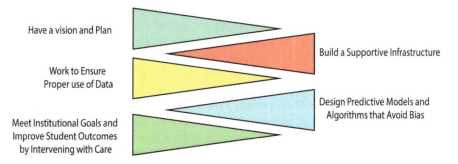

Fig. 4.2 Predictive analytics in higher education: guiding practices for ethical use

Guiding Practice 1: Have a Vision and Plan Establishing a strategic goal and plan for data application might assist in pointing the way for a predictive analytics project. Without proper planning, predictive analytics could be employed in a way that is counterproductive to student achievement, excludes essential members of the staff who should be included, and/or fails to define how success will be determined.

Here are some suggestions for developing a vision and plan:

Convene Key Staff to Make Crucial Decisions It is essential to involve and gain the support of key personnel and stakeholders as you formulate your plan. By involving them early on, you can ensure that predictive analytics is being used in a way that does not cause harm to the people whose information is being studied.

When formulating the plan, keep in mind the following three factors:

1. *The purposes of predictive analytics:* Both the questions you seek to answer and the outcomes you desire should be outlined in the plan. The group needs to make sure the information is not used for any bias. The paper must also consider the possible drawbacks of utilizing student and institutional data.
2. *The unintended repercussions of predictive analytics:* Your institution and its partners (including third-party vendors) should identify potential unintended outcomes and strategies for mitigating them in the strategy.
3. *The outcomes to measure:* Measurable goals for using predictive analytics should be outlined in the plan.

Guiding Practice 2: Build a Supportive Infrastructure By having protocols and other supports in place to aid the data endeavor and ensuring campus stakeholders are aware of and receptive to the benefits of predictive analytics, a campus may create a supportive infrastructure for the analytics to thrive.

Communicate the Usefulness of Predictive Analytics and Foster an Environment Where Its Use Is Encouraged Using information from students and schools, predictive analytics can prompt urgent action. The stakes of ensuring students graduate on time may be too high for many educational institutions to have expertise using data in this way, at this speed. Well-thought-out plans may not get the necessary backing if the benefits of using predictive analytics to improve campus life are not communicated. It would be best if you took the initiative to inform your campus's administration, faculty, and students why predictive analytics is so crucial to the future of your school and your education. The VP of PR and marketing could be of use here.

Create Effective Change Management Processes Changes to workflows, reporting mechanisms, personnel, and collaboration partners, all of whom bring unique expertise, are common when introducing new technologies. When decision-makers gather to discuss data use, they may also ensure that the necessary infrastructure is in place to accommodate the ongoing transformation on campus. For those in charge of implementing predictive analytics on campus, this can lead to pandemonium or, at best, bewilderment.

Assess Institutional Capacity Evaluate how well predictive analytics can be implemented at your institution. Institution-wide data cleaning, sharing, and decision-making rely on the interoperability of many data systems; keeping this infrastructure in good working order is essential. It is crucial to have access to high-quality data and the necessary hardware, software, personnel, resources, and knowledge of how to analyze that data. The project's success could be increased by adding staff members who are experts in information technology, student data legislation, and contract drafting with vendors.

Guiding Practice 3: Work to Ensure Proper Use of Data Supporting enrollment efforts or assisting students in making academic progress requires data to develop predictive models (demonstrating how different data points are related) and algorithms. Moral development and use of these technologies require considering data quality, data interpretation, privacy concerns, and security vulnerabilities.

Ensure the Information Is Comprehensive and Accurate Enough to Respond to Specific Inquiries Having complete and accurate information about students and how the school operates is essential. Evaluating students thoroughly also entails taking into account any and all pertinent information about them.

Quality data is precise, exhaustive, and up-to-date, acquired from reliable sources through clearly established procedures, and easily understood by a broad audience.

Ensure Data Are Accurately Interpreted Data analysts need to keep the context in mind. Ensure that you have personnel familiar with your organization's data and can correctly understand the prediction models based on this data. It is crucial to educate teachers on how to use dashboards that show how students utilizing adaptive technologies are doing in their classes. Finally, even though they may be included in datasets used for predictive analytics, look for measures to preserve data integrity for reporting reasons. Imagine that analysts at a large institution have been tasked with gathering data for use in reports and conducting analyses for predictive analytics initiatives. If the information is being put to creative use on campus, then there is no reason to doubt its veracity for reporting purposes. Your institution must maintain compliance with federal funding requirements, and predictive analytics should not compromise the quality of the data it reports.

Guarantee Data Privacy Students, employees, and others whose data are gathered should be informed of their rights, including how their data may be used for predictive analytics and how long it will be held. Inform employees and students that their data will be used for predictive analytics and obtain their permission to utilize sensitive data like health records.

Take precautions to ensure your data is secure, as this will prevent it from falling into the wrong hands. It is also crucial to safeguard the personal information of students who are particularly at risk, such as those who are underage and engaged in college-level coursework while still in high school, undocumented, and disabled.

Furthermore, ensure that all policies regarding who owns what and who can access student and school data are communicated clearly.

Monitor Data Security Unexpected security incidents often occur. Security becomes more of an issue as institutions gather and store more data on students and staff and as more gadgets that keep data on the teaching and learning process are utilized in classrooms. This highlights the importance of thorough monitoring of data privacy and security by educational institutions. Threats and dangers need to be tracked frequently. You and your vendors must implement security processes that comply with student privacy regulations and industry best practices to keep sensitive data safe.

Get the IT department involved in data security at your organization. Officers tasked with data security and privacy are invaluable to any organization. One of the most important things you can do to protect your data is to provide your IT and other employees with regular training on data security.

Guiding Practice 4: Design Predictive Analytics Models and Algorithms that Avoid Bias Predictive models and algorithms can aid in deciding how much effort should be put into student support and recruitment. Therefore, it is essential that predictive models and algorithms are developed to minimize bias instead of amplifying it and that these models and algorithms are rigorously evaluated for efficacy. When developing models and algorithms, ensure that you work with suppliers willing to guarantee that they will not be designed to codify prejudice inadvertently and that their efficacy can be verified through testing.

Create Predictive Models and Algorithms that Reliably Deliver the Outcomes you Need No classification of people should ever be the goal of an algorithm. The use of algorithms that create discriminatory results should be prohibited, and it is vital to eliminate bias in predictive models and assure the statistical significance of forecasts beyond race, ethnicity, and socioeconomic position.

Therefore, it is necessary to build or understand the process by which predictive models and algorithms are developed in order to guarantee the success of their vision and goal. If this precaution is not taken, unfair treatment may result.

Predictive Models Must Be Put to the Test and Made Transparent Before using predictive models in algorithm development, it is essential to evaluate their correctness, possibly with the help of an outside party. The predictive models should incorporate new realities and aims for the campus. You should try to ensure algorithms can be understood by those they will affect, and you may wish to restrict the variables used in predictive models to those that can be described. Such actions promote openness and simplify identifying and punishing those responsible for discriminatory consequences resulting from poorly conceived models or algorithms.

Choose Vendors Wisely If a university needs assistance developing models or predictive tools, it typically contracts with a third party. It would help if you were directly involved in or informed about constructing prediction models and algorithms to guarantee their soundness, transparency, and lack of bias. This may be more challenging if you opt to work with third-party vendors.

Some vendors make their models and algorithms transparent, giving universities more agency in the design process or letting them seize the reins entirely. However, not all sellers act in this way. Because of this tendency to treat models and algorithms as intellectual property, many institutions are either not participating in the design process or are actively excluded from it. The level of openness between you and the vendor should be high on your list of priorities.

Guiding Practice 5: Meet Institutional Goals and Improve Student Outcomes by Intervening with Care Predictive analytics' actual test is how your organization uses the information it gathers. Even if they do not see or understand how the algorithm-based judgments are produced, they will experience these actions or interventions firsthand. Even with modern aids, human beings are still necessary for most involvement. Therefore, it is essential to consider interventions in the context of other supports provided at your institution and spread information about them thoughtfully. It is essential to verify the efficacy of treatments after implementation and provide proper training to staff members who will implement them.

Inform Teachers and Students About the Change in Intervention Practices An institution's culture may shift if data-informed interventions become increasingly central after adding predictive analytics to the toolkit for student achievement. Faculty, staff, and students must be aware of the positive outcomes that can be achieved through implementing interventions that are informed by predictive analytics to achieve widespread buy-in for this shift.

Incorporate Predictive-Driven Interventions into Existing Programs Aimed at Improving Student Performance Predictive analytics is a valuable tool, but it is only one component of a more extensive set of resources, including first-year orientation programs, that can guarantee students' and institutions' success. All your efforts to improve student achievement should be interconnected and build upon one another, so keep an eye out for ways to use predictive analytics to advance other initiatives.

Predictive-Driven Interventions Might Cause Harm If Not Handled with Caution There will always be room for error in decision-making, no matter how detailed an institution's data, models, algorithms, processes, and training are. For this reason, it is essential to fine-tune any treatments you take in response to predictive analytics to ensure no students are harmed. In response to student data and predictive models, educators may increase outreach to a specific student based on his predicted likelihood of enrolling, mandate a meeting with an adviser at the suggestion of an early-alert system, or modify the practice problems assigned to a student using adaptive technology.

Colleges must know the potential downsides of using algorithms for strategic enrollment management, early alerts, recommender systems, and adaptive technology. However, one must carefully consider the risks involved before employing such methods. Protecting students from damage might be accomplished by shifting our perspective from illness and lack to wellness and asset. In this model, each and every student is seen as having limitless potential. Furthermore, it allows for the possibility that a student's dropout risk may be affected by factors unique to the institution. Finally, it will be smart to determine how people will be punished for inappropriately utilizing or manipulating student and institutional data and how to restore trust after a damaging incident.

Here are some cautious applications of predictive tools:

- Early-alert systems.
- Recommender systems.
- Adaptive technologies.
- Enrollment management.

When Implementing Interventions, Make Sure to Keep Everyone Informed Communicate effectively and make the intended audience can reach sure of interventions. It is essential that the words you deliver do not discourage students and that the tactics you use to get the word out about interventions reach as many students as possible.

Educate Employees on Implicit Bias and the Limits of Data Confront implicit bias and learn to recognize the limitations of data. Intervention strategies for at-risk students may be hampered by staff members' implicit biases or a lack of complete data. They inadvertently hurt the pupils they are trying to help because of their prejudices or an unhealthy obsession with school data. Staff members who have received adequate training should gladly accept their responsibility to use student and institutional data to benefit their pupils.

Instruct Students on How to Make Effective Use of Their Data An example would be students using the data they produce in adaptive learning tools to figure out what works best for them as far as studying goes. Staff members may also seek to instruct pupils on properly using data to shape their time at school.

Evaluate and Test Interventions A successful intervention should not be declared before it has been tried and proven to work.

- *Which interventions are most effective, when, and why?* It would help if you evaluated how well your interventions are working. This evaluation can reveal whether or not these interventions have different effects on different groups, allowing for re-tuning. The research into the therapies' efficacy may also shed light on unforeseen outcomes.
- *Verify the claims made by tool vendors before making a long-term investment:* One of the biggest questions surrounding adaptive technology is whether or not the techniques are helpful. There must be a steady stream of new tools and validated claims in technology-enabled student learning. There is minimal third-party confirmation for many companies' claims that their solutions are adaptive and would boost student achievement. Demand that providers team up with objective academics to verify the efficacy of their products and services.

4.11 How to Implement Predictive Analytics for Education: Best Practices

Predictive analytics in classroom implementation is complex. However, there is a standard rule of thumb (Kyianovska 2022) you can follow to ensure success:

- Determine the metrics that data analytics should concentrate on after you have identified the bottlenecks in your operations.
- Identify relevant data sources.
- Methods for boosting students' grades should be digitized.
- Applying statistical methods to find some insights.
- Set up an automated system for gathering and analyzing data; create a system for getting notifications including the findings of this analysis; and establish rules for following up on these alerts.

Developing and implementing this new product into your business has potential pitfalls. The following best practices (Kyianovska 2022) can assist you in meeting these difficulties head-on.

Give Students Access to Their Data There may be privacy issues with implementing predictive analytics in the educational sector. That is why data collection needs to be as open as possible. Students should have the option to participate or not. Get their permission by explaining the value of opting in and being transparent about how you use their data.

Keep in mind that you do not need to provide any identifying information. Some universities collect information on entire classes to understand student behavior better.

Make Sure Your Data Is Safe A school must ensure the security of its students' data if it gathers it in massive databases. If not, the information could be vulnerable to hacker assault. Predictive analytics can be used to enhance the educational experience of students and can also be used to strengthen cybersecurity.

More than that, schools should have rigorous guidelines for managing student data. Some employees may care only about attendance records in the workplace, while others would need detailed information on how often the library is used. Only a select few faculty members need access to all student information.

Search for Implicit Biases in the Algorithms One common expectation placed on algorithms is that they will render fair assessments. However, their biases may be introduced by the people who made them. In order to achieve this, they can use biased information to teach the model. Therefore, the effect of a structural bias can be amplified by an algorithm.

It has been argued that the prediction model can become skewed if indicators such as secondary school, race, and zip code are included. For example, in the case of Georgia State University, these considerations are omitted on purpose.

4.12 Advantages of Predictive Analytics in Education

Predictive analytics has great potential to improve the educational experience for everyone involved, including students, parents, and teachers (Saranya 2020).

- Predictive models can help teachers anticipate academic difficulties and intervene with interventions like tutoring or supplementary classes for students who are at risk of falling behind.
- When applied to areas of the institution where problems have been identified, predictive analytics can aid administrators and educators in making positive changes, such as:
  - Identification of factors that lead prospective students to decide against enrolling.
  - Predicting which departments have the highest attrition rates and using that data to inform efforts for keeping enrollment consistent.
  - Keeping the school in a solid academic and financial position requires constant analysis of student feedback to determine what is working and what needs to be changed.

- Students' participation in sports and other forms of physical activity can be predicted and improved with predictive analytics. The same is true of schoolwork and extracurriculars.
- Predictive analytics can be used to spot patterns that improve accessibility and adaptability in the classroom, such as the increased popularity of weekend online classes and last-minute cram sessions before exams. Once a new teaching method is implemented, its effectiveness can be evaluated and tweaked to benefit all students.

4.13 Examples of Predictive Analytics in Education

If you are on the fence about whether or not the implementation of predictive analytics into the educational system is worthwhile, consider the following (Kyson 2021):

- *Causes of absenteeism can be identified:* It is well known that a student's level of attendance has a significant impact on both their salary and return on investment. The higher the number of students absent from class, the more critical it is for schools to investigate why this is happening, such as the student's health or financial situation, to accommodate these students better.
- *Promotes in-depth, individualized focus:* Every learner has a different learning pace and/or ability to grasp new material. You cannot judge their comprehension of your lesson from the looks on their faces. Neither hunches nor gut feelings have led them anywhere. You can figure out which youngsters require extra help by using predictive models. Foreseeing and preparing future issues through specific data metrics is now possible by deploying such measures and scheduling tailored seminars.
- *Helps reduce college dropouts:* US dropout rates for 16–24-year-olds are at a record high of 5.4%. The working class bears unemployment's social and financial weight, diminishing student return on investment. Should any division in a university see a spike in the dropout rate, predictive analytics can be a valuable tool. The data from these forecasts can be used to increase enrolment in that area year after year.
- *Competes effectively in retaining students:* Due to the high level of competition, universities and colleges are under significant strain to maintain and grow their student body and faculty. Instead of focusing on increasing semester enrollment, institutions should work to increase graduation rates, boost the quality of their studies, and make students more aware of their academic progress. By encouraging a proactive response from the student, predictive analytics aids retention and development.
- *Analyses of feedback from students and teachers:* The main issue with written or vocal comments is that they can easily get lost in the shuffle. Here is where the institution's operations may be fine-tuned with the help of technology, which can collect feedback from across the web and compile it into usable, well-structured

data. Finally, schools can modernize their academic and financial offerings to fill gaps and better serve their students and employees.
- *Encourages adaptive learning:* Adaptability in the classroom is crucial in today's ever-changing world. With everything documented, educators may spot areas for improvement in their lessons and adjust their delivery to reach their students better. Similarly, predictive analytics in education can use information about students' knowledge gaps to encourage institutions to develop more cutting-edge educational practices and create individualized curricula for each student. Therefore, in the end, adaptive learning provides a more fulfilling and well-rounded college experience.
- *Encourages participation in physical activities:* Many schools have a terrible reputation for misplacing students based on their athletic records and failing to recognize students' prior achievements. On the other hand, this technology uses past data to encourage students to continue their education and choose a career path. Predictive models and algorithms can be reused in the classroom and the real world.
- *Identifies emerging educational trends:* Like any other organizational practice, educational practices need metrics to measure their instruction's efficacy and impact on students' learning. Institutions must determine what is beneficial and what is not for their students. However, without concrete data, many organizations struggle to assess the efficacy of their systems. Good thing there is predictive analytics to help us find the most recent productive patterns and evaluate system responsiveness. You can use it to see if pupils are better off with a specific grading scheme or to compare the effectiveness of online and traditional classroom settings. After recognizing and implementing the recommended educational trends, you may evaluate your current teaching methodology to determine how it might be enhanced to provide the most beneficial learning opportunities.
- *In other ways, predictive analytics can be used in education:*
  - Specialized support for low-income students, ethnic minorities, and students of color.
  - A deep dive into KPIs with actionable recommendations for improvement.
  - Making wise choices during the learning process.
  - Improvements in student motivation and retention rates are vital to ensuring their success in the long run.

4.14 Case Studies

This section presents case studies (Ekowo and Palmer 2016) on various universities' use of predictive analytics.

Finding at-Risk Students at Temple University Temple University in Philadelphia, Pennsylvania, developed an early alert system based on statistical analysis to anticipate better which students are at risk of dropping out. Peter

R. Jones, the university's senior vice provost for undergraduate studies, was a crucial figure in the system's development. Jones had utilized datasets to make predictions before. For his previous employer, a criminologist, he employed such models to forecast which formerly incarcerated individuals would commit new crimes. Temple's "intrusive, or even forceful, advising," as Jones put it, is provided to students flagged as "at risk" by the university's early-alert system.

Predictive analytics at Temple is similar to the Global Positioning System at Georgia State. Predictive modeling helped Temple administrators discover surprising information about Temple's student body. For instance, they discovered that low-income students who got the federal Pell Grant at its whole reward level had a lower dropout rate than those who received a smaller Pell payment. The highest degree of education a student's mother attained is considerably more predictive of that student's odds of academic achievement than the highest level of education his or her father attained, as was discovered by Temple officials. There was also a significant disparity in the high school dropout rates between students who did and did not take 4 years of a foreign language.

Temple's retention and graduation rates dramatically increased after implementing the early alert system.

- The percentage of students who came back for their second year of high school increased by 12%.
- There was a 24% boost in the university's 4-year graduation rate.
- The percentage of students who complete their degrees within 6 years at the university increased by 11%.

While the initial investment in an early-alert system may seem high, the return on investment is often more than justified, as was the case at Temple University.

Helping Students Select Courses at Austin Peay State University Degree Compass is the course recommendation system used at Austin Peay State University (APSU), a public 4-year university in Clarksville, Tennessee. The program analyzes current students' transcripts against those of previous students (almost 100,000) to provide advice tailored to each individual. Based on the success of streaming services like Netflix, Amazon, and Pandora, Degree Compass helps existing students find the right major and coursework.

The algorithm ranks the courses based on how they will help the student complete her program, using information such as grades and enrolment. The following criteria are taken into account while making course recommendations:

- The suggested order of courses for completing a given degree.
- Their potential for academic success and significance to the university's overall curriculum means they may count toward graduation requirements in more than one major.

To help students choose classes where they have the best chance of succeeding, Degree Compass calculates the likelihood that they will receive a specific grade.

According to university data, students' success at APSU has improved by five standard deviations since the implementation of Degree Compass. For instance, students who receive the federal Pell Grant have had their chances of graduating college improve by 4%.

My Future, introduced in the 2012 academic year, is an additional resource for students deciding to major at APSU. Using Degree Compass's predictive analytics, My Future identifies the majors where students have the best chance of succeeding based on their courses, including courses for all of Austin Peay's majors.

My Future guides fields of study and career outlooks for students who have previously declared a major. Students who have not declared a major might use My Future to see which fields they would be most successful in.

More than 40,000 students have had access to Degree Compass since its debut at Austin Peay University in 2011.

Adaptive Learning at Colorado Technical University Career Education Corporation, a publicly traded company, owns Colorado Technical University (CTU), making it a for-profit institution. It focuses on providing online education at all levels, including undergraduate, graduate, and doctoral programs in business, nursing, and information technology. In 2012, CTU began testing adaptive learning in introductory-level science and mathematics classes. The university claims that its intellipath adaptive learning system evaluates what students already know, predicts what they need to learn, and provides them with that knowledge as rapidly as possible.

To create intellipath, CTU collaborated with Realizeit, a leader in adaptive learning. Intellipath leverages CTU faculty-created personalized content and Realizeit's Adaptive Intelligence Engine to tailor instruction to each student's strengths and weaknesses. The Adaptive Intelligence Engine at Realizeit utilizes machine learning to learn individual students' skills and thought processes as they interact with the tool.

Officials said using intellipath led to higher test scores, more active class participation, and higher student retention rates. They claim that by using intellipath, an additional 27% of their students successfully finished Accounting I; 95% of those who enrolled in the course ended up taking it, and the average grade earned by those students increased from 69% to 79% (a very high C). Furthermore, the passing and staying rates in Accounting II and III increased.

In 2015, CTU had 63 courses and over 34,000 unique student users of intellipath. Over August 2016, over 30,000 and 28,000 online students used the technology. CTU trained students, staff, and almost all faculty on intellipath. This process did not happen overnight. According to Connie Johnson, chief academic officer, and provost, it took about "four years to reach 15 percent of its total course offerings" at CTU.

Proprietary Predictive Modeling at the University of South Florida USF (University of South Florida) has been committed to student achievement since 2010, dramatically increasing its retention and graduation rates through several initiatives. By 2012, most of the reforms and new policies had been implemented, and progress had halted, with retention and graduation rates being around the same.

Interest grew in utilizing data to foretell first-year student persistence as a means of moving the needle. Student Affairs professionals have been using an in-house strategy to identify at-risk student populations, coordinating interaction with them through its staff and student employees like Resident Assistants, and developing specialized programming to pique their interest.

Following the success of in-house modeling, USF officials realized the value of using data to learn about the patterns and habits among the student body. In 2014, the institution contracted with Civitas Learning, a leader in the field of higher education technology, to implement a predictive analytics platform that would create predictors of persistence for all students to broaden its programs and increase its retention rates.

Using data from the university's student information and learning management systems, Civitas' cutting-edge predictive analytics modeling software identifies at-risk students in real-time, allowing the institution to assist them better and keep them on track for academic achievement.

4.15 The Benefits of Predictive Analytics in Higher and Further Education

The ability to quickly access and understand data on outcomes and accomplishments is crucial to the strategic planning of any educational institution, and this is where predictive analytics can be a powerful tool. Although predictive analytics results are not immediately apparent, their value cannot be understated. Improvements in quality across the board are an undeniable outcome of a more comprehensive and methodical approach to data use.

There is little doubt that higher quality control throughout the organization is driven by a more comprehensive and methodical approach to data use. Predictive analytics' many advantages in postsecondary education include the following (Fisher and Mulroy 2021):

- Providing stakeholders with the data they need to make educated decisions at the strategic level.
- The process of distilling data into understandable evidence, reports, and dashboards for dissemination to decision-makers.
- Contributing to overall institution-wide performance management planning.
- Monitoring academic progress and increasing awareness of potential dangers allows for early, well-informed intervention.
- Building models to learn how different factors contribute to students' final grades.
- Finding and helping students in danger of dropping out or not performing up to their potential is a top priority.

- Bringing attention to underserved areas by analyzing broad patterns of student achievement and speculating on where further resources are needed.
- Gaining a deeper familiarity with usage patterns might help you run your services more effectively.
- Consolidating funding and improving services to enhance the educational experience for students.

4.16 How Colleges Should Go About Selecting a Predictive Analytics Vendor

Universities use models more frequently to forecast student behavior and implement corrective measures. Because of this, it is more crucial than ever to pick the best vendor to work with on projects that require a collaborative effort. Using predictive analytics through a partnership with a vendor is no different from buying any other technological product. However, the complexity of the algorithms and the forecasts they provide adds another layer to the decision-making process.

Today, many colleges select vendors through informal networks. Colleges can learn about the vendors' client retention rates by talking to other colleges about their experiences. However, colleges must also weigh some moral weights in this age of big data.

The best predictive analytics services will promote responsible data use across the educational spectrum. Vendors who check that data are comprehensive and integrated correctly can reduce the likelihood of incorrectly identifying students. They can be open and honest about their algorithms and conduct experiments to determine whether they disproportionately affect specific student populations. When protecting students' personal information, they can be lenient with permits and employ acceptable security methods. They can aid in assessing programs to ensure that no subsets of students are harmed. Further, they can educate employees on correctly understanding data and the perils of unconscious bias.

Of course, not all vendors operate in this manner. Some researchers have claimed that their algorithms and models are unique. Regarding data integration, many people only accomplish the bare minimum. Some people do not care about students' right to privacy and safety. However, many oppose both assessment and development.

This section (Palmer 2018) intends to equip administrators with the knowledge to examine and evaluate predictive analytics vendors effectively. It will ensure that vendors ethically use early warning systems and other forms of predictive analytics.

Do Your Analytics, or Hire a Vendor? Once colleges have determined their data-use capabilities, they should proceed with the following steps:

- *Cost:* Does your college set aside funds specifically for this?
- *People:* How well do your various offices (registrar, financial assistance, academic advising, registrar, and IR) work together? Can we expect college administration to back efforts to alter institutional culture to better use data?

- *Level of analysis:* In what ways have data analytics been explored thus far? Can you effectively connect with other colleges using analytics and ask about their experiences?
- *Institutional capacity to act on the data:* If your college cares about student performance, how much experience do you have using data to make decisions?

You Have Finally Settled on a Vendor Partnership Colleges have varying requirements based on their aims and profiles when looking to work with a predictive analytics vendor. These requirements, too, will evolve with time. Schools must consider technological and ethical factors to guarantee that the vendors' data and tools are adaptable enough to meet those requirements. Please ensure the data and tools can be adjusted to fit your needs.

- Determine the degree of tool integration.
- Assure true interoperability.
- Determine data needs.
- Set goals for the future.
- Check the interface.
- Ensure that these tools are easily accessible.
- Plan out the implementation timeline.

Ensure Transparent Use of Data For colleges, one of the most challenging parts of selecting a predictive analytics vendor is being unable to inspect the inner workings of the vendors' algorithms. The system's administrators are interested in learning more about the prediction process but are unsure of the types of answers to expect. Administrators without a technical background may be particularly confused by salespeople who do not fully understand the system and do not know what questions to ask to get the information they need about the algorithm. Due to a lack of shared knowledge between the vendor's technical personnel and the university, missteps are more likely to be made. There should be some accountability for the algorithms colleges use, so knowing how they function is an ethical obligation. There are a few things universities should require their vendors to disclose about their algorithms:

- Inquire about the data that was utilized in the prediction.
- Enquire about training data.
- Inquire about the model's effectiveness.
- Ask that vendors do tests on their algorithms.
- Request for a Disparate Impact Analysis.
- Inquire about what factors cause the prediction.
- Inquire about the frequency of algorithm updates.

Concerns with Predictive Analytics Vendor Agreements Colleges, like any vendor, should check that any contract with a predictive analytics firm adequately safeguards student privacy and keeps college ownership of collected data. It is crucial when dealing with vendors who rely on cloud services. Even though FERPA sets a floor for compliance, additional factors must be considered when selecting a

4.16 How Colleges Should Go About Selecting a Predictive Analytics Vendor

vendor. There are a few things that administrators should bear in mind, even if institutions' legal and IT departments likely know what contracts with vendors should look like. This is not an all-inclusive checklist, but it covers some essential points:

- Who owns the data after it has been cleaned, after it has been reused, and after it has been created as a byproduct?
- The practice of changing vendors.
- Vendor bankruptcy, closure, or acquisition.
- Using external suppliers.
- Disaster mitigation, recovery, and breach plan.
- Commitment to service standards.
- Security.

Ensure Security and Privacy Ethical data use and vendor selection depend on the presence of privacy and information security safeguards. Typically, CIOs and IT teams are aware of the criteria that must be met by vendors in order to gain access to student information. The Higher Education Cloud Vendor Assessment Tool has over 300 data security and privacy questions that vendors must answer. However, non-technical decision-makers should have a few considerations in mind. All concerns about a vendor's administrative, technological, and physical security and privacy protections should be answered. It may hint that they must further investigate their security and privacy procedures if they have trouble responding to these questions.

- Administrative safeguards.
- Technological safeguards.
- Physical safeguards.

The Promotion of Research and Evaluation Efforts Colleges that use predictive analytics will consistently work to enhance their intervention procedures. However, the tools themselves require verification from the outside world through studies.

- Check the product's research base.
- Assist with intervention design and evaluation.

Facilitating the Growth and Application of Professional Skills Among Employees Implementing a new tool into the daily routines of academics and staff can be challenging. Consider how the vendor will aid in deployment and troubleshooting to determine if they can be trusted to help you overcome this obstacle.

- Implementation consulting.
- Technical support.
- Communities of practice.
- User training.

4.17 Using Predictive Analytics in eLearning

Predictive analytics may sound like a complex and arcane field of study, but its core idea is straightforward. Below, we will discuss how predictive analytics can be applied to eLearning (Edly 2022).

The rising popularity of distance education has contributed to the demand for predictive analytics in educational institutions. Monitoring student progress in traditional classrooms and online learning environments is crucial to guarantee that everyone is learning what they should be.

- *Implementing adaptive learning:* The advantages of online education lie in its adaptability and individualization. Top-notch online education programs recognize that each student learns uniquely. Predictive analytics, which examines historical student data to identify the material, assessments, and learning paths most likely to be successful for an individual student, enables schools to construct adaptive learning measures in this way. Predictive analytics in adaptive learning also enables teachers to identify and swiftly fix their student's weaknesses. Courses can be designed more effectively for individual students by considering their preferred learning environment, assessment methods, and study speed. Learners are also afforded a degree of agency through adaptive learning strategies. Students can select their courses of study, quickly moving beyond the material they already know and focusing on areas where they need more practice. Students are more invested in their education when they have a hand deciding what will be covered in class.
- *Recognizing strengths and interests:* Institutions of higher learning can better cater to their student's individual needs by analyzing data from previous enrollments to identify common areas of interest and academic achievement. The use of predictive analytics in this approach greatly aids targeted academic advising. A student's probable success in future classes can be predicted by analyzing the types of grades they received in their previously taken classes. With this data, schools can better guide students in selecting electives and majors that best serve their professional goals.
- *Addressing performance issues:* Data on student achievement gives schools a rare chance to pinpoint those students most likely to struggle academically. Colleges can use predictive analytics to properly assess whether a student is on track, at risk, or performing moderately by using large amounts of student data. Purdue University's "Signals" project implements this idea; it uses visual cues reminiscent of traffic lights to convey information about a student's performance in a specific course. In another illuminating example, analytics alerts have been used to significantly increase graduation rates at Georgia State University by intervening with students early on.
- *Managing enrollment:* The number of students enrolling in universities consistently rises each year. Institutions need to be sure they are making informed enrollment decisions in light of the high demand for courses with low enrollment caps. Predictive analytics help the pupils and the school as a whole. Predictive analytics can estimate the total number of incoming students, the proportion of

those applying to specific colleges, and the cost of meeting individual students' financial aid requirements. It is also helpful for colleges and universities since it allows them to focus their recruitment and marketing efforts on the students who are most likely to be interested in the programs they provide.

4.18 The Future of Predictive Analytics in Education

Predictive analytics in EdTech is a part of the more significant shift occurring in the educational industry. Let us examine a few current tendencies (Kyianovska 2022) that are likely to have an impact on the market soon:

- The development of tailored education will be aided by predictive analytics. As a result, the trend in education is away from a universal curriculum and toward individualization. In contrast to the latter, which considers each learner's unique characteristics and circumstances, the former was developed with the average student in mind. Teachers and lecturers can better anticipate their students' performance and intervene at the correct times by analyzing their learning habits. Consequently, the learning outcomes for students and teachers will increase thanks to personalized education. The need for flexible learning platforms and adaptable pedagogical resources is only expected to increase over the following years. In addition, these resources will have to cater to the needs of students with special needs, such as those with dyslexia. Individualized education will be almost instantaneous when meeting each student's needs.
- COVID-19 will hasten the spread of data analytics programs at universities. The pandemic highlighted the adaptability of digital teaching methods. These tools, which may include predictive analytics models, can be sufficiently robust to implement distance learning rapidly. Teachers can gain knowledge to assist their students better, while executives and administrators can use the information to make more informed decisions. The educational system was not immediately transformed by COVID-19.
- Nonetheless, it highlighted the importance of digital resources and online education. Using data analytics tools has become increasingly popular in pre-schools, schools, colleges, and universities because it helps them use their resources and create better learning results. As a result, the foundations for a new education model are becoming more apparent.
- As with every technological advancement, predictive analytics will focus on the user experience. There will be a further honing of the algorithms. However, they are insufficient for fully realizing analytics' potential benefits. The administration's reaction to the data discoveries is also crucial to the project's outcome. Increased student retention rates result from using predictive analytics in higher education. This is because universities can better tailor their student assistance programs. In other words, setting up a program to notify the student automatically that "you have earned a low grade in..., you should do..." is not the answer. As part of this effort, the institution should "design" its campus culture so that fac-

ulty and staff are more likely to proactively engage at-risk students and introduce them to available resources.

4.19 How to Prepare for the Future of Predictive Analytics for Education

As institutions become more data-led when making strategic decisions, and as the findings, reports, and insights gained from predictive analytics become more available, many organizations will naturally use predictive analytics.

As more people inside an organization access data, predictive analytics are becoming increasingly important in various settings. Decisions can be made swiftly and efficiently based on evidence, allowing for early action and resolution of issues as soon as they are recognized.

Furthermore, in the future, students may have direct access to the results of reliable predictive analytics. In their education, it might help them make informed decisions by revealing, for instance, the likely employment outcomes of completing specific modules or programs.

Predictive analytics will be crucial in bringing about meaningful change by integrating predictive models into the strategic decision-making process. Predictive analytics is expected to increase in the education sector, leading to the deeper and more precise analysis of student performance data. Predictive models and the data they use to make predictions will develop over time better to suit the specific context of each educational institution.

Predictive analytics is the future, and universities and colleges can get ready for it (Fisher and Mulroy 2021):

- *Intuitively knowing what you want to accomplish:* Think carefully about the information you must collect and analyze to help achieve your organization's strategic goals and improve the student experience.
- *Gathering the right data:* To ensure the success of your predictive analytics models, you will need a reliable and safe internal database to store all of the necessary data.
- *Guaranteeing the optimum data quality:* High-quality data is crucial for reliable analysis. To avoid needing to clean or reformat the data later, you should ensure that everyone in your organization responsible for data collection and input enters the correct data values in the specified format.
- *Selecting the best predictive analytics approach:* Educational institutions can use readily available predictive models that provide quick and straightforward access to their data.
- *Evaluate your predictive model at regular intervals:* The predictive model should be evaluated and validated regularly to ensure it is error-free and to identify and fix any potential problems. Having faith in your organization's prediction models will let you make smarter business choices.

4.20 Conclusion

Opportunities abound for academic institutions in the realm of predictive analytics systems. Institutions of higher education continue to benefit from the improvements in graduation rates made possible by predictive analytics. They can foresee students' results, identifying those at a higher risk of dropping out. Schools can prepare for the future by knowing which pupils require extra support. An individualized training program for educators could help to raise motivation levels. Thereby, universities and colleges can boost their retention rates, student satisfaction, and financial gains.

References

Edly. (2022). *Using Predictive Analytics in eLearning*. Edly. https://edly.io/blog/using-predictive-analytics-in-elearning/

Ekowo, M., & Palmer, I. (2016). *The Promise and Peril of Predictive Analytics in Higher Education* (Issue October).

Ekowo, M., & Palmer, I. (2017). *PREDICTIVE ANALYTICS IN HIGHER EDUCATION: Five Guiding Practices for Ethical Use* (Issue March).

Fisher, M., & Mulroy, S. (2021). *GUIDE TO PREDICTIVE ANALYTICS IN EDUCATION: the benefits and practical applications* (pp. 1–13).

Judge, L. (2021). *Predictive analytics in education: an introduction*. Tribal. https://www.tribalgroup.com/blog/predictive-analytics-in-education-an-introduction

Kyianovska, H. (2022). *Predictive analytics in education: use cases, best practices, and perspectives*. Menklab. https://www.menklab.com/post/predictive-analytics-in-education-use-cases-best-practices-and-perspectives

Kyson, C. (2021). *Predictive Analytics in Education: Improving Educational Offerings with Big Data*. InData Labs. https://indatalabs.com/blog/predictive-analytics-in-education

McGavisk, T. (2022). *Using Predictive Analytics to Improve Student Education*. TimeDataSecurity. https://www.timedatasecurity.com/blogs/using-predictive-analytics-to-improve-student-education#:~:text=For

Moraes, N. (2018). *A Provost's guide on how to use Predictive Analytics in Education*. Talismatic. http://www.talismatic.com/blog/a-provosts-guide-on-how-to-use-predictive-analytics-in-education/

Palmer, I. (2018). *CHOOSING A PREDICTIVE ANALYTICS VENDOR: A Guide for Colleges* (Issue September).

Saranya, K. (2020). *Role of Predictive Analytics in Transforming Education*. Bold BI. https://www.boldbi.com/blog/role-of-predictive-analytics-in-transforming-education#:~:text=Predictive analytics can help identify,learning experience for all students.

Worcester Business Journal. (2011). *Predictive Models Give Recruiting Edge | Colleges seek to optimize marketing*. Worcester Business Journal Online. https://www.wbjournal.com/article/predictive-models-give-recruiting-edge-colleges-seek-to-optimize-marketing

Chapter 5
AI for Mobile Learning

5.1 What Is Mobile Learning, and How and Why Did It Become Widespread?

M-Learning or mLearning, short for mobile learning, is a novel approach to online education that uses mobile devices such as smartphones, tablets, digital notebooks, and laptops. With the click of a button, students can access many paid and free resources.

Microlearning, augmented, virtual reality's impact on eLearning, and the growing reliance on smartphones have contributed to a sea change in how students deliver and process information. There has been a considerable shift in the eLearning market because of the rise of mobile learning.

Many premium mobile learning apps now include features like performance assessment, grading, and attendance rate, making it easier for students and their parents to keep tabs on their academic progress.

When creating content for mobile learning apps, developers keep students' unique requirements in mind. This allows students to learn at their own pace and focus on areas where they struggle.

When mobile learning is combined with microlearning, there is a startling increase in the completion rate, from 20% to as high as 80% (Mushavvirkhan-Balooch 2022).

Seventy percent of academic leaders believe online education is as successful as traditional classroom instruction. Another study shows that the retention rate can be increased by 25%–55% when using online learning (Mushavvirkhan-Balooch 2022).

Cretx's chief marketing officer and co-founder, Mushavvirkhan Balooch, has observed that "major changes have been brought to the eLearning business as a result of technological breakthroughs and innovations in the mobile app development industry" (Mushavvirkhan-Balooch 2022). It is now clear that mobile learning has enormous promise because of its adaptability, interaction, and low cost.

Mobile learning will thrive if people have a burning desire to learn.

For several compelling reasons, mobile learning is gaining popularity among students worldwide (Mushavvirkhan-Balooch 2022).

- Study whenever and wherever you like. More people can finish their courses as a result.
- The level of interest from students is boosted through a customized curriculum.
- It is learner-centered.
- Being accessible around the clock adds versatility.
- Content that can be consumed in small bites speeds up the learning process.
- It is cost-efficient.
- Supports a collaborative learning environment.
- Graphically rich content.

Incorporating the possibilities of mobile technology into information and curriculum is genuinely altering education worldwide.

5.2 Why Adopt Mobile Learning?

The excitement and interest that mobile learning has inspired among students worldwide are worth investigating. Here are some vital benefits (Mushavvirkhan-Balooch 2022) (see Fig. 5.1) of adopting mobile learning.

- *On-the-go learning:* Students are no longer required to be physically present at their desks to pursue their academic interests. In addition, mobile learning provides access to carefully curated content in videos, audio, and podcasts at any time and from any location.
- *Dynamic learning:* Every single kid has his or her unique learning style. Some people learn best by listening, while others do better by seeing. Instead of relying on the tried-and-true method of reading and writing, modern mobile learning has

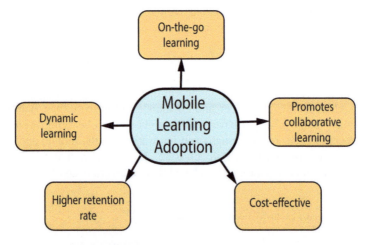

Fig. 5.1 Benefits of adopting mobile learning

brought more exciting and engaging learning formats such as pictures, videos, audio, and slide shows. It is safe to assume that a more innovative and interactive approach to education has become the standard.

- *Higher retention rate:* The goal of providing courses optimized for mobile devices is to make even the most complex subjects more accessible. "Microlearning" refers to breaking down large amounts of content into smaller, more manageable pieces that are then presented aesthetically appealing formats. Because of this, learning as a whole is efficient, helping students retain more information.
- *Promotes collaborative learning:* Mobile learning platforms aim to facilitate a pleasant educational environment by connecting teachers and students in a virtual space to exchange ideas and work together to achieve a common goal. The exchange of information between the teacher and the student is two-way since the latter can contribute their thoughts and ideas to the former.
- *Cost-effective:* It is no secret that mobile learning's low price tag is one of its most appealing aspects. Teachers may create and distribute web and mobile app content using a web-based authoring system, making it accessible to students anytime and anywhere.

5.3 Key Characteristics of mLearning

The following are some of the main characteristics (see Fig. 5.2) features of mobile learning (Simplilearn. 2022) that make it useful for training and education:

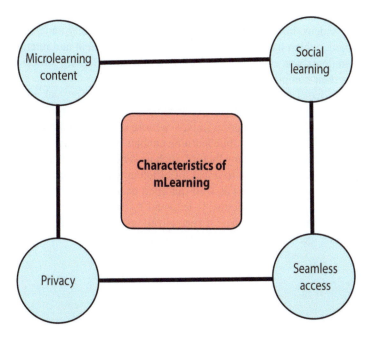

Fig. 5.2 Key characteristics of mLearning

- *Microlearning content:* Microlearning, typically delivered via mobile learning, lasts two to five. Learners' interest is sustained, and the information's clarity and relevance enhance their retention.
- *Social learning:* Using social learning in mobile learning has
- increased student participation. The newsfeed, forums, chat feature, or comments area can all be used to facilitate student-to-student communication and exchange ideas and information.
- *Seamless access:* To reduce barriers and boost participation, many mobile-based training systems integrate course materials directly into the native app, bypassing the need for users to log in first.
- *Privacy:* Nobody can snoop on them and see how they are doing or access any information they want to keep private.

5.4 What Are the Challenges That Mobile Learning in Education Overcomes?

Some of the most significant challenges (Hurix 2019) that can be overcome with the aid of m-Learning include:

- *Lack of tailored learning approaches:* No matter how advanced a university or school is, there is always room to improve how it engages its students. As a goal, catering to each student's unique learning requirements and preferred methods of instruction is sometimes impossible in the standard classroom setting. However, mobile learning can be more participatory and customized to learners' preferences. Students using M-Learning can select from various instructional media, including videos, infographics, and audio, to help them easily understand a specific subject, which has been shown to increase engagement and retention. As a result, students are more actively involved in the learning process, which improves their comprehension.
- *Lack of analytics and data to benchmark performance:* The lack of sufficient data and analytics to compare student accomplishments is a problem most educational institutions face. In order to have a more complete and nuanced picture of each student's progress, mobile learning enables educators to track and benchmark performance across many factors, such as student history or subject.
- *Less qualified teachers:* Due to a lack of efficient teaching methods and lesson plans, instructors who are not as well-qualified or training cannot make significant contributions. This difficulty is lessened by mobile learning in the classroom because of the availability of specialized resources that facilitate trainers' and teachers' exchange of successful teaching methods.

5.5 Role of Mobile Learning Solutions in the Education Industry

There are many more contexts in which the term "mobile" can be applied than just in telecommunications. The same is used in education, with a recent example being "learning during the lockdown."

Mobile learning (mLearning) was 90% efficient in a 2019 study (Sugermint 2019). Due to this, the mobile learning solutions market reached $27.32 billion in 2019 (Sugermint 2019). With its rising popularity and bright future, companies are creating their mLearning solutions or teaming up with a mobile learning services provider.

The mLearning industry is proliferating, incorporating new features to improve the quality of its daily interactive lessons. It is important to remember that mobile learning is a subset of eLearning that has expanded nine hundred percent over the past two decades. You may also be wondering what role, if any, mLearning courses played in the evolution of the educational sector.

Positive Impact During the Lockdown Nearly eighty-five percent of businesses experienced a learning crisis due to the COVID-19 pandemic. Everyone wants to know how to close the learning gap. Mobile learning made it possible to have dynamic classes on mobile devices. Remember that students of all ages, from all walks of life, and in various organizations take mLearning courses.

One study found that half of all businesses saw an improvement in performance after implementing mLearning solutions. mLearning offers numerous advantages, like ease of use and customization for different learners.

Accessibility According to the data, nearly a billion students could not get any schoolwork done during the lockdown. There is a universal fear that the learning issue may worsen during this pandemic.

So, most benefited from the education provided through mobile learning solutions. Smartphones' use extends beyond making calls; they may also be used for research and education.

Nearly 91 percent of smartphone users who are also students spend between 5 and 6 hours daily studying (Sugermint 2019). Using media like online videos, live sessions, and customized mobile apps, educational institutions were better able to manage learning content by demand. Indeed, if we infer that mLearning is an efficient tailor-made learning solution, we would not be wrong!

Collaborative Learning The rise of online socializing is an emerging trend in education. Some examples of social media learning environments include online discussion boards, real-time chats, and dedicated learning community websites.

The convenience of their incorporation into mobile apps is another plus. With just a few clicks, you may access learning modules and work with students worldwide, regardless of their language, culture, or background.

This is one of the many advantages of mLearning programs. As things are right now, there is no shortage of mLearning courses that include social media in their instruction.

Learning reports can be shared on social media, or educators can be contacted to provide information. As a result of its success, this strategy is employed by 60% of academic institutions and 80% of businesses. It has also been shown that 52% of students in grades 6–9 have access to tablets and smartphones for collaborative learning (Sugermint 2019).

Multi-device Support Smartphones and tablets are becoming more popular than personal computers and laptops. The reality remains that 30% of all mobile students still favor desktop or laptop computers as their primary learning devices.

Also, mLearning courses are compatible with more devices than any other type of eLearning module. This is why mLearning accounts for 21.45% of the total eLearning market (Sugermint 2019).

Many different mLearning modules are available, including videos, PDFs, gamification courses, and more. All devices and storage options are compatible with mLearning courses, so you may keep them on a flash drive or the cloud.

Productivity Undeniably, people who use mobile devices like you are more efficient than people who use computers. This is because people are more likely to actively participate in games and apps on their smartphones than on their laptops.

Data shows that those who use the Internet through their mobile devices are 43% more productive than those who use a computer. This is why BYOD (Bring Your Own Device) has been adopted by 70% of US organizations (Sugermint 2019).

This in no way discredits the usefulness of computer machine learning. However, students expect adaptability in their education, and mobile devices are convenient for on-the-go study. That means that studying continues unabatedly regardless of the time of day.

The Information Is Available at the Fingertips In this age of instant information, nobody has time to waste on library research. The online repository of books is on the rise. It is easy to access any and all modules. As a result, mLearning apps compile all available educational resources into one convenient digital library.

One piece of evidence suggests that mobile learning has a 40% higher completion rate than traditional approaches. Moreover, it can be learned in half the time it would take using traditional approaches.

5.6 Key Benefits of Mobile Learning for Higher Education Students

Some of the most forward-thinking universities are capitalizing on mobile learning because it improves learner engagement and increases graduation rates. We will go over each of these (see Fig. 5.3) in more detail below (Hurix 2019):

- *On-the-go learning:* The portability of mobile devices makes it possible to study whenever and wherever is most convenient. Using audio, video, podcasts, and other multimedia assets on mobile devices, m-Learning allows users to tailor their education to their unique learning preferences.
- *Better collaboration:* Using mobile devices in the classroom facilitates student participation and group projects that strengthen the online learning environment. This is a significant benefit of mobile learning compared to more traditional methods of education when student interaction is typically limited to the classroom.
- *Multi-device support:* Multi-device compatibility is another major perk of mobile learning in the classroom. In contrast to previous forms of online education, the mobile learning environment allows for a unified course experience across multiple platforms and devices.
- *Higher retention and better completion rates:* Learners have much freedom with m-Learning platforms because the content is broken into small, manageable chunks. As a result, students are more likely to finish their courses, retain more information, and have a profoundly positive experience with mobile learning.
- *Engaging design formats to learn from:* Diverse and engaging design forms, such as interactive videos, animated movies, and so on, are featured in M-Learning and are often favored by students. This kind of customization in education increases motivation and keeps students on track with their training.
- *Driving performance:* Given the proliferation of mobile Internet access, schools have turned to m-Learning to serve their student's educational needs better and boost their academic standing. Online training courses consisting of videos and images can be broken down into bite-sized segments and delivered to mobile devices. These quick courses' content can be exciting to provide just-in-time pedagogical aid.

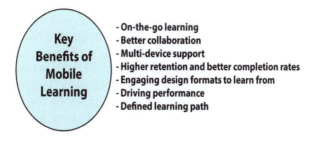

Fig. 5.3 Key benefits of mobile learning for higher education students

- *Defined learning path:* One reason why m-Learning programs are so well-liked is that they offer a flexible and adaptable curriculum that can be tailored to each student. Students appreciate the practicality of m-Learning platforms that incorporate course organizers and push notifications for reminders on their mobile devices. In addition, they get constant access to the latest information on courses and suggestions.

5.7 The Impact of Mobile Learning on the Future of Education

As a result of our constant connectivity to nearly endless volumes of raw data and information, mobile devices like smartphones and tablets are drastically altering how we access our collective knowledge sources. From quick culinary videos on YouTube to full college degrees available at your fingertips, fast access to specialized knowledge is at an all-time high. Exciting new kinds of learning are capturing people's attention worldwide, but the established educational system still fails to take advantage of the many possibilities in this field.

This section introduces ten overarching concepts (Sergio 2012) that will likely inspire new approaches to mLearning's development.

- *Continuous Learning:* Until recently, "education" was seen as something that happened only once in a person's life, from the time they started school at age five until they graduated from college. There was a time limit on schooling before it was on to the working world. This approach, developed during the industrial era, is becoming increasingly outdated and irrelevant to modern life. Increasingly, we cannot go about our day without encountering educational content. People of all ages, from 11-year-olds to retirees, are taking advantage of free online courses to learn about cutting-edge topics like artificial intelligence, computer science, and game theory in their leisure time. We learn how to utilize new professional software or how to mend our broken equipment by reading articles on our phones, tablets, and computers. Today's children are among the first to be born within touching distance of a connected personal gadget, so continuous learning will be taken as read.
- *Educational Leapfrogging:* People constantly learn new things, even in less-advanced societies. A portable classroom allows students to study whenever and wherever they like, whether during brief breaks in the day, late at night, or as background "music" as they get work done. Many students in low-income areas who are engaging in technological leapfrog will also be able to bypass antiquated formal school systems due to the widespread availability of inexpensive computers, tablets, and cell phones. This is especially important for kids from low-income homes who may have to start working at a young age to help support their families or who may not reside in a neighborhood with access to exemplary educational opportunities.

- *A New Crop of Older, Lifelong Learners (and Educators):* The continuous learning phenomenon has a side effect: today's grandparents, watching their grandchildren grow up with a touchscreen in their hands, are more interested than ever in mLearning. Tablets and other touch-enabled gadgets have drastically lowered the computer's perceived complexity, making it easier for seniors to keep in touch with their middle-aged children and grandchildren through digital mediums like email, Facebook, Twitter, and Skype. This segment of the population has the leisure and interest to take online classes for fun, but they also present an untapped market for more practical use of that spare time: In many parts of the world, there is a severe shortage of trained teachers, but this problem could be solved if retirees took up teaching, especially if they did so remotely through mLearning.
- *Breaking Gender Boundaries, Reducing Physical Burdens:* mLearning has the potential to provide girls and women of all ages with access to high-quality education on their own time in settings where this may not have been possible in the past due to centuries-old cultural practices. Similarly, mLearning facilitates access to higher education for individuals who, due to severe impairments, cannot regularly visit a traditional classroom or campus. Therefore, members of these communities are empowered to make decisions about their academic and occupational futures. In either instance, previously hidden liberties become accessible.
- *A New Literacy Emerges: Software Literacy:* The advent of mLearning has the potential to spark a renaissance in the study of software programming languages, which have all the makings of a global lingua franca. This is already taking place; numerous new online firms, such as Codecademy, provide interactive education to help individuals learn to comprehend and create computer programs. Codecademy has more than a million "students" and has raised roughly $three million in venture money. This is especially true in developing nations, where a skilled software development workforce may open up new avenues for economic growth and equip communities to meet previously unmet demands. When considering fostering software literacy and local entrepreneurship, one needs to consider the success of organizations like Ushahidi, which has been sponsoring a high-tech social accelerator called iHUB in Nairobi.
- *Education's Long Tail:* A wealth of educational resources could be available through mLearning solutions. YouTube, Vimeo, and other video-sharing platforms provide helpful guides, tutorials, and complete lessons that can be re-aggregated by topic and packaged as educational content. The latest TED-Ed project is an excellent example of the possibility presented by the innovative repurposing of established, high-quality teaching materials. It was popularized by Salman Khan, an MIT grad whose eponymous academy "flips" the traditional education approach by having students learn new material at home and then apply it in class through practice and discussion. Others have used social platforms to share videos to disseminate spontaneously produced instructional content. Materials for mobile learning can come from various sources, from grandparents explaining how to make traditional foods to businesses exhibiting how to place solar panels on mud huts, and the knowledge they impart is invaluable. Having a video-capable smartphone is not always necessary, as the type and

difficulty of educational resources might vary substantially. Many humanitarian organizations, like MAMA, have successfully used text messages to educate expectant and new mothers in underdeveloped countries on pregnancy, childbirth, and infant care. These instances demonstrate the potential of mLearning to cater to a wide variety of specific user groups.

- *Teachers and Pupils Trade Roles:* The same portable, Internet-connected gadgets that provide children and adults access to existing edtech allow them to record and distribute their insights. Imagine a 12-year-old boy teaching nurses, doctors, and parents how to communicate health information to him in a way he can understand. Imagine, then, a world in which young children are taught to code and produce videos from an early age, and these children go on to create and teach their educational materials to their peers and even adults, whose perspectives on the world are thus broadened by being exposed to those of children.
- *Synergies with Mobile Banking and Mobile Health Initiatives:* Others working on new mLearning ecosystems would study the experiences of those who came before them in mobile banking and mobile healthcare. It is possible to combine mLearning, mHealth, and mFinance in more fruitful ways than simply adapting unique ideas, such as sending short lessons, teacher feedback, and grades by text message. In whatever order, the product of these three variables will be greater than the sum of their parts. This positive feedback loop has excellent promise to boost local, national, and global economies, whether applied on a small or large scale. After all, a higher standard of education is a simple way to boost people's standard of living and even their health.
- *New Opportunities for Traditional Educational Institutions:* Harvard and MIT's announcement that they will partner to provide open online courses through their nonprofit firm edX presented an intriguing new concept. The rise of mLearning will not replace traditional education but will enhance and broaden the scope of what is already available. The two schools want to use the students' reactions to the courses to inform their future remote education strategies. Established universities, perhaps realizing they missed specific opportunities in the early 2000s, are now looking at mLearning to find new prospective students or study how people learn. By tapping into their enormous and established networks of students, staff, and alums, traditional institutions can aid mLearning solutions' rapid expansion. Global Industry Analysts produced a report, "The business potential could also be big," in February 2012, predicting that the global online and other electronic distance learning market will reach $107 billion by 2015. This indicates substantial commercial potential.
- *A Revolution Leading to Customized Education:* Successfully directing the mLearning revolution will need more than automating today's educational practices. MLearning indeed has enormous commercial potential, but what makes these solutions truly exciting and rewarding is the possibility that they will enable students of all ages and walks of life to pursue and acquire meaningful, relevant, and practical knowledge to help them succeed in their own lives. The true allure lies in individuals' freedom to chart their courses, make the most of their gifts, and pursue their true calling.

5.8 Pros and Cons of Mobile Learning

Let us check out (see Fig. 5.4) the pros and cons (Simplilearn. 2022) of mobile learning.

Pros of Mobile Learning

- *Availability:* Students can quickly and easily access relevant resources whenever needed.
- *Usability:* When using an M-Learning platform, the focus is on completing specific tasks. It offers practical advice through tutorials, step-by-step guidelines, and exercises designed to put newly acquired knowledge into practice.
- *Convenient size:* The lessons and assignments can be easily incorporated into busy schedules.
- *Social touch:* Students can consult with one another and their teachers when they need help or advice. They have the option of commenting and maintaining a sense of community.
- *Engagement:* For the student, it adds no further work. There is more interaction between teachers and students.
- *Cost-effective:* This method of education is less expensive than the standard classroom setting. It reduces the need for a physical location, equipment, trainers' salaries, and transportation costs. Since students can use their gadgets during instruction, costly computer classrooms can be avoided.

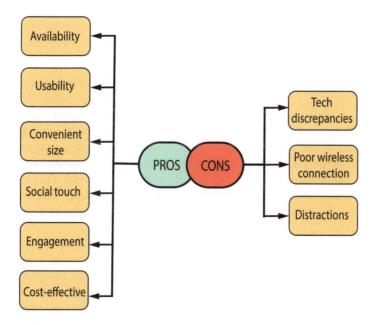

Fig. 5.4 Pros and cons of mobile learning

Cons of Mobile Learning

- *Tech discrepancies*: The mobile learning experience is hindered by mobile devices having wildly different storage and processing capacities.
- *Poor wireless connection:* In many outlying areas, there is a lack of cell phone service and, consequently, poor Internet connectivity.
- *Distractions:* Distractions during training include checking phones and social media, which might lessen the efficiency of the training.

5.9 How Are Mobile Learning Apps Taking Advantage of AI?

One of the most important factors influencing the expansion of many markets, including the online learning industry, is the rise of AI.

It is also being put to good use in the development of novel mobile applications that provide consumers with expanded capabilities. This technology has gradually become an essential part of the educational system and has brought about profound changes in teaching and learning.

Mobile learning apps with the assistance of artificial intelligence are helpful not only for children in elementary school through university but also for professionals and businesses. The outcomes of learning and productivity both benefit from this.

This section discusses how artificial intelligence (AI) revolutionizes mobile learning apps (Kizhakedath 2021). In addition, you can use these apps to learn not only in the classroom, at university, in the workplace, or in your day-to-day life. Instead of taking traditional piano lessons, you may learn the instrument with the help of artificial intelligence at Skoove.

- *Improving Administrative Operations:* The automation of routine administrative duties in educational institutions is a promising area of application for artificial intelligence in mobile learning apps. One example of such work is the faster and more precise marking of essays and exams. The same principle can be applied to the admissions process to ensure that all applicants are objectively evaluated and considered. With the help of AI-powered intelligent assistants, we can close the communication gap between schools and their students. This is used in mobile learning apps using chatbots, which provide students with answers to their questions and direct them to the appropriate admissions or support departments.
- *Connecting Students with Teachers:* Mobile learning apps driven by AI can potentially revolutionize education from kindergarten to graduate school. Most programmers focus on making AI-powered learning apps for students who struggle to articulate their needs to their instructors and tutors. Students with unique needs, disabilities, or circumstances that prevent them from attending a traditional classroom can benefit from AI-assisted, individualized instruction. As a bonus, mobile learning apps can single out students who could benefit the most

from supplementary materials and pinpoint individual areas of difficulty. This provides an opportunity for a more tailored education to aid their development as students. Moreover, it helps students and teachers connect and work collaboratively.

- *Flexibility in Course Development:* Mobile learning apps powered by AI are helpful for students and instructors in designing lessons. Educators can better pinpoint students' areas of weakness with the help of these apps' intuitive and insightful suggestions for enhancing their teaching content. Some educational apps for mobile devices can send notifications to teachers if multiple students submit incorrect answers to a question or attempt an assignment using the wrong strategy. So, the software can help students better grasp the ideas they are struggling with. They can also access sample exams and supplementary readings to help them prepare for future assessments and enrich their knowledge.

- *Smart Lessons and Experiential Learning:* Traditionally, a teacher would instruct a big class in physical activity, and all students would be expected to follow along and absorb the material. Students have the right to ask questions, but most lack confidence in doing so in class. Plus, not every student will absorb information at the same rate. This is where educational apps for mobile devices come in helpful. As a result of advancements in AI, these apps may now be utilized to automatically create insightful and tailor-made courses for each student. Students can use the classes to meet their individual educational goals. They can access reading materials in various disciplines, from mathematics and physics to history and geography. The AI-driven platform can evaluate student work and provide feedback through reports and comparisons, allowing for easier self-evaluation. As a result, students who require supplementary instruction can progress at their own pace and without unduly stressful pressure.

- *Microlearning:* In a traditional classroom setting, students commit to a lengthy two- to five-year course or degree program. They will not be able to take individual lessons or receive individualized instruction in areas needing improvement. Here is where artificial intelligence-powered mobile learning apps come in handy. Several online learning apps allow you to sign up for a single course or class to acquire new knowledge and abilities. The popular term for this strategy is "micro-learning," which refers to how professors and instructors present information to students in bite-sized chunks and packages that improve retention and comprehension. Text, pictures, videos, music, and even games can all be used to deliver microlearning content to students, including the youngest ones. Furthermore, it allows students to learn at their own pace and in their manner. They are also less time-consuming and cheaper for educators to prepare.

- *Professional Education and Training:* Professional education and training is another area where AI is utilized for mobile learning apps. This is where businesses train their staff and provide them with courses and learning content to advance in their jobs. In addition, the learning curve presented by these digital learning apps for professionals may be easily negotiated.

5.10 How AI Is Changing the Mobile Learning Education Game

Today's tech-driven world has helped every industry. There has been a recent uptick in businesses and individuals who see the potential in implementing AI-powered software to improve their daily operations. Effects of AI are also being felt in the mobile education sector, as younger students are increasingly turning to digital devices for their education.

Artificial intelligence (AI) allows teachers to tailor their lessons to each student, ensuring their attention is focused on the presented material. As a result of this shift, there has been a meteoric rise in the popularity of educational apps designed for mobile devices.

Let us look at the revolutionary impact of AI (see Fig. 5.5) on the mobile learning industry (Sales POP Guest Post 2021):

- *Personalized Learning:* According to Gates/RAND Studies (Herold 2016), students do better when given greater freedom in their educational setting. A personalized learning program can help the most academically challenged students reach their full potential. Each student has unique strengths and weaknesses, requiring a unique learning approach. Through AI, course materials may be adapted to each student's learning style and pace, improving their overall performance in class.
- *Tailored Content:* Online courses are ineffective if they only require students to watch videos and memorize material. They have a limited attention span and will soon stop listening to their teacher. Artificial intelligence can be used to reorganize the course content into more manageable chunks to aid students' retention and comprehension. In addition, lectures can be turned into videos and podcasts to keep students interested for much longer.

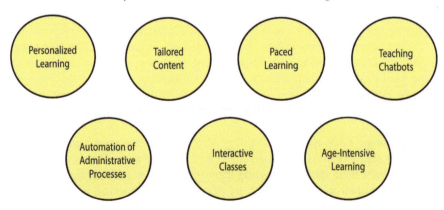

Fig. 5.5 Impact of AI on the mobile learning

5.10 How AI Is Changing the Mobile Learning Education Game

- *Paced Learning:* Rather than being forced to adhere to a rigid schedule, students can take their courses and progress through the material at their leisure with the help of AI-powered mobile learning platforms. They can go over each lesson as often as needed before moving on to the next because the course materials and lectures are online and accessible at any time. This is especially helpful for students who cannot attend traditional lectures due to illness or are enrolled in online courses from another country and physically located in a different time zone. Furthermore, AI can translate the subject matter into any language, allowing anyone to take classes and study from the convenience of their own home.
- *Teaching Chatbots:* Artificial intelligence (AI)-driven chatbots have exploded across all sectors, including education and mobile learning. If you have questions about a topic or subject on the learning platform, you can contact a chatbot for help. The chatbot will provide a thorough response based on its extensive database and will do it in a matter of seconds. To avoid missing out on the opportunity to ask a question, you can do so before the next class session begins. This is a massive boon to those who take classes online.
- *Automation of Administrative Processes:* Students are not the only ones who can benefit from AI. In contrast, AI-powered mobile learning solutions can also be helpful for teachers. Even in a virtual classroom, teachers still have much administrative work, such as keeping track of students' attendance and test scores. If an AI-based platform could automate these tasks, educators could devote their full attention to what they do best, i.e., teaching. Moreover, AI can help teachers with grading exams. As soon as students log into an online class, their presence will be noted, and their grades will be added automatically.
- *Interactive Classes:* A few years ago, it would have been impossible to imagine doing something with the help of automated procedures. Still, it is now possible because of the significant advancements in artificial intelligence. People with smartphones can now learn about things like music theory and even more specialized things like piano chords (Shipp 2021) that they could not before. With mobile learning, students have access to all course content, which makes it simpler to follow along with each lesson and remember what they have learned. One example of this trend is the rise of music apps powered by artificial intelligence (AI) that give instant feedback and tailor each class to the user. Adding interactive courses, which enable students to remain actively engaged in each class, is another way AI is upping the ante. You may have noticed that on some educational platforms, a question appears on the screen after the teacher has finished a subtopic, and you can choose an answer by tapping it.
- *Age-Intensive Learning:* One of the primary contributions of AI in the mobile learning education game is that it gives the students age-specific lessons and course content. This means that it may serve everyone interested in expanding their skill set through online instruction, from infants to adults in their forties. You cannot have too many words for little children, so you need films, sounds, and interactive learning games. This can only be made achievable with AI.

5.11 Application of AI in Mobile Learning

Artificial intelligence's (AI's) particular use in mobile education (Liu et al. 2010):

Mobile Intelligent Teaching Expert System (MITES) MITES is a novel form of educational technology that draws from the fields of cognitive and thinking science, integrated artificial intelligence technology, educational psychology, and other related areas of study. A MITES-enabled classroom can be a highly-intelligent one. The approach creates an open, interactive classroom by modeling the minds of professors and professionals and employing cutting-edge tools like artificial intelligence and mobile media. Students can access knowledge from the system on their mobile devices. The system may adapt lessons to students' background information, skill level, and preferred learning style. It has the potential to provide adaptive learning for each student.

MITES aims to investigate the features and methods of study to find a cognitive model of education that will help students learn more quickly and efficiently.

The following forms of intelligence (Liu et al. 2010) are typical of MITES systems:

- It can mechanically produce a wide range of problems and exercises.
- Choose relevant learning content and modify teaching progression by students' varying skill levels.
- As a result of comprehending the course material, the system can solve the problem mechanically and on its own.
- With the ability to generate and interpret natural language, users can easily ask and receive answers to system-related questions, improving human-computer interaction.
- Capable of providing a meaningful context for course material.
- Identifying student mistakes, investigating their root causes, and implementing effective solutions are possible.
- Ability to judge student performance.
- Capable of enhancing one's pedagogical practices indefinitely.

Mobile Intelligent Decision Support System (MIDSS) The MIDSS system comprises several fundamental parts: a database, model base, method base, man-machine interface, and intelligent components. The four-base and fusion structures are two examples of system architectures that can be constructed using these elements. The future of MIDSS in mobile learning applications is promising; as such, it can aid in the identification of decision-making problems, the clarification of decision-making goals, the establishment or modification of a decision-making model, the provision of alternative courses of action, the evaluation and selection of excellent features of human-computer interaction, and the determination of the best course of action.

5.11 Application of AI in Mobile Learning

Mobile Intelligence Information Retrieval Engine (MIIRE) Most information resources used in mobile learning are discovered by students surfing the web. Therefore, one of remote support's crucial aspects is providing information retrieval services of a high standard. The intelligent engine is the foundational technology behind the evolution of the mobile intelligent information retrieval system. Mobile intelligent retrieval aims to power the learning engine with intelligence. Current search engines are server-side programs without intelligence; furthermore, the high-precision retrieval engine needs a formatted input string. If relocating the search engine for the mobile client gives them the ability to self-analyze to grasp the interest of intelligent learners, then they can glean data from the web per the users' desires. MIIRE is a vital component of the navigation system. Personal intelligent navigation systems built on Java, for instance, feature a self-learning function that automatically collects and records the user's browsing habits and, based on the preferences of different users in different navigation, makes recommendations to help users find the relevant resources.

Mobile Intelligent Induct-learning System (MTIS) MTIS provides support services. Mobile education relies heavily on its accompanying support services. Creating, managing, and implementing projects to support mobile learning requires setting up and maintaining a reliable, adaptable, and robust support services subsystem. Effective learning environments are fostered by various services designed to make it simple for students to access the help they need from various sources. The AGENT Mobile Intelligent Guidance System can take the reins when it comes to developing and implementing different learning strategies and leading the charge when it comes to providing personalized services; these objectives are at the very core of distributed artificial intelligence, which seeks to minimize the need for complex software and the implementation of burdensome, repetitive tasks to maximize productivity. A diagnostic function, error diagnosis through the study, analysis, and enhancement of the reasons; automatic correction of guiding strategy through feedback to make it more in line with the learner's knowledge base and cognitive characteristics; and a focus on the learner's future and goals are all hallmarks of effective guidance.

Intelligent Hardware Network (IHN) Employing the IHN is prudent in light of current affairs to make the mobile network smarter. In this context, intelligence refers to "operational intelligence" and "service intelligence." A mobile network's "operational intelligence" refers to its capacity for smooth operation, ongoing upkeep, and expert management. What we mean by "service intelligence" in the context of mobile networks is providing information processing expertise and decision-making tools to end users. In terms of hardware, mobile education relies on the mobile network. With the proliferation of networks and the increasing importance of information in modern society, mobile education online will soon necessitate the integration of multimedia information processing capabilities and the network's provision of high-level information-processing capacity, that is, concerning the processing power of knowledge.

5.12 Using AI to Create Personalized Learning Paths in Mobile Learning

Today's students need on-demand, individualized instruction. L&D professionals may better organizational support objectives by tailoring training and education to each learner's preferences and interests. Using a personalized approach, you may effectively teach your students what they need to know and provide the skills they will use in their careers. It offers students a sense of their educational needs and encourages them to participate actively.

With the help of personalized education, students can get the skills they need to advance in their chosen fields. The term "personalized learning" refers to altering and modifying one's course of study based on specific needs and goals. Personalized learning routes consider the individual learner's preferences, knowledge, experience, and needs, making them superior to a one-size-fits-all approach.

Because of its convenience and efficiency, mobile learning has quickly gained in popularity. You can more effectively teach, re-skill, and up-skill your learners at scale by combining individualized learning paths with mobile training delivery.

Let us look at four approaches (Kumar 2021) to developing personalized learning paths for your students through mobile learning.

1. *Understand Learner Preferences:* Students have different needs and preferences for when, where, and how they study. Some students find infographics, films, and scenario-based instruction helpful in absorbing new knowledge and abilities. Some people learn best by seeing demonstrations or reading guides written by experts in their field, while others learn best by listening to podcasts or watching instructional videos. It is possible that some students would instead learn new material through testing and quizzes. When designing training sessions, keeping students' preferences in mind is crucial. Determine each student's preferred method of receiving information by doing a needs analysis using a self-assessment tool, techniques, and questionnaire.
2. *Use a Learning Experience Platform:* Organizations adopt learning experience platforms (LXPs) to facilitate efficient, personalized training. Learning experience platforms (LPs) are being viewed as a viable replacement for legacy learning management systems (LMSs). Employees can benefit from LXPs' just-in-time and hands-on training as they do their day-to-day job. Newer LXPs facilitate the distribution of dynamic rather than static course materials and aid in managing students' development toward their objectives. The tracking and reporting capabilities of many up-to-date LXPs have also vastly enhanced in recent years. The L&D professionals can use the information in these reports to fill in the gaps in their students' skill sets by creating content specifically designed to address those areas. An LXP allows you to combine internal and external training resources into unified learning paths. These learning pathways can be modified to suit the learner's goals and existing knowledge, making them suitable for personalized learning. Future iterations of LXPs will undoubtedly incorporate even more functions tailored to students.

3. *Use Artificial Intelligence:* To meet the needs of today's students better, consider using AI to design individualized paths for instruction. Learning paths can be effectively tailored by leveraging data created by AI and assessing it. AI aids in detecting knowledge gaps and providing valuable recommendations for filling them. You can also get more accurate information on how students' learning affects their performance: Information such as which courses students are taking, how long it is taking them to finish them, which training delivery mode they prefer, how well they do on exams, and evaluations, and any comments or feedback they have on the effectiveness of the modules can all be gathered by AI. Ultimately, AI can aid L&D professionals in providing tailored content based on their learners' requirements and unique preferences, making courses more relevant to the learners' future work needs.
4. *Obtain Feedback From Your Learners—And Use It:* Learning and development professionals need to understand how to tailor mobile learning paths to the individual needs of their students. Educators can better understand each student's preferred learning style, areas of interest, and requirements using self-assessment tools and artificial intelligence. However, getting honest critiques from your students is also crucial. So, L&D professionals should constantly ask for feedback from students after they finish a program so that they may make any necessary adjustments. Training more tailored to individual students' specific skills, interests, and goals is made possible through personalized mobile learning paths. Using the methods above, you can increase productivity and student interest in your mobile learning paths.

5.13 The Challenges of AI-Based Mobile Learning

This section investigates two significant issues (UKEssays 2018) related to AI-based mobile education. The evolution of soft tools and the resolution of technical issues come into play.

- *Technical problems:* The success of mobile learning enabled by artificial intelligence depends on the quality of the mobile learning environment, as well as the speed and precision of the enabling technology. There are still technical challenges with this learning style, which may persist for the foreseeable future. Regarding wireless communication, the latest and greatest is, without a doubt, third-generation (3G) technologies. As mobile wireless technology continues to make an indelible impression on the next generation, it, too, necessitates a maximum transfer rate. The rising demand for cellular networks has resulted in an additional cost to Internet use that will not go away overnight. Wireless Internet service is prohibitively expensive for the typical consumer. To their dismay, this stymied their plans to utilize wireless Internet. Although the tools for creating mobile apps are expanding rapidly, they still do not do enough to help students study using their devices. Mobile communications equipment will influence future advancements in mobile learning.

- *Development of soft tools:* Due to the early development of AI for mobile learning, the soft tools for AI-powered mobile learning are pretty limited. Most modern software is designed for a different purpose, yet some can be used for private information management. The increasing complexity of these technologies has made using them more cumbersome in many situations. In the long run, educational institutions can only effectively promote mobile learning. However, this challenge presented by mobile learning is best met by collaborative effort. The growth of the mobile business will necessitate the involvement of governments, mobile device makers, and the creators of educational software. Because of this, the advancement of tools could satisfy the requirements of artificial intelligence in mobile education. The progress of AI is accelerating at a rapid pace, and its implementation in mobile learning would usher in a new era of learning that simplifies the process for students.

5.14 Conclusion

We have come a long way in the past decade thanks to advances in artificial intelligence, which have made the seemingly impossible conceivable. Education is the foundation of any society's development, and by adding AI to mobile learning apps and online classrooms, we will be able to produce an entire generation of imaginative thinkers who will carry the technological revolution to new heights.

References

Herold, B. (2016). *Personalized Learning: What Does the Research Say?* https://www.edweek.org/technology/personalized-learning-what-does-the-research-say/2016/10#:~:text=TheGates%2FRAND Studies&text=They found that 11%2C000 students,the greater their achievement growth

Hurix. (2019). *Mobile Learning in Education is Changing the Overall Landscape.* Hurix. https://www.hurix.com/mobile-learning-in-education-impact/

Kizhakedath, B. (2021). *How mobile learning apps are taking advantage of AI.* InfotechLead. https://infotechlead.com/artificial-intelligence/how-mobile-learning-apps-are-taking-advantage-of-ai-70415

Kumar, S. (2021). *4 Ways to Create Personalized Learning Paths in Mobile Learning.* Training Industry.

Liu, Q., Diao, L., & Tu, G. (2010). The application of Artificial Intelligence in Mobile Learning. *2010 International Conference on System Science, Engineering Design and Manufacturing Informatization*, 80–83. https://doi.org/10.1109/ICSEM.2010.28

Mushavvirkhan-Balooch. (2022). *Mobile Learning has Brought Huge +ve Impact on eLearning Industry*. ELearning. https://elearning.adobe.com/2022/02/mobile-learning-has-brought-huge-ve-impact-on-elearning-industry/

Sales POP Guest Post. (2021). *How AI is Changing the Mobile Learning Education Game*. Sales POP. https://salespop.net/artificial-intelligence/how-a-i-is-changing-the-mobile-learning-education-game/

References

Sergio, F. (2012). *10 Ways That Mobile Learning Will Revolutionize Education*. FaST CoMPANY2. https://www.fastcompany.com/1669896/10-ways-that-mobile-learning-will-revolutionize-education

Shipp, A. (2021). *Piano chords for beginners: all basics explained in detail*. Skoove. https://www.skoove.com/blog/piano-chords/

Simplilearn. (2022). *Mobile Learning: Definition, Benefits, Types and More*. Simplilearn. https://www.simplilearn.com/mobile-learning-benefits-types-article#key_characteristics_of_mlearning

Sugermint. (2019). *Role of Mobile Learning Solutions in the Education Industry*. Sugermint. https://sugermint.com/role-of-mobile-learning-solutions-in-the-education-industry/

UKEssays. (2018). *Artificial Intelligence In Mobile Learning Information Technology*. UKEssays. https://www.ukessays.com/essays/information-technology/artificial-intelligence-in-mobile-learning-information-technology-essay.php

Chapter 6
AI-Enabled Gamification in Education

6.1 What Is Gamification?

Focus and concentration can profoundly affect the quality of the learning experience. With gamification, classes can become more exciting and engaging, leading to better student results.

The term "gamification" needs to be defined first. "Gamification" refers to "a strategy that implements game-like elements into non-gaming activities to enhance engagement and motivation" (FutureLearn 2021).

The designers of video games strive to create experiences that are both immersive and enjoyable. It is not unusual to get so engrossed in a game that you cannot stop playing until you have unlocked every possible level.

However, what about video games draw us in and keep us returning for more? Dopamine, also known as the "feel-good chemical," has been related to playing video games (Koepp et al. 1998), which can cause addiction.

This is because games' elements like points, rankings, and rewards all work to keep players engaged. The gamification approach uses game mechanics to improve non-game contexts, such as learning environments.

Intrinsic Motivation . Gamification fosters intrinsic motivation, defined as "the want to accomplish something due to one's interest in the work" (FutureLearn 2021). Thanks to this enticement, students will be interested in their study material.

On the other hand, extrinsic motivation refers to the desire to act in response to an external incentive or factor, such as a command from an authority figure. Learners should be careful not to rely too heavily on extrinsic motivation, even though most people will have a healthy balance of the two types.

A student who relies solely on external incentives to drive their work will do so for the wrong reasons. Educators should emphasize to their students that learning is rewarding, and they can do so by offering various incentives for successful academic performance.

6.2 Reasons to Implement Gamification

Engagement, or how much interest and effort a person puts into anything, is the best predictor of success in learning. Students are more likely to remember what they have learned if they are actively involved in learning. According to research on gamification, including gaming elements in the classroom can enhance participation and interest. Keeping students interested is paramount, so here are some things to consider (Solanki 2022) when deciding whether to introduce gaming into your classroom.

- Gamification boosts competition, which can boost engagement.
- With gamification, students are more invested since they have more agency in their learning.
- Students may easily keep track of their progress toward academic goals with the help of gamification, which provides instant feedback (via peer comments, progress bars, badges, teacher responses, etc.).

Because of these benefits, gamification can be a powerful technique for enhancing the educational process for students.

6.3 Gamification in an Educational Context

Games encourage problem-solving, an increasingly important ability in the modern world. Several components of games make them effective tools for teaching and learning. Depending on the game, players may be encouraged to share information, work together, or even compete against one another. The most engrossing games are in-depth stories that inspire players to use their imaginations (TeachThought Staff 2017). Last but not least, games can function as both a learning tool and an assessment tool for their players depending on their structure. They are fantastic pedagogical, instructional, and evaluative bundles.

Additionally, the games' frameworks suit today's students' needs. The practice of incorporating game elements like story-telling, puzzle-solving, aesthetics, rules, collaboration, competition, rewards, feedback, and trial-and-error learning into non-game contexts has been called gamification (or gameful design, in Jane McGonigal's terminology) and has seen widespread adoption in fields like marketing, training, and consumerism with runaway success (TeachThought Staff 2017).

The use of gamification in the classroom is gaining popularity. Game-based learning has the potential to extend to more schools, especially with pioneers like Classcraft, Class Dojo, and Rezzly paving the way (TeachThought Staff 2017). A subset of the education community also creates its own "gameful-designed" classrooms.

6.4 How Can Gamification Benefit Education?

Adding games and incentives to the classroom can radically improve student engagement and retention. Now, the question becomes, "How can we use gamification to improve education?"

Many of us have developed an expectation of instant gratification due to the frequent use of social media, mobile apps, and video games (FutureLearn 2021). Because of the habitual dopamine release from destructive behaviors, it might be challenging to maintain concentration on something constructive.

Because they spend so much time online, this is especially important for the younger generations. According to studies, more than half of all members of Gen Z use their smartphones for more than 5 hours daily (Vuleta 2022).

When we apply the same gamification principles to education, we may help students develop a similar addiction to success in their studies.

Gamified learning has been demonstrated to improve academic performance (Smiderle et al. 2020). Though gamification has been shown to boost student performance in the classroom (Legaki et al. 2020), this has not been linked to increased student engagement.

Motivation The introduction of progress indicators may greatly inspire students. When used in the classroom, gamification can help keep students motivated by rewarding them for incremental progress toward a larger goal (FutureLearn 2021). Motivating yourself is far more straightforward if you work toward something you can achieve.

Social learning, which may be a powerful motivator, is greatly enhanced by gamification in education. To encourage maximum growth in knowledge, certain apps and websites let users connect with their social networks and compete against one another.

Fun Learning Aiming for a higher level or a specific accomplishment can motivate you to put more effort into your studies. By incorporating game mechanics, gamification transforms learning from a chore to a pleasure (FutureLearn 2021).

Like any good video game, pursuing a higher score or a more challenging objective may be much more fun. With the help of gamification, students can shift their perspective on school from drudgery to anticipation.

Teachers are always looking for new methods to capture the attention of their young students. It is no secret that today's classrooms use technology and other innovative techniques. However, outside of school, many members of Gen Z enjoy playing video games. Designing a curriculum based on what they already know and are familiar with makes perfect sense.

Control and Encouragement Students can familiarly and enjoyably achieve their objectives using motivators such as point systems and levels. Using gamified learning materials can help students and learners feel more responsible for their education (FutureLearn 2021).

Gamified learning makes students feel more in charge of their own learning experience and motivates them to keep trying even if they first fail. Traditional education approaches can be very discouraging for students who do not achieve their goals.

Because of the playful character of the gamification model, it can be simpler for students to see how to try again and progress toward their goals. Points encourage progress toward a level rather than working toward a grade or result that can be failed. Taking this constructive tack results in a more encouraging atmosphere in the classroom.

E-Learning Business in the field of providing education online is booming. Additionally, gamification complements online education. Online learning platforms are the best places to implement gamified education.

Due to the pandemic and the demand for online education options, the popularity of e-learning has exploded in recent years (FutureLearn 2021). Software and the web are well-suited to house gamification elements like leaderboards and point systems.

When compared to traditional classroom settings, learning online has its drawbacks. Younger students may find it challenging to focus and pay attention during online lectures and lessons due to the abundance of distractions. Using game mechanics, online education may be just as engaging as classroom instruction.

Disadvantages of Gamification in Learning Apps and websites rely on technology and are frequently used in gamification strategies. By emphasizing technology so heavily in the classroom, we risk isolating some pupils who are not adept with it. Gamification is a great educational tool but comes with challenges (FutureLearn 2021).

Students' attention spans can decrease if gamification is introduced into the classroom. Today's youth crave immediate satisfaction; gamifying education could appeal to this need. Combining game elements with more conventional forms of education could help us fight this problem. This will ensure pupils have access to more solemn settings conducive to learning and work.

6.5 How Can Gamification Transform Education?

The motivation to study is essential to academic success and long-term retention of lessons learned. However, the conventional classroom environment undermines this goal by emphasizing memorization over critical thinking and discussion.

A person's professors and books were once the primary means of gaining information. These days, it is the online world with countless courses and a global community of peers. Even so, the trend toward the homogenization of all educational materials persists. New ways of teaching and learning, like game-based instruction, are desperately needed (Agrawal 2021).

How It Helps Gamification of learning" refers to utilizing game elements and dynamics to improve educational outcomes (Agrawal 2021). In the past, students were motivated to study because their teachers gave them high marks for their work. The goal of gamifying the educational process is to exchange traditional letter grades for numerical scores based on how well students do at various milestones in the learning process. When a student reaches a specific point total, a badge is awarded as a visible indication of achievement. When students complete a section of material, an assignment, or an exam and receive feedback about their performance, they are more likely to continue learning and improving.

Games are developed to have the same responsiveness and interactivity. The relevance and significance of the topic are brought home to players in a very tangible way. Students are given immediate feedback on their performance in gamified learning instead of in a traditional classroom setting. They can better correct their errors and learn from their explorations and discoveries of new knowledge and methods of approaching their objectives when they receive these when they make them. Students are pushed to learn and can retain more information when they use it in a dynamic, real-time environment.

Additionally, collaboration is boosted by gamification. Students are more likely to learn from each other and share their knowledge and ideas when placed in competitive groups.

With a gamified system, students may move through the material at their own pace, making it more effective and adaptable (Agrawal 2021). Each player can have an equal chance at learning a topic because games can be adapted to their native language, region, and age range. In addition, with the help of ed-tech-enabled competency-based learning, students can learn and acquire skills based on the demonstration of learning outcomes.

As a result of students' increased participation and enthusiasm for the material, teachers' workloads are reduced thanks to gamification. More than that, users are given multiple means of gauging their progress in a course rather than just one, thanks to the availability of alternative paths to completion. They will be able to tailor their instruction to the specific requirements of each learner.

It is expected that gamification will usher in a new era of education as it becomes more commonplace in K-12 classrooms, colleges, universities, and corporate training and development programs.

6.6 Gamification and Artificial Intelligence

The widespread application of games in education, as defined by and shown by game-based learning (Homer et al. 2020), has led to the creation (Dingli and Seychell 2015) and implementation (in schools) of educational video games (Panoutsopoulos and Sampson 2012), (Sykes 2018). Compared to traditional didactic teaching approaches, studies show that using games as a teaching tool might help students learn more and be more enthusiastic about it (Posso 2016). Recently, a new conceptual layer has been added to using games in education (Bezzina et al. 2021).

The theory behind gamification, also known as the "use of game design elements in non-gaming contexts" (Deterding et al. 2011), shifts the emphasis from the use of actual games in educational settings to the use of specific design elements, such as game mechanics and thinking, to captivate and motivate learners and generate innovative solutions to challenges (Pfeiffer et al. 2020). Preliminary empirical research on gamification's use in the classroom indicates a favorable impact on students' interest and effort (Kingsley and Grabner-hagen 2015), (Leaning 2015).

Conversely, detractors of gamification point out that its primary motivators—such as points, badges, and leaderboards—are overly simplistic and exploitive of game design characteristics that lead to a phony sense of accomplishment (Woodcock and Johnson 2018). As there is currently only a small amount of scientific research about the use of gamification in education, most of it relates to the effects of gamification on students' motivation and engagement rather than on their cognitive development and learning (Alsawaier 2018) (Jayalath and Esichaikul 2020).

Artificial intelligence (AI) is an interdisciplinary topic with applications in many fields and disciplines, including medicine, law, linguistics, and education (Goksel-canbek and Mutlu 2016). Grading automation, adapting to students' needs, predictively analyzing their learning, differentiating and personalizing learning activities, real-time learning analytics, anytime, anywhere support from AI tutors, and targeted individualized feedback are just a few of the many advances made in the field of artificial intelligence in education (AIEd) over the past two decades (Bezzina et al. 2021). There has been a recent uptick in classroom implementations of AI-based algorithmic and systemic initiatives. Therefore, artificial intelligence has the potential to enhance the quality of instruction and learning as a leading-edge developing technology that is breaking new ground in the academic world (Chen et al. 2020). It is important to note that while many AIEd systems have been developed throughout the years, there is currently scant scientific evidence of their effect on student learning (Goksel-canbek and Mutlu 2016).

Students' cognitive learning, insight acquisition, and risk prediction can benefit from using AI-supported adaptive learning objectives, feedback, and rewards to foster intrinsic motivation (Bezzina et al. 2021). Access to a stimulating learning environment that allows for individualization and adaptation of instruction is even more critical in mobile learning and evaluation.

6.7 Educational Gamification Powered by AI

A fundamental requirement of Educational Gamification is a familiarity with digital games and gameplay. Imagine hiring a consultant with no background in gaming yet who gives you in-depth instructions on how to use gamification but has no idea what you are talking about because they have no experience with digital games. In most cases, gamification entails some metamorphosis, as seen in (Friedemann et al.

2015). It is grounded in students' prior learning, skills, and established pedagogical procedures (Jantke 2018).

Educational Gamification Beyond Game Elements and Mechanics People's interest in playing digital games is consistently high. After only a few years, the digital games industry has already shown to be more successful than the film industry. Furthermore, it cannot be denied that playing digital games might become a habit-forming behavior. Educational gamification seeks to maximize the potential of digital games for teaching and education by capitalizing on the entertainment value and the potential for addiction they present.

Video games are a form of popular entertainment that can give humans unique opportunities to engage in meaningful activities. A range of psychological aspects, such as the gratification of overcoming a challenge or difficulty or the relief of escaping a potentially dangerous situation, can set the stage for emotionally moving and fulfilling experiences. It could be exciting or surprising. Those working in the film industry are familiar with dramaturgical methods like Mitaffekt and Eigenaffekt, both famously used by Alfred Hitchcock.

Parasocial experiences, which are difficult to separate from social experiences in multiplayer games, may emerge through interactions with non-player characters (NPCs). Even a novice player in flow (Jantke 2018) does not control a digital system through an interface, nor does he or she have to work through technical difficulties to have fun while exploring a virtual world through touch. To "gamify" a classroom or other learning space means changing it into an atmosphere where students can have positive learning outcomes while having fun.

Whether instructive or not, various humans see gamification results differently due to the sheer nature of digital games and gameplay. In light of this, the teaching and instructing occasions may differ considerably.

The Need for Artificial Intelligence for Educational Gamification Educators, aware of the allure of digital games and eager to respond to the increasing digitization of society, seek to maximize their impact on as many students and trainees as possible. Results from gamification are often misinterpreted. Only by enhancing AI in educational gamification can this problem be solved. The key to making Educational Gamification flexible and, thus, more effective for varying human learners and trainers is artificial intelligence, which allows a digital system to learn about users. The ideas and procedures of AI make digital systems eminently edifying. A digital system based on AI might be able to pick up on the nuances of its user, such as the player's goals, the learner's misconceptions, or even the human's current emotional state (Jantke 2018).

As can be observed from case studies (Jantke 2018), gamified education has advantages over conventional approaches due to its personalized, adaptable nature and its attractiveness based on playfulness.

Concepts and Technologies of Artificial Intelligence Implementation One of the biggest challenges with gamification is that it is hard to predict how people will react to it, which is true even outside the classroom. This dynamic planning challenge calls for the anticipation of future courses of action.

Storyboarding is essential for preparing for various user experiences (Jantke 2018). Digital storyboards are required for direct integration into the deployed system. Technically speaking, storyboards are graphs; more specifically, they are families of graphs with a hierarchical structure. The strategy works well for sophisticated, realistic training applications (Jantke 2018).

Scenes and episodes are typically represented as separate nodes in storyboard graphs. Scenes are fundamental nodes with application-specific meaning, such as a cutscene, downloadable file, text or audio file to be read or listened to, or menu options from which to choose. Each episode is a stand-in for a different subgraph. The various subgraphs have new substitution criteria introduced in each episode. Interaction history, the application's setting, and the user's role are all factors the conditions can influence. Through the use of the information implied by the substitution conditions, dynamic adaptation is achieved. What we now call "storyboard interpretation technology" has its syntactic foundation in storyboards. In technical parlance, this is the idea of reading and using storyboards during actual gameplay, practice, or instruction.

Graphs depict many instructional notions that can be interpreted as patterns (Jantke 2018). It is possible that changing out episodes for different graph nodes can stand in for entirely new pedagogical ideas. There is empirical evidence that this method works (Jantke 2018). Effective Educational Gamification is made possible by AI's storyboarding, storyboarding software, and storyboarding interpretation technologies.

6.8 Incorporating AI Into Educational Games

General education manager at Microsoft Dan Ayoub (Ayoub 2020) claims that the use of AI in education is not a new phenomenon but that the technology is set to change how teachers teach radically and students learn.

How can educational game makers apply machine learning to educational games, as artificial intelligence plays an increasingly important role in the status of education? Let us examine a few cases (Jantke 2018) in point:

Personalized Learning Adaptive learning, in which content is automatically and constantly adapted to the learner's competence and knowledge depending on their input, is one significant way artificial intelligence supplements game-based learning. This can be achieved in a game-based learning setting by collecting and analyzing information about the player's actions, skills, and preferred learning methods and then delivering tailored content to the player. It could be more complex game mechanics activated when the player progresses quickly through content and seeks a more significant challenge, or it could be the activation of supplementary aids if a student is having difficulty grasping a particular subject.

Task Automation Scholastic and the Bill and Melinda Gates Foundation polled teachers in 2013, finding that they spend an average of 53 hours per week on the job, with much of that time spent on things like home grading and staff meetings. However, by outsourcing all grading-related chores to artificial intelligence systems integrated within learning games, educators will have increased time and availability to engage directly with learners – especially 1-on-1 encounters with individuals who require additional attention and support. Learning games with added AI features can also help with task automation.

Support Beyond the Classroom Many parents nationwide struggle to provide enough at-home learning support for their children for various reasons, including a lack of financial resources or educational experience. The use of AI in games is one way to address this issue, as it can enable the game itself to provide individualized assistance to players, thus leveling the playing field and guaranteeing that student always have access to the guidance they require, regardless of the setting in which they are learning. Using AI in educational games makes them adequate resources for both in-class and at-home learning.

6.9 Conclusion

The purpose of the in-depth analysis and evaluation of the novel application of AI-powered gamification to the educational setting is to contribute to and shape the development of future thought and practice in the field of education. This chapter provided additional insight into how AI facilitates efficient educational gamification.

References

Agrawal, A. (2021, June 12). How gamification can transform education. *The Hindu*, 1–10. https://www.thehindu.com/education/how-gamification-can-transform-education/article34796220.ece

Alsawaier, R. (2018). The effect of gamification on motivation and engagement. *The International Journal of Information and Learning Technology*, 35(1), 56–79. https://doi.org/10.1108/IJILT-02-2017-0009

Ayoub, D. (2020). *Unleashing the power of AI for education.* https://www.technologyreview.com/2020/03/04/905535/unleashing-the-power-of-ai-for-education/

Bezzina, S., Pfeiffer, A., & Dingli, A. (2021). AI-Enabled Gamification for Learning and Assessment. *International Conferences on Mobile Learning and Educational Technologies*, 189–193.

Chen, L., Chen, P., & Lin, Z. (2020). Artificial Intelligence in Education: A Review. *IEEE Access*, 8, 75264–75278. https://doi.org/10.1109/ACCESS.2020.2988510

Deterding, S., Sicart, M., Nacke, L., O'Hara, K., & Dixon, D. (2011). Gamification: Using Game Design Elements in Non-Gaming Contexts. *CHI EA '11 Extended Abstracts on Human Factors in Computing Systems*, 2425–2428.

Dingli, A., & Seychell, D. (2015). *The New Digital Natives: Cutting the Chord*. Springer. https://doi.org/10.1007/978-3-662-46590-5

Friedemann, S., Baumbach, L., & Jantke, K. P. (2015). Textbook Gamification: Transforming Exercises into Playful Quests by Using Webble Technology. *7th International Conference on Computer Supported Education*, 116_126. https://doi.org/10.5220/0005489101160126

FutureLearn. (2021). *What is gamification in education?* FutureLearn. https://www.futurelearn.com/info/blog/general/gamification-in-education

Goksel-canbek, N., & Mutlu, M. E. (2016). On the track of Artificial Intelligence: Learning with Intelligent Personal Assistants. *Journal of Human Sciences*, *13*(1), 592–601. https://doi.org/10.14687/ijhs.v13i1.3549

Homer, B. D., Raffaele, C., & Henderson, H. (2020). Games as Playful Learning: Implications of Developmental Theory for Game-Based Learning. In *Handbook of Game-Based Learning* (pp. 25–52). MIT Press.

Jantke, K. P. (2018). *Educational Gamification & Artificial Intelligence*.

Jayalath, J., & Esichaikul, V. (2020). Gamification to Enhance Motivation and Engagement in Blended eLearning for Technical and Vocational Education and Training. *Technology, Knowledge and Learning*, *27*, 91–118. https://doi.org/10.1007/s10758-020-09466-2

Kingsley, T. L., & Grabner-hagen, M. M. (2015). Gamification: questing to integrate content, knowledge, literacy, and 21st-century learning. *Journal of Adolescent & Adult Literacy*, *59*(1), 51–61. https://doi.org/10.1002/jaal.426

Koepp, M. J., Gunn, R. N., Lawrence, A. D., Cunningham, V. J., Dagher, A., Jones, T., Brooks, D. J., Bench, C. J., & Grasby, P. M. (1998). Evidence for striatal dopamine release during a video game. *Nature*, *393*(May), 266–268.

Leaning, M. (2015). A study of the use of games and gamification to enhance student engagement, experience and achievement on a theory-based course of an undergraduate media degree. *Journal of Media Practice*, *16*(2), 155–170.

Legaki, N., Xi, N., Hamari, J., Karpouzis, K., & Assimakopoulos, V. (2020). The effect of challenge-based gamification on learning: An experiment in the context of statistics education. *International Journal of Human-Computer Studies*, *144*(November 2019), 1–14. https://doi.org/10.1016/j.ijhcs.2020.102496

Panoutsopoulos, H., & Sampson, D. G. (2012). A Study on Exploiting Commercial Digital Games into School Context. *Educational Technology & Society*, *15*(1), 15–27.

Pfeiffer, A., Bezzina, S., König, N., & Kriglstein, S. (2020). Beyond Classical Gamification: In-and Around-Game Gamification for Education. *19th European Conference on E-Learning*, October, 415–420. https://doi.org/10.34190/EEL.20.007

Posso, A. (2016). Internet Usage and Educational Outcomes Among 15-Year-Old Australian Students. *International Journal of Communication*, *10*, 3851–3876.

Smiderle, R., Rigo, S. J., Marques, L. B., Coelho, J. A. P. de M., & Jaques, P. A. (2020). The impact of gamification on students' learning, engagement and behavior based on their personality traits. *Smart Learning Environments*, *7*(3), 1–11. https://doi.org/10.1186/s40561-019-0098-x (2020)

Solanki, V. (2022). *Gamification in Education | Learning, Benefits & Strategies*. Study.Com. https://study.com/academy/lesson/what-is-gamification-in-education-definition-research-strategies.html

Sykes, J. M. (2018). Digital games and language teaching and learning. *Foreign Language Annals*, *51*(December), 219–224. https://doi.org/10.1111/flan.12325

TeachThought Staff. (2017). *12 Examples Of Gamification In The Classroom*. TeachThought. https://www.teachthought.com/the-future-of-learning/examples-gamification/

Vuleta, B. (2022). *Generation Z Statistics*. 99Firms. https://99firms.com/blog/generation-z-statistics/#gref

Woodcock, J., & Johnson, M. R. (2018). Gamification: what it is, and how to fight it. *Sociological Review*, *66*(3), 542–558. https://doi.org/10.1177/0038026117728620

Chapter 7
AR, VR, and AI for Education

7.1 What Is AR and VR?

These days, people spend time in front of devices. We now rely heavily on computers, smartphones, and televisions for our news, social media, entertainment, and other daily needs. As a result of technological advancements in virtual reality (VR) and augmented reality (AR), we can now enjoy a whole new level of interactivity with our devices.

What Is Augmented Reality (AR)? The term "augmented reality" (AR) refers to the process of creating a synthetic environment that combines the digital and physical worlds in an ideal way (Martin 2022). Apps for smartphones and computers that use augmented reality to superimpose computer-generated imagery over a physical setting.

What Is Virtual Reality (VR)? The term "virtual reality" (VR) refers to any technologically created simulation of an external environment (Martin 2022). It is the technology behind those eye-popping 3D movies and games. Combined with computers and sensory gear like headsets and gloves, it allows for creating simulations that are very close to the real world and effectively "immerse" the viewer. Virtual reality is not just for fun and games; it has severe applications in education, science, and training.

How Does AR Work? With the help of computer vision, mapping, and depth monitoring, AR can display relevant content in the right place at the right time (Martin 2022). Due to this feature, cameras may now gather, transmit, and process data to display digital material tailored to the subject being viewed.

By superimposing pertinent digital information over the user's real-world surroundings in real-time, augmented reality provides a richer, more meaningful experience. You may enjoy augmented reality (AR) with a smartphone or specialized equipment.

© The Author(s), under exclusive license to Springer Nature Switzerland AG 2023
M. Kurni et al., *A Beginner's Guide to Introduce Artificial Intelligence in Teaching and Learning*, https://doi.org/10.1007/978-3-031-32653-0_7

How Does VR Work? The primary goal of VR is optical illusion simulation (Martin 2022). The user must position the virtual reality headset's screen in front of his or her eyes. In this way, it becomes impossible to have any contact with the outside world. In virtual reality, the screen is sandwiched between two lenses. The eyes must be adjusted by the user for their eye movement and posture. An HDMI cable linked to a laptop or mobile device can display the images on the screen.

It employs head-mounted displays, audio, and, in some cases, hand-held devices to create an artificial environment. Virtual reality creates a natural environment using visual, aural, and haptic (touch) input.

7.2 How Does VR/AR Fit into the Education System?

The potential influence of VR/AR deployment in the educational system may be summed up in four words: harder, better, faster, and stronger (Tkachenko 2022). The educational system requires cutting-edge technological advancements to adapt to a constantly evolving world. The education system will unavoidably progress toward more cutting-edge technologies like virtual and augmented reality shortly.

Virtual reality (VR) and augmented reality (AR) solutions for education offer readily transferable business models, which are an attractive feature for potential investors (Tkachenko 2022). On the one hand, you will not have to worry about developing a long-term profitable business strategy. There is no way it could ever happen because rules are handled differently in public education.

In augmented and virtual reality (AR/VR) businesses, one of the biggest challenges is developing a sustainable business model; removing this variable frees up significant time for focusing on creating compelling content (Tkachenko 2022). However, that is when things start to get serious. Virtual reality (VR) instruction requires more than just a well-crafted reproduction of a bodily function; teachers must also consider pupils' backgrounds and skill levels.

7.3 Reasons to Use AR and VR in the Classroom

Incorporating cutting-edge technologies like augmented and virtual reality (AR and VR) into the classroom has increased student participation and retention.

Recent years have seen a rise in the use of augmented and virtual reality (AR/VR) technology in STEM education. Teachers use exciting new technologies to introduce their students to new worlds and prospects in their studies and careers.

There are several reasons (Wilson 2019) why these immersive technologies will affect students, and they are becoming increasingly apparent (see Fig. 7.1).

7.3 Reasons to Use AR and VR in the Classroom

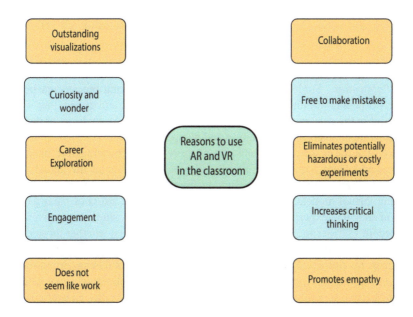

Fig. 7.1 Reasons to use AR and VR in the classroom

1. *Great visualizations:* Most children may encounter limited prospects because of their location, especially in rural areas with poverty rates above the national average. However, by adopting the vision of offering the finest possible experiences through superior instructional technology, students can access thousands of models they may interact with, virtual field trips to exotic locations, and potentially transformative simulations. It gives the students what they can accomplish, motivating them to work more.
2. *Curiosity and wonder:* In the classroom, students using augmented and virtual reality (AR/VR) technology is a beginning, not a conclusion. Unlike what may be found in a lecture or textbook, these interactive activities pique students' enthusiasm for learning. Many students indicate that their interest in a topic was aroused during classes in a virtual environment, leading them to do more research outside of class.
3. *Career exploration:* Experiences in augmented reality (AR) and virtual reality (VR) can show students many career options and assist them in finding their passions, giving them a head start in deciding which course of study or profession to pursue. CTE programs provide students with hands-on training in their chosen field even before they graduate high school by using AR and VR in the classroom, expanding students' access to academic pursuits and opportunities.
4. *Engagement:* Virtual reality models can pique their curiosity and facilitate their conceptualization of complex ideas by putting students in charge of their learning. Because AR and VR allow students to go deeper into topics, alter virtual models in novel ways, and even build their designs and experiments, they can maintain interest and concentration throughout the class.

5. *It does not seem like work:* Students have a great time using AR and VR for study and exploration. These interactive activities make students feel like they are playing, but they are learning through discovery and exploration in ways impossible in a traditional classroom setting.
6. *Collaboration:* Students are likelier to initiate and contribute to teacher and peer-to-peer communication when engaged, interested, and driven. Pair work is typical in the classroom; students work with the instructor to discover new content while exchanging information and perspectives.
7. *Free to make mistakes:* Students can be more safely encouraged to make mistakes and learn from them in virtual science labs than in the actual world. Students can make mistakes, gain valuable insights, and swiftly recover when using virtual models, all without incurring the cost or stress of having to perform an actual experiment. With this paradigm shifted, students are given more freedom to experiment and grow from their experiences, whether those experiences are successful or not.
8. *Eliminates potentially hazardous or costly experiments:* Using virtual models, middle and high school students can learn about complex topics that would be out of reach in a traditional classroom setting, such as roller coaster construction and heart dissection. Virtual reality (VR) provides students of all ages with high-tech, risk-free, and cost-effective educational experiences, from introducing them to the inner workings of the human and animal bodies to letting them experiment with mechanics and robotics.
9. *Increases critical thinking:* Students can ask "what if?" questions and generate constructive hypotheses in a virtual context, leading them to more credible conclusions. Students are encouraged to use their imaginations to investigate and address issues by manipulating models to observe how different outcomes result from human or environmental actions.
10. *Promotes empathy:* Using virtual reality in the classroom can increase students' capacity for empathy and positive outlooks on various social groupings and real-world circumstances. Students gain a more nuanced and empathetic understanding of diverse cultures and lifestyles by putting themselves in another person's virtual shoes.

7.4 The Present Applications of VR and AR in Education

As state of the art in immersive technologies advance, novel applications in the classroom are constantly being developed, and learning at all levels and fields benefits significantly from AR/VR technologies. To help pave the way for the next generation of immersive educational technology, this section highlights recent breakthroughs laying the groundwork for that future.

7.4.1 K-12 Education: Enriching Classroom Experiences and Expanding Opportunities

Immersive Learning Curricula and Resource Collections Many augmented and virtual reality (AR/VR) solutions for K-12 education come with pre-made lesson plans and libraries of immersive experiences that can be tailored to meet the needs of individual classrooms. Publicly available resources from government organizations, libraries of immersive content with an educational focus, and specialist services from companies specializing in applying AR/VR in immersive experiences (Dick 2021) are just some of the options currently available.

1. *Public Resources:* The Smithsonian Institution maintains a database of freely available 3D models that visitors can use to see Smithsonian Museum objects in their natural environments through augmented reality on a mobile device. These models enhance scale and interaction in three-dimensional space, which are superior to print or digital two-dimensional representations. These materials are ideal for teachers supplementing environmental and American history lessons. Any mobile device with a camera can access the collection via the web-based Voyager platform, which features ten artifacts, such as full-size skeletons, cultural relics, and statues. The National Aeronautics and Space Administration (NASA) provides teachers with interactive educational materials that can be incorporated into lessons or expanded upon in a museum or planetarium setting. NASA launched a virtual reality (VR) experience in 2018 that puts users in the center of a rocket blast-off. The agency also provides 360-degree videos that can be seen online via a VR headset, desktop computer, or mobile device. This virtual reality (VR) experiences can transport students to far-flung locations and give them a taste of what it would be like to live on the International Space Station or explore distant planets.
2. *Content Collections: The New York Times* has published a guide titled "VR in the Classroom," which features lesson plans that use the publication's collection of 360° videos. Teachers with little experience incorporating immersive content into their courses will benefit from the guide's detailed lesson plans and step-by-step directions covering STEM and humanities topics. In addition to the lesson plans, 360° videos can be used independently in the classroom. You only need a computer, smartphone, or VR headset to see the videos. Many features once available in the Expeditions app—which lets educators create and conduct virtual field trips—are now available on the Google Arts and Culture platform. Artwork, space travel, natural history, musical events, and cultural and historical landmarks worldwide are just some of the 360-degree experiences available on the platform. Teachers can use these activities as building blocks for larger virtual field trips or supplementary materials for existing sessions.
3. *Edtech Services:* Avantis, a provider of educational technology, has released a virtual reality (VR) platform for schools called ClassVR. The service includes the necessary gear (plastic VR headsets) and a library of immersive instructional

content that teachers can manage from a centralized administration system on a single computer. This approach allows teachers to integrate virtual reality into guided classes, which is impossible with decentralized libraries because teachers have no control once students put on the headsets. Access to field excursions and other extracurricular activities outside the classroom is only one of the many educational inequalities that inspired the creation of Kai XR, a subscription-based virtual reality (VR) learning platform. The service provides multilingual, instructor-led virtual tours of real-world attractions like museums, landmarks, and outer space. The platform not only provides students with access to immersive locations and virtual experiences but also provides students with the means to create their own.

Subject Specialization Some K-12 products provide experiences for various courses and learning goals, while others focus on a narrower set of topics.

Designed to educate middle school students about marine biodiversity, BioDive by Killer Snails is a virtual reality (VR) experience accessible over the web. Students take on the role of marine scientists as they use the app to investigate a marine ecosystem and are then asked to record their findings and hypotheses in an electronic notebook. A student needs a web browser and Internet connection to participate in the interactive experience and keep a digital journal. In this way, educators can better monitor and direct their students' academic development.

In order to include Black experiences in middle school textbooks, Movers and Shakers have created an augmented reality tool. Recently, the group released an app called Kinfolk, which has augmented reality (AR) replicas of prominent Black leaders, including Frederick Douglass, Harry Belafonte, and Shirley Chisholm, and allows children to learn about and connect with these figures. Users can check out the digital "monument" for each person of note and view further information about them, like their biography, items from that time period, and even related music.

Special Education Students of all abilities, including those with cognitive and learning challenges, can benefit from the tailored learning solutions made possible by AR/VR. Furthermore, special education children with autism spectrum disorder (ASD) can access intensive programs designed for their unique needs.

The University of Kansas's Center for Research on Learning and Department of Special Education runs the Virtual Reality Opportunities to Implement Social Skills project, abbreviated as VOISS. Students in middle school with learning difficulties are targeted for this initiative, which employs virtual reality experiences to teach and practice social skills. The program gives kids and educators a safe space to experiment with various uses of a headset or Internet-connected gadget.

Young people on the autism spectrum can benefit from Floreo's virtual reality (VR)-based social and life skills instruction. The activities are designed to help participants develop their social skills, prepare them for real-world encounters, and give them opportunities to exercise control over their emotions. The user can practice communication and social cues through story-based interactive scenarios in a gamified setting. Teachers and other adults in authority can monitor students' development and shape their learning with the help of an app on a mobile device.

Higher Education: Putting Theories into Practice and Preparing Students for Their Futures Immersive learning has traditionally been at the forefront of STEM and healthcare. However, higher education institutions are increasingly looking to AR/VR solutions to improve instruction in traditionally "soft" subjects like the humanities, the arts, and even hard sciences like law and business. The benefits of AR/VR for learning are combined with their use in higher education to break through geographical obstacles. Many colleges and universities are less hierarchical than K-12 schools, allowing students more freedom to learn and explore independently under the guidance of faculty (Dick 2021).

STEM Education More and more professors in the STEM fields and educational technology professionals are developing innovative ways to convey the field's notoriously difficult-to-explain topics through AR and VR. In STEM education, immersive experiences can be beneficial since they provide students with hands-on opportunities that would otherwise be impractical or unattainable.

Researchers from Arizona State University, Northern Arizona University, the University of Arizona, and the University of Colorado Boulder collaborated to create Polar Explorer, a virtual reality (VR) teaching tool for teaching undergraduate students about the effects of climate change on polar environments. This initiative allows students to go on virtual field trips to the Arctic, something few people would ever be able to do due to a lack of funds or physical ability.

Teachers at Spain's Universidad Católica San Antonio de Murcia created a virtual reality (VR) environment using the web-based Mozilla Hubs to provide students with experience with the coronavirus. When in-person collaboration was impossible owing to COVID-19 safety requirements, students could still work with their professors and peers in real time using virtual environments to explore learning materials like a larger-than-life virus model.

Purdue University's astronomy students have access to a virtual, collaborative space where they can interact with 3D models of *astronomical* objects. Via a computer and a headset, students and the professor can enter the virtual space and learn about faraway, complicated phenomena that would otherwise have to be explained using two-dimensional images.

Through a new platform called HoloChem, the Air Force Academy is incorporating MR solutions into chemistry classes. The platform, built by GIGXR (a manufacturer of augmented reality, virtual reality, and mixed reality learning systems for STEM and medical education), enables cadets to perform complex chemistry experiments that would be too risky for less experienced learners to perform in real labs.

Medical Training Hands-on, in-person training is essential in the medical field, from learning how to communicate with patients to performing intricate procedures. AR/VR solutions are becoming increasingly popular among medical and healthcare instructors because they offer low-cost, low-risk, and frequently more participatory alternatives to conventional methods of instruction.

The COVID-19 epidemic severely hampered medical education, but the collaborative, MR-based approach proved invaluable for distant learning. Case Western Reserve University has created a medical education program, HoloAnatomy, which uses Microsoft HoloLens MR equipment to improve traditional anatomy teaching methods. HoloAnatomy replaces cadavers with 3D anatomical models that can be interacted with and evaluated in real-time.

Oxford Medical Simulation is a virtual reality (VR)-based medical simulation platform that allows students to practice patient care situations such as taking a medical history and giving treatments. If a class cannot access headsets, the software can be used remotely on a computer. Students can re-experience a simulation as often as they like to learn from their mistakes and improve each time.

The School of Medicine at Imperial College London has begun using Microsoft HoloLens for remote clinical instruction in preparation for the 2020 COVID-19 pandemic. Clinicians wear HoloLens devices to record a live stream of patient interactions during rounds, representing the hands-on clinical experience necessary for medical education. In the same way, students can ask questions in person during rounds; they can do so virtually during virtual rounds. Because of the prevalence of virtual learning environments, opportunities previously limited to a small group of students are now available to a much larger audience.

Arts, Humanities, and Other Disciplines AR/VR in higher education goes beyond the hard sciences to improve instruction in all fields. Academics and experts in all fields increasingly utilize these tools to create more interactive and informative learning environments for students.

In 2018, a visiting professor at Hamilton College taught a class titled "Dream a Little Dream: Virtual Realities and Literature," which required students to create their own VR worlds based on literary books. Students learned the principles of virtual reality production while also gaining valuable humanities skills like critical thinking and literary analysis.

The Center for Immersive Media at the University of the Arts was established in 2019 to integrate virtual reality (VR), motion capture, and spatial audio into the institution's stellar performing arts curriculum. Teachers and students can use the space to experiment with virtual and augmented reality for performing arts education.

The Virtual and Augmented Reality Language Training (VAuLT) initiative was established in 2018 at the University of Oregon's Center for Applied Second Language Studies. VAuLT is an alternative to more conventional methods of teaching a new language that gives students real-world experience in a safe environment. Foreign language learners can use the app to practice more natural conversations and put classroom concepts into context while abroad.

Soft Skills and Career Development In addition to their utility in specialized courses, AR/VR tools can teach students the "soft critical skills" they will need to succeed in the real world. This is especially helpful for future law, business, and healthcare professionals, where soft skills like communication, negotiation, and critical thinking are as crucial as technical know-how.

Bodyswaps, a platform for digitally delivering training in "soft skills," has created a virtual reality (VR) simulation called Career Mindset Development in collaboration with UK's *further education colleges*. New employees can use the 15-minute session to hone their verbal and nonverbal communication skills and receive constructive feedback.

Faculty at the University of Michigan has received funding from the university's Innovation Fund for many immersive technology-based soft skills and leadership development initiatives. Some projects span academic disciplines and learning goals, such as those that teach future lawyers how to provide constructive feedback in the courtroom, those that help nursing students become more effective leaders, and those that train the next generation of social workers.

Technical Education and Specialized Training In order to better prepare students for real-world fieldwork, immersive experiences might expose them to highly specialized and possibly *hazardous* activities. Technical education and specialized training can benefit from AR/VR since it provides a low-risk, low-cost learning environment, much like soft skills training. To further broaden participation in technical education, augmented and virtual reality technology might lessen the burden of acquiring or traveling to training facilities.

Health sciences, advanced manufacturing, agriscience, and transportation are just a few industries that might benefit from the immersive learning tools provided by zSpace, an ed-tech provider that creates interactive AR experiences for specialized hardware. In 2019, zSpace teamed with NOCTI, a provider of resources and credentials for technical and vocational education, to allow students to use the platform to acquire up to thirty-three certifications in various fields. Over fifty US technological universities have adopted zSpace software, the company claims on its website.

The Synthetic Training Environment (STE) is used by the United States Army to give its leaders the tools they need to train and simulate in artificial environments employing augmented reality (AR), virtual reality (VR), and mixed reality (MR). This feature liberates training from being restricted to a particular physical place or terrain, paves the way for more iterative and information-rich training simulations, and equips leaders with the analytical tools they need to tailor training to meet their unique goals.

The FerrisNowVR Initiative at Michigan's Ferris State University is a virtual reality (VR) program that provides innovative STEM instruction to high school students in underserved areas of the state. The program will use funding from the US Department of Agriculture's Distance Learning and Telemedicine program to equip twenty high schools and career and technical education centers across 11 counties with the necessary equipment. Students can get college credit for IT or other technical credentials through dual enrollment in university-level synchronous courses without leaving their home district.

Teacher Training: Preparing Educators for Success There are many potential users for educational virtual reality experiences besides schoolchildren and college students (Dick 2021). The same features that make these technologies useful in primary, secondary, and tertiary settings also put them in a prime position to aid in the professional development of teachers.

The University of Central Florida's Center for Research in Education Simulation Technology created TeachLivE, an interactive classroom simulation. The program offers a safe space for new and aspiring educators to practice high-pressure handling situations to prepare them for classroom challenges. Teachers can learn about their actions and reactions in a safe, no-risk environment by playing out scenarios in a simulation.

The gender and racial prejudices that may affect instructors' interactions with their female and minority students are discussed in Teacher's Lens. Participants use virtual reality headsets to experience a simulated classroom interaction in which they are asked to raise their hands and call on students of varying racial and gender identities. Using the Harvard Implicit Association Test results as a starting point; the program analyzes the participant's responses to determine whether or not they exhibit unconscious preference. It then provides constructive feedback to help them recognize and overcome any biases.

7.5 Examples of VR and AR in Education

This section will look at ten favorite ways AR/VR is used in the classroom (Marr 2021) to help students learn and stay engaged:

1. Using augmented reality to visualize scientific concepts. With the help of augmented reality, we can now generate a funnel cloud and transport it into the classroom, where the students may have an up-close look at one of these catastrophic storms. Alternatively, kids can use augmented reality (AR) to tour a beehive and learn more about the bees' vital role in maintaining a healthy ecosystem.
2. SkyView is an augmented reality app that superimposes night sky images, allowing students to travel across space virtually. Anyone with a mobile device and SkyView may look up and learn about the night sky, from stars and constellations to planets and satellites.
3. Dissecting frogs to learn about their internal anatomy was a repulsive procedure to us, and it was probably even worse for the frogs. Students may examine a frog's interior anatomy with the augmented reality technology built into the Froggipedia app.
4. Microsoft HoloLens has created a mixed-reality method for medical students and practitioners to study the human body. To better learn anatomy and how to treat various medical disorders, students can now really "flow through the bloodstream," isolate, magnify, and even walk inside the various parts of the human body.

5. The Berlin Blitz in 360°, created by Immersive VR Education for the BBC, allows viewers to experience what it was like to be a part of a nighttime raid on Nazi Germany in 1943.
6. Even though most educators lack the resources to transport their students to places like Mount Everest's Base Camp or the Louvre, those institutions' collections can be experienced through immersive Google Expeditions virtual field trips.
7. If you have ever wanted to rehearse a speech in front of a fake audience before delivering it to real people, you can now do so by strapping on a pair of VR glasses. With VirtualSpeech, you may train your public speaking abilities using cutting-edge VR simulations.
8. The Mona Lisa and other masterpieces are now accessible without the hassle of crowds or glass barriers at Steam's Virtual Museum of Fine Art.
9. In the business world, extended reality can also be used by training businesses. For the benefit of both the public and police, many police departments are beginning to use virtual reality (VR) to prepare officers for dealing with riots and making arrests under specific circumstances.
10. Reading a book to learn a new language can feel very theoretical, but with the help of virtual reality and educational software like Mondly, you can get a more realistic feel for the language even if you cannot visit the nation itself. Virtual reality (VR) environments like those provided by Mondly allow for natural dialogue with native speakers, making learning a language easier and more enjoyable.

You should be excited about the potential of augmented and virtual reality in education after seeing these beautiful examples.

7.6 Advantages and Challenges of Using AR in Education

Here are the advantages and challenges of augmented reality in education.

Advantages of Augmented Reality in Education Educators that have experimented with augmented reality software have found several benefits. What follows are the most important ones (Program Ace 2021)!

- *Access to learning materials:* Many students are left to rely on out-of-date materials or research at home because of a dearth of teaching resources in educational institutions. The most up-to-date information can be downloaded and presented engagingly via an augmented reality app.
- *Access to virtual equipment:* When you need to get familiar with new machinery or learn how to use it, augmented reality software can show you a 3D model of the device and provide helpful instructions. This is an excellent supplement to more conventional textbooks.

- *Higher student engagement:* Students learn more and better retain information when immersed. Many people will find this to be a refreshing break from the norm.
- *Faster learning:* A novel presentation method can speed learning and reduce preparation time. This allows us more time to focus on mastery and exploration in specialized areas.
- *Safer practice:* Anatomy classes, for example, no longer necessitate the dissection of live animals because the process can be accurately simulated in software. Students can acquire the same amount of practice without using harmful materials or equipment.

Challenges of Augmented Reality in Education Although there are many positive aspects to using online learning resources, there are also some drawbacks (Program Ace 2021):

- *Proper hardware is needed:* Older phone models and those running older versions of operating systems do not support the immersive nature of augmented reality applications; hence they cannot be loaded on such devices. Buying smartphones or smart glasses for students might not be feasible for schools that are not known for having cutting-edge technology.
- *The lack of teachers' experience with tech:* A minority of teachers either do not see the value in or are uncomfortable using digital tools. When the instructor is tasked with demonstrating the tool's use and assisting struggling students, this can become a problem.

The advantages of utilizing augmented reality apps in the classroom outweigh the disadvantages. The difficulties above, moreover, are solvable with little exertion.

7.7 Advantages and Challenges of Using Virtual Reality in Education

Here are virtual reality's advantages (Fig. 7.2) and challenges (Fig. 7.3) (Hicks 2016) in education.

Advantages of Virtual Reality in Education

- *Excellent visuals that would be impossible in a regular classroom are available here.* One of the many benefits of virtual reality is the ability to experience new worlds and scenarios in rapid succession. When you put on a virtual reality headset, you are exposed to realistic images that can leave an impression.
- *Creates interest.* Virtual reality (VR) technology is fascinating because it makes possible experiences that would be impossible to "live" in the actual world. The utilization of this technology will inspire students to learn. No matter how old they are, students prefer to sit back and watch anything rather than read.

7.7 Advantages and Challenges of Using Virtual Reality in Education

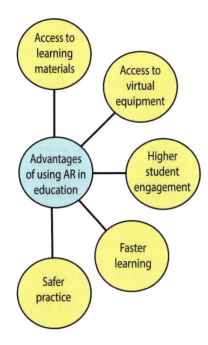

Fig. 7.2 Advantages *of VR in education*

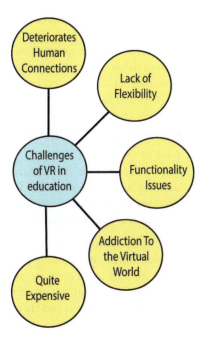

Fig. 7.3 Challenges *of VR in education*

- *Increases students' engagement.* Engaging students in meaningful ways is a challenge for today's educators. This will no longer be an issue thanks to the widespread use of VR technology in classrooms; students will not be able to resist the temptation to discuss their immersive experiences.
- *It does not feel like work.* Putting on a headset, having information whiz by in front of your eyes as you watch videos and incredible visualizations do not appear like work. Young people will be more motivated to study and learn if they see school as a positive experience. This is a rule of thumb. Generally, while having fun, we pay closer attention, improve our performance, and do not view the activity as a chore.
- *Enhances learning across a variety of disciplines.* Consider the field of medicine. Several forward-thinking medical professionals used virtual reality (VR) equipment in 2016 to expand their horizons and improve their ability to teach others. One more would be the area of writing and editing material. In many cases, VR may aid in correcting content errors and provide fantastic new tools for editing.
- *Eliminates the language barrier.* The inability to communicate effectively is a common impediment to learning. Learning the local tongue is a prerequisite for attending college abroad. Virtual reality allows for incorporating every conceivable language into the system's software. Because of this, students can pursue their educational goals without being limited by language.

Challenges of Virtual Reality in Education

1. *Deteriorates human connections.* Virtual reality has the potential to benefit many current fields of endeavor greatly, yet it also presents severe drawbacks in some situations. Historically, schools have relied on face-to-face interactions between teachers and students. In a virtual reality experience, you are completely isolated from the outside world. This can disrupt students' interpersonal interactions and undermine effective human commun**ication.**

2. *Lack of flexibility.* Using a VR headset is a new and exciting experience if you can be adaptable in the classroom, ask questions, and get answers. If you are utilizing a piece of software designed to perform a single task, you cannot do anything besides that. Since learning is not a constant process, pupils may struggle due to a lack of adaptability. That number is continually changing.

3. *Functionality issues.* Errors are to be expected in every computer program. When problems arise, the learning process for your students is halted until the tool is repaired. This is not only uncomfortable but may also be very costly. Therefore, if a student has examinations tomorrow and his VR headset explodes, he cannot study for them. This is merely an illustration; real-world occurrences may vary.

4. *Addiction to the virtual world.* The risk of young people becoming dependent on their online environments is equally substantial. We have observed the effects of extreme events and video games on people. We may even use drugs as an example; if the high is preferable to everyday life, users are more likely to grow dependent on them.

5. *Quite expensive.* The price tag of cutting-edge gadgets might be hefty. There must be a massive investment of billions of dollars in these capabilities if the virtual reality movement is to grow and become mainstream. To add insult to injury, only the wealthy can afford a cutting-edge education that uses the VR platform. Inequality in educational opportunities will result since the poor cannot afford it.

7.8 AI Meets VR and AR

Virtual reality (VR), augmented reality (AR), and artificial intelligence (AI) can collaborate to create content for entire curricula and lesson plans, with AI handling the technical, nuts and bolts details, and VR/AR crafting the immersive, interactive experiences (Liu 2020). Students may find these tools, coupled with AR, exciting.

The realm of virtual reality (VR) and artificial intelligence (AI) simulations provides endless chances for students to escape the conventional classroom setting and enter a realistic, immersive virtual experience (Liu 2020). This helps students become ready for the real world by providing them with experiences as similar as possible, and it also makes learning about the subject fun because they get to live out their studies in a realistic setting.

Create STEM content, build apps, and bring them to life with the help of your students and their teachers. Using the virtual reality (VR) and augmented reality (AR) platform CoSpaces Edu (https://cospaces.io/edu/), educators can provide students with real-world coding experience while crafting immersive 3D classroom environments. By using the spatial computing technology of the Merge Cube (https://mergeedu.com/l/engage), students can interact with 3D digital content (including virtual reconstructions of ancient artifacts, plant cells, and sculptures) at any time and from any location.

Google Sky Map is another example of a virtual reality (VR), augmented reality (AR), and artificial intelligence (AI) program. This app transforms the user's smartphone into a portable planetarium, allowing them to explore the night sky and keep tabs on stars, planets, nebulae, and more.

As Susan Fourtané writes on the website Interesting Engineering (Fourtané 2022), studies have shown that incorporating technologies like these into the classroom can have a wide variety of positive effects on students.

7.9 How AR, VR, and AI Technology Make Education More Accessible

Due to the COVID-19 epidemic, students of all ages have been forced to seek alternative methods of instruction, and the term "edtech" has entered the general lexicon to describe these new tools for teaching and learning.

One of its primary advantages is reducing geographical constraints on education, which assists students with special needs.

This section will examine three technological developments influencing educational practices (Web Desk 2021).

Augmented and Virtual Reality The primary advantage of augmented and virtual reality (AR and VR) technologies in education is that they make learning more dynamic and exciting, even adding gaming elements to traditional textbooks. Curiscope Virtuali-Tee is a shirt and accompanying app that provides an interactive anatomy lesson. While the other dons the garment, they may use an augmented reality app on their phone to visually peel back the layers and investigate what is happening inside. Some research suggests that this technology could potentially help students with neurological differences. Virtual reality (VR) headsets are used in the Floreo telemedicine platform (https://www.floreotech.com/) to provide social and behavioral therapy in institutional settings like schools.

Artificial Intelligence Learning may be made more exciting and personalized with the help of AI technology because it allows students to study on their own time and receive feedback virtually. A rudimentary form of AI called statistics and machine learning is used by Mathematics Sparx (https://sparxmaths.com/) to assist educators in assigning student-specific math problems. The UK-based software developer claims that an average of 4 hours of weekly use can improve GCSE maths exam outcomes by one grade. Additionally, Sparx can help youngsters from underprivileged backgrounds catch up to their more privileged peers, thus closing the achievement gap. In the meantime, KidSense.AI (https://www.diffzy.com/) has developed a deep learning-based automatic voice recognition system for kids. The Ryobi robot (https://roybirobot.com/), an AI-based toy that teaches language and STEM fundamentals, is powered by a system called KidSense, which was trained using samples of children's voices.

7.10 Benefits of Using VR, AR, or AI in a Classroom Setting

The most apparent advantage is higher levels of student involvement. Virtual reality (VR) and augmented reality (AR) make it easy to create engaging educational environments where students may delve deeply into subjects. Moreover, virtual reality and augmented reality have the potential to enhance communication by creating a more engaging setting for education. Lastly, AI can free up teachers' time by automating assessment activities and providing individualized comments to their students (ACTE 2021).

Technology like this is revolutionary because it paves the path for students to engage with concepts in previously impossible ways. With these tools, students can personalize their avatars and explore subjects uniquely (ACTE 2021). Technology's ability to give pupils more control over their learning is one of its most significant advantages. This greater degree of control inspires students and makes learning enjoyable.

Furthermore, this technology can potentially motivate students by allowing them to play and study—by using a system of incentives. Assessments are taken and graded on the platform(s). In addition, students can advance in levels to access more customization options for their characters (ACTE 2021).

7.11 How VR, AR, and AI Will Transform Universities?

Undoubtedly, the future of education will be altered by the arrival of cutting-edge technologies like virtual reality (VR), augmented reality (AR), and artificial intelligence (AI). The future classroom will be an all-digital, fully immersive experience that caters to experiential learning needs and encourages teaching and learning reminiscent of face-to-face encounters (Shenoy 2021).

Whether it is through the simulation of whole environments in virtual reality, the blending of digital and real-world elements in augmented reality, or the application of machine learning in artificial intelligence, new technologies are set to impact education on all fronts, with a particular emphasis on professional and continuing education, as well as distance and online learning (Shenoy 2021). As a head of a university, are you prepared to make use of these game-changing educational tools?

From Virtual Tours to Medical Marvels Virtual reality (VR) applications within the classroom are anticipated to expand rapidly. That is understandable, after all. Virtual reality (VR) has been around for decades and has enjoyed widespread success in the gaming sector; leading market research firm Grandview Research (Grand View Research 2022) predicts that the VR market size will reach $48.5 billion by 2025. Thousands of universities now provide virtual reality tours of their campuses, using the technology to replicate an immersive experience. However, the potential influence of virtual reality on online learning programs is enormously significant, especially given the rising cost of graduate school. Virtual reality can help us connect teachers and students. With distance learning tools, instructors and their students can appear together in the same virtual space, allowing them to guide one another through the experience.

The price of virtual reality consumer products has decreased as mobile phone-powered VR headsets and VR-compatible laptops have dropped below $1000, as reported by eLearning Inside (Kronk 2017). As a result of these innovations, many organizations can afford to adopt virtual reality technology.

The inability to communicate with classmates and professors is a significant drawback of remote education. Understandably, students would grow discouraged and lose interest if they encounter difficulty grasping an idea and receive no assistance. However, virtual reality (VR) has the potential to alter that. Students may feel more engaged in distance learning if they have a greater sense of "presence." They could put on a headset and join a virtual classroom with other students and a teacher instead of studying alone at home.

While visiting Averett University in Danville, Virginia, I used their virtual reality equipment to "virtually" investigate human anatomy.

Students at Averett University in Danville, Virginia, may use the virtual reality equipment to "virtually" investigate the human anatomy, make appropriate motions to zoom inside the chest, view the chest muscles, and then click to view the interior cavity. They can then examine the heart on a more microscopic scale, down to the level of individual cells. Along with the virtual reality (VR) investigation, textual information describes the organs and anatomy.

Using this technology, one can practically immediately use anatomical knowledge. Using virtual reality to practice medical procedures allows mistakes to be made without the potentially fatal outcomes of natural treatments. Virtual reality can also help medical students practice for actual procedures. Please think of how this would affect students in continuing education or other professional programs where they are working to develop particular abilities. A professor of physical therapy and anatomy at the University of California, San Francisco (UCSF), recently gave an interview with the UCSF News Center (Baker 2017) about the benefits of virtual reality (VR) for education and training. "Virtual reality can move us to the next level of experience to go from generic anatomy study to a world where anatomy has been disrupted, and the learner has to act on it."

Virtual reality (VR) technology has the potential to revolutionize several fields by giving students access to extraordinary experiences. Students can practice their language abilities and receive immediate feedback in a setting where they are less likely to feel nervous. It is also possible for students to practice their language abilities with virtual reality scenarios starring animated characters powered by artificial intelligence (AI) rather than by taking a costly trip. Using virtual reality, students in Nicole Mills' French language and culture lessons in Cambridge, England, can "meet native speakers at parties in their homes and eavesdrop on discussions in Parisian cafés, all without leaving Cambridge," according to a blog post (Rota 2018) by Educause. This initiative uses virtual reality (VR) film narratives to immerse students in the 11th arrondissement of Paris, a well-established method for teaching foreign languages.

In the future, what is now considered science fiction will be ordinary, such as Tony Stark employing virtual reality to design his Iron Man armor in the Iron Man films. Modern virtual reality allows scientists to explore the inner workings of their creations, such as new medications, robots, or machines. University medical experts are still investigating how virtual reality (VR) can aid in treating a wide range of conditions, from agoraphobia to burn wounds to stroke. Virtual reality can improve and lower research and education costs if embraced correctly and given sufficient network capacity.

Distance Learning, Now Up Close Modern students frequently switch between online and face-to-face learning. Augmented reality (AR) takes this form of immersive learning to the next level by simulating artificial items placed in real-world

7.11 How VR, AR, and AI Will Transform Universities?

settings to enrich students' perceptions of such settings and boost student engagement. Virtual items can be interacted with or explored by students in the same way as real ones. Consider how well-liked this technology has become in games like Pokémon Go and improved retail environments. These insights will inform future teaching practices that increase student interest and achievement.

Any field, from the hard sciences to the arts, can benefit from augmented reality. Imagine a chemistry lesson where students can learn what happens if they mix the wrong organic compounds without being exposed to a dangerous lab setting or a physics class where students can scan their textbook to see the Thrust Equation brought to life with a rocket's takeoff. Students in other classes can experience historical battles as if they were happening right in front of them, travel back in time to hear Franklin D. Roosevelt deliver speeches from his desk in the Oval Office during World War II, witness the Trojan War unfold, or even travel to the moon in the role of astronauts. It is currently possible for students to employ augmented reality (AR) in their study of astronomy by aiming their phones at the night sky and allowing software to see planets and galaxies using location-based technology.

For instance, humanities classes at Duke University (Lester 2018) have used virtual reality to visit historical structures and archaeological sites. At the Western University of Health Sciences in Pomona, California, students can learn about anatomical functions using a virtual dissection table (Brereton 2018). To teach clinical anatomy and physiology and to improve surgical visualization and planning, MEDIVIS (https://www.medivis.com/) has created a similar augmented reality (AR) platform for use in medical schools, nursing schools, and hospitals. This tool allows students to explore the three-dimensional tissue structures of the body.

There has been a recent shift toward the "blended" paradigm among traditional and nontraditional students. First-time visitors can benefit significantly from augmented reality applications. Visitors can get directions to their destination, and as they walk, they can use their cameras to gather information on buildings and activities, bringing the campus "to life," much like the future of Google Maps (Nieva 2023). A visitor to the engineering lab might notice a dance class or a debate club convening at the building on their right at 9:00. By being able to approach walls honoring the college's benefactors and reading brief biographies of the contributors, students are provided with an experience that can strengthen their emotional ties to the institution.

These methods can be used in traditional classroom settings and online learning environments, giving students of varying learning styles more opportunities to interact with course materials. Students can see a real classroom and walk freely and interact with their surroundings thanks to the advent of remote-controlled robots. Student-athletes commonly utilize tabletop versions to keep up with their studies when away from campus for sports or matches, but larger robots allow them to participate in a broader range of classroom activities. More students will pay attention in class if AR is used to provide them with interactive experiences. Improved student outcomes are the result.

Leading Higher Education Through Artificial Intelligence All sorts of problems that demand "thinking" from humans or machines may now be tackled with the help of machine learning tools and methodologies, and deep learning is at the forefront of this development. Utilizing machine learning technology, such as AI tools used in self-driving cars or image identification, educational applications range from giving machines "vision" to speech recognition, machine translation, medical diagnosis, etc. Universities would do well to take the lead in adopting and pioneering deep learning as the new scientific infrastructure for research and education. The implications for research in academia and the professional world are immense (Shenoy 2021):

- Not only is melanoma extremely dangerous, but a proper diagnosis is not always easy to make. One institution employs cutting-edge picture recognition technology (sometimes known as "computer vision") to help diagnose an aggressive but curable form of cancer. The scientists trained a neural network to identify moles and worrisome lesions based on their unique properties (texture and structure).
- The University of California, Irvine, is among the leading medical research institutions in the world, and its researchers are collaborating with gastroenterologists to enhance colonoscopies (UCI Health 2018). Massive volumes of data will be collected in the future to detect polyp growth and make predictions about its development. Depending on whether or not a growth is safe, the scope will display "green, orange, and red" boxes.
- AI aides have been employed in computer classes for Georgia Tech's undergraduates for several years. There is no need for a human TA to address questions regarding grades or due dates when you have AI, and your students cannot tell the difference. Although artificially intelligent TAs are limited in responding to in-depth topic queries, they can be helpful because many students have the same inquiries.

What Do We Need to Make This Happen? High prices are still a problem, and the day is not far off when AI and VR/AR tools will be as affordable as smartphones and desktop PCs (Shenoy 2021). We need to ensure adequate wireless network capacity to support these incredible applications, powerful enough personal computers, and locations designed for the specific needs of VR and AR. As a society, we overlook the interconnected nature of the sensors, cameras, microphones, cellphones, glasses, and other gadgets that make immersive technology possible. Not only that, but virtual reality/augmented reality and deep learning are among the most bandwidth-hungry tools employed in universities today. Colleges and universities should begin planning for their potential adoption of virtual reality, augmented reality, and artificial intelligence, including what resources and setup will be needed.

Colleges and universities will be better able to adapt their teaching and learning environments to the demands of today's students if they can fully take advantage of the technological tools at their disposal. Virtual reality (VR), augmented reality (AR), and deep learning (DL) advances can enhance learning in a variety of contexts, from one-on-one tutoring to improved distance education to enhanced research capacities and more integrated student life. The value of a college education can only rise if students are given opportunities to engage more deeply with the subject matter they are studying. Universities will be able to meet the needs of their students in today's rapidly developing technology environment if they take advantage of the opportunities presented by the wide range of programs and services available to them. The truth, in whatever form it takes, is a swift ride. In the past 3 to 5 years, the concept of BYOD (Bring Your Device) has exploded in popularity, with many companies allowing employees to use their smartphones to access company data (Shenoy 2021). Teaching and learning are set to be revolutionized by the combination of virtual reality/augmented reality (VR/AR) and artificial intelligence (AI), coupled with students' demands for access to various devices and personalized platforms. In addition, it is not too late to start preparing right away.

7.12 Conclusion

Virtual reality (VR), augmented reality (AR), and artificial intelligence (AI) are more than just buzzwords; they also offer the potential to individualize each student's educational experience and shift away from the cookie-cutter model of schooling to which we have all been accustomed. VR, AR, and AI are technologies that rapidly expand the possibilities for teaching and learning while also providing novel and innovative ways for administrators to monitor student performance, bridge gaps, and collaborate with specialists from around the globe to achieve a centralized way of helping children track and bridge gap areas and accelerate upon areas of excellence. Using virtual and augmented reality, for example, educators can provide students with a more hands-on learning experience with the help of artificial intelligence.

References

ACTE. (2021). *Leveraging VR, AR & AI for CTE student success*. ACTE. https://www.acteonline.org/tech-changes-how-we-learn/

Baker, M. (2017). *How VR is Revolutionizing the Way Future Doctors are Learning About Our Bodies*. UCSF. https://www.ucsf.edu/news/2017/09/408301/how-vr-revolutionizing-way-future-doctors-are-learning-about-our-bodies

Brereton, E. (2018). *How College VR is Transforming Teaching and Learning*. EdTech. https://edtechmagazine.com/higher/article/2018/05/4-ways-colleges-are-embracing-virtual-reality

Dick, E. (2021). *The Promise of Immersive Learning: Augmented and Virtual Reality's Potential in Education* (Issue August).

Fourtané, S. (2022). *Augmented Reality: The Future of Education*. Intresting Engineering. https://interestingengineering.com/innovation/augmented-reality-the-future-of-education

Grand View Research. (2022). *Virtual Reality Market Size Worth $87.0 Billion By 2030*. https://www.grandviewresearch.com/press-release/global-virtual-reality-vr-market#

Hicks, P. (2016). *The Pros And Cons Of Using Virtual Reality In The Classroom*. ELearning Industry. https://elearningindustry.com/pros-cons-using-virtual-reality-in-the-classroom

Kronk, H. (2017). *Educating with VR is still pricey, but costs are dropping*. ELearning Inside. https://news.elearninginside.com/educating-with-vr-is-still-pricey-but-costs-are-dropping/

Lester, S. (2018). *Duke's New Reality*. Pratt.Duke.Edu. https://pratt.duke.edu/about/news/dukengineer/2018/virtual-reality

Liu, A. (2020). *Back to the Future Classroom: VR/AR/AI Transformation*. EqOpTech. https://www.eqoptech.org/publications/2020/8/22/back-to-the-future-classroom-vrarai-transformation

Marr, B. (2021). *10 Best Examples Of VR And AR In Education*. Forbes. https://www.forbes.com/sites/bernardmarr/2021/07/23/10-best-examples-of-vr-and-ar-in-education/?sh=1987ae5a1f48

Martin, B. M. (2022). *Augmented Reality (AR) vs Virtual Reality (VR)*. Guru99. https://www.guru99.com/difference-between-ar-vr.html

Nieva, R. (2023). *Google begins testing AR walking navigation for Maps*. CNET. https://www.cnet.com/tech/tech-industry/google-begins-testing-ar-walking-navigation-for-maps/

Program Ace. (2021). *Using Augmented Reality in Education: Key Concepts and Benefits*. Program Ace. https://program-ace.com/blog/augmented-reality-in-education/

Rota, A. (2018). *Three Examples from the Field: AR and VR in Teaching and Research*. https://er.educause.edu/blogs/2018/8/three-examples-from-the-field-ar-and-vr-in-teaching-and-research

Shenoy, R. (2021). *VR, AR and AI will Transform Universities. Here's How*. Unbound. https://unbound.upcea.edu/online-2/online-education/vr-ar-and-ai-will-transform-universities-heres-how/

Tkachenko, I. (2022). *Augmented and Virtual Reality in Education*. The App Solutions. https://theappsolutions.com/blog/development/ar-vr-in-education/

UCI Health. (2018). *Making colonoscopies "smarter" with artificial intelligence*. UCI Health. https://www.ucihealth.org/blog/2018/03/artificial-intelligence-colon-cancer

Web Desk. (2021). *How AR, VR and AI Technology Makes Education More Accessible After Covid*. Tech Bollyinside. https://www.bollyinside.com/news/technology/how-ar-vr-and-ai-technology-makes-education-more-accessible-after-covid/?amp=1#

Wilson, A. (2019). *10 reasons to use AR and VR in the classroom*. ESchool News. https://www.eschoolnews.com/2019/09/10/10-reasons-to-use-ar-and-vr-in-the-classroom/

Chapter 8
AI-Based Online/eLearning Platforms

8.1 What Is an AI-Based eLearning Platform?

An AI-based eLearning platform is a machine or system that can carry out many tasks requiring human intellect. It continues to be able to develop answers for problems relating to humans, such as speech recognition, translations between languages, decision-making, and many other things (Neelakandan 2019).

An artificial intelligence engine is even built into our mobile devices to help analyze our texting behaviors and generate plausible ideas (Neelakandan 2019). Although most learning organizations still do not use the AI-based eLearning platform as their standard learning strategy, it is still essential.

Despite its limited utility, artificial intelligence is moving in the right direction to improve the efficacy of eLearning instruction. An AI-based eLearning platform can shape the industry's future and positively impact its growth.

8.2 Why Use AI in eLearning?

Some typical problems with the conventional training model include the following (SHIFTelearning 2022):

- *Too much content and long:* Long-form modules make up most traditional learning programs. Additionally, it takes too many hours to create an hour's worth of this training material. People are easily overwhelmed by this!
- *Lack of personalized experiences*: Because it takes time to create content, eLearning courses frequently lack customization and are too general to meet the unique needs of each employee.
- *Do not track the program's effectiveness*: Traditional training ROI calculations need laborious data gathering and entry procedures.

- *The demands and aspirations of the digital workforce are not met by it:* Training is now an ongoing activity rather than a one-time or biannual initiative. According to a LinkedIn Learning report, millennials and Gen Z workers want to self-manage their learning experiences.

Artificial intelligence can solve many problems in training and eLearning courses.

8.3 How Are ML and AI Enhancing Online Learning?

An enormous amount of people are taking classes online. Furthermore, face-to-face training boosts knowledge retention rates by 25–60% compared to face-to-face training. Machine learning (ML) and artificial intelligence (AI) are significant contributors to the success and efficacy of online learning.

One size fits all is a thing of the past. Learning has become more individualized and adaptable because of ML and AI (Ray 2019).

Each student has a unique educational background and set of cognitive skills. Giving them case studies and examples they can most easily relate to is critical for them to learn more effectively.

With a Learning Management System (LMS) with machine learning capabilities, such a high level of personalization is possible.

Leveraging Big Data Personalized adaptive learning is a potent tool for retaining today's workforce. AI offers insights based on the vast quantity of data it has gathered and examined, which makes it easier to create personalized learning programs more quickly than before (Ray 2019). Thanks to these insights and data, online learning platforms can better comprehend student behaviors and anticipate needs by proposing and positioning content based on prior behavior.

Personalized and Adaptive Learning Along with personalization, AI and ML help to improve course content and delivery (Ray 2019). A cloud-based LMS online course is not a one-time task. Based on the input you receive from the students, you may need to change the course material. Feedback can come from qualitative student surveys or comments and quantitative information like test scores, ratings, and other course metrics that the LMS gives the students.

Gamification Businesses like BYJU'S, Collegify, and QuoDeck are doing fantastically well. Gamification is a significant additional aspect that makes straightforward tasks easier, from documentation to client engagement (Ray 2019).

For SMEs, startups, and educational institutions, QuoDeck's DIY LMS is a product that offers cutting-edge technology at a reasonable price. It is designed on a mobile and game-based SaaS platform. The platform can be implemented in a company with a staff size ranging from 30 to 1000 employees working in various conditions.

To find trends, correlations, and other insights, QuoDeck uses a multivariate model that includes clickstream data, time spent on the system, distribution of course utilization, and devices used, among many other characteristics.

AI and ML have significantly increased employee learning customization, partner resource allocation, and course efficiency for QuoDeck workers. The business plans to use AI and ML techniques to offer learners a pre-designed course based on their profiles before they start their e-Learning experience.

While offering self-paced SAT/ACT preparation classes, Collegify also developed several intriguing features that interest users.

Students can choose avatars as part of a "gamified" work-and-reward strategy that appeals to the target age group and promotes steady progress. According to our methodology, which balances performance with a challenge while avoiding overstimulation, this includes gradually releasing the content.

The content is organized into progressively more challenging tiers, and the AI is programmed to adapt to each student's unique learning and performance trends in real-time. This flexibility helps students maximize their time on the platform while allowing educators, mentors, and parents to provide the most helpful guidance possible.

BYJU'S also utilizes data, ML, and AI to provide individualized instruction. Instead of relying solely on theoretical frameworks, the emphasis is on providing a visual and contextual framework for education. Students benefit from this since they understand when, how, and how much they should study. Its method of instruction can be adapted to suit the individual student's needs. There is no need to memorize anything anymore; review the material on your phones or tablets as much as necessary till you understand it.

Everyone who has access to the Internet today makes use of online education.

8.4 Benefits of Using AI and ML in eLearning

The followings are some of the most salient benefits (as shown in Fig. 8.1) for using AI and ML in eLearning (Kurkina 2022):

- *Adaptive learning:* Some people learn best by reading text, some learn best by watching videos, and others learn best by listening to audio recordings. AI-driven analytics enables course complexity level adjustment and content personalization for learners. Learners' motivation and engagement are considerably increased when their instruction is customized to their preferences, improving learning outcomes.
- *Advanced analytics:* Only using test outcomes to gauge student participation is challenging. The instructor learns very little from it, which takes time. Contrarily, analytics backed by AI can evaluate the amount of time spent completing the test, the number of tries, and other performance-related aspects. This can be used to

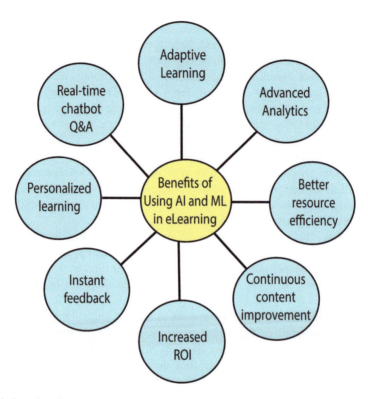

Fig. 8.1 Benefits of using AI and ML in eLearning

assess a student's progress, pinpoint any flaws in the course material, and decide how to enhance it.

- *Better resource efficiency:* With AI-based eLearning systems, managing and updating the content takes minimal human labor. eLearning systems use fewer system resources when they are deployed in the cloud. They also guarantee improved training effectiveness, which results in learners reaching company objectives more quickly and requiring less time to learn new skills.
- *Continuous content improvement:* Identifying patterns of successful and unsuccessful learning outcomes is possible by analyzing the data on student performance gathered throughout the course's duration. This makes changing the course's content possible, swapping out more difficult-to-understand elements for simpler ones, etc. In order to increase learning outcomes, educators may maintain the currency and usefulness of their course materials while also giving their students long-lasting, satisfying customer experiences.
- *Increased ROI:* The ROI evaluation of eLearning effectiveness is most heavily influenced by time gains. Your staff can use their newly gained talents more quickly the less time they spend training. As a result, the eLearning system pays for itself far quicker than you would have anticipated and increases the productivity and adaptability of your entire organization.

8.5 Solutions for AI/ML in Online Education

- *Instant feedback*: By combining the factors above, it is possible to give each user individualized real-time feedback. As a result, each learner views comments like this as a personalized development plan that highlights his or her strengths and areas for progress rather than as a form of public intimidation.
- *Personalized learning*: Every training group in the present era consists of persons from various backgrounds and with gaps in their expertise. Each student can have a unique learning path created for them by using AI solutions in eLearning and analyzing the responses to determine their level of topic mastery. While some students will need to go through the fundamentals, more seasoned students can speed through them by answering tests to demonstrate their proficiency.
- *Real-time chatbot Q&A:* Many students find it difficult to understand certain concepts fully. Being able to replay watching the videos or listening to the audio till they figure everything out is a benefit of pre-recorded content. However, many people refrain from asking their "stupid" questions during live webinars and other training sessions. This problem is also resolved by AI-powered chatbots, which allow students to ask as many queries as they like without interfering with the lecturer and receive in-depth responses as often as necessary.

8.5 Solutions for AI/ML in Online Education

AL/ML will deliver the following solution (Kurkina 2022) for online education (see Fig. 8.2).

- *eLearning chatbots:* Chatbots can be set up to respond to questions about the course, give detailed comments on each learner's development, and deliver analytics on possible course material updates.
- *Machine translation:* By employing machine translation, users can better understand the language, grasp its grammatical quirks, learn proper sentence construction, and expand their vocabulary.

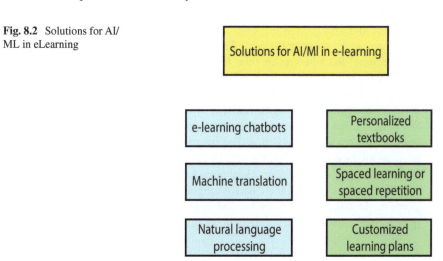

Fig. 8.2 Solutions for AI/ML in eLearning

- *Natural language processing:* By using AI technologies to convert speech into text, enable voice recognition, and enable translations, educators may now instruct students anywhere in the world, greatly enhancing the potential of eLearning as a teaching tool.
- *Personalized textbooks:* The learning outcomes are considerably improved, and rewarding experiences are created when the eLearning materials are customized to each student's unique training preferences.
- *Spaced learning or spaced repetition:* Most language learning software employs this method. To promote greater topic comprehension, the system continuously provides the terms the learner could have problems recalling based on an analysis of their progress.
- *Customized learning plans:* Applying AI in eLearning guarantees that instructors may create varied, in-depth, and focused learning programs because of detailed analytics on individual learner progress and course-wide statistics. This makes it simpler to update or reuse the current eLearning content.

8.6 Various Ways AI-Based eLearning Platform Can Shape Online Learning

Today's eLearning is benefiting more from artificial intelligence. These five strategies (Neelakandan 2019) will help us mold online learning and improve its effectiveness. The way training is provided at work will likewise alter due to AI.

- *Real-Time Questioning:* Many students encounter obstacles when seeking clarity on a particular subject during learning. While some students are brave enough to ask questions during their studies, others are not. However, introducing AI into your learning program may give students an excellent way to get an explanation whenever and however they choose. A vital function of an AI-based eLearning platform is its capacity to serve as a tutor and offer solutions to problems as they arise. With AI, students may ask questions about unclear material and receive prompt responses.
- *Generate Fresh Learning Content:* Creating course content is one of the aspects of eLearning that takes much time for SMEs and eLearning experts. Suppose properly trained AI systems can extract useful information and transform it into intelligent material for digital learning. This enables professionals to concentrate more on designing a fun digital learning environment for their students. One of the most challenging aspects of digital learning is creating eLearning courses because it takes various abilities. The ongoing development of AI can assist in bringing all the necessary abilities together to offer an excellent eLearning course.
- *Natural Language Processing:* How often have your students asked to speak to your learning program in their native tongue? A machine with artificial intelligence could make this a reality for you. Natural language processing is artificial intelligence's fundamental component (or sub-field). It focuses on making it pos-

sible for systems to process human language rapidly and effectively. Therefore, by incorporating AI into your eLearning program, students can communicate with the system and ask questions in the dialect/style of their choice. This will save time, contribute to creating effective and exciting eLearning, and make learning more accessible.

- *Personalized Tutoring Session:* eLearning has been a considerable benefit for educators due to the ability to develop content that can be shared with various learners. In a perfect world, it would be nearly impossible for a teacher to meet every student's needs simultaneously. Of course, corporate training frequently uses this one-size-fits-all strategy. It is not the most excellent strategy because different learning styles should be considered before providing content to diverse audiences. Artificial intelligence is essential for identifying a learner's learning style and reviewing a learner's prior performance. AI modifies the updated course materials to provide the individualized instruction that today's students need.
- *Gamification:* To engage and inspire learners to learn new information, gamification is a crucial strategy employed in online learning. Tactical game design for online training materials is simple with AI. Processing much data is helpful because it allows for the behavior of learners to be predicted and for them to be informed about how their learning is going.

8.7 Different Ways That AI Is Being Used in eLearning

This section has included six applications (Denton 2022) of artificial intelligence in the eLearning sector (see Fig. 8.3).

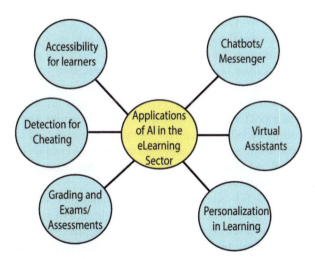

Fig. 8.3 Applications of AI in the eLearning sector

- *Accessibility for learners:* The way that the eLearning sector has improved accessibility for distance learning for virtually everyone, everywhere, at any time, is one of the most beneficial consequences on students' education and learning experience. It is no longer confined to a physical classroom or corporate training session. Anyone with Internet access can immediately start mobile learning on almost any subject by logging on to their computer or mobile device. The phrase "continuous learning" describes the process of learning over time. A never-ending thirst for knowledge drives continuous learners, and the steady flow of information exposes them to a dynamic educational lifestyle. Nowadays, many companies provide programs for lifelong learners, including webinars, podcasts, digital publications, training modules, workshops, or sessions on specific subjects.
- Additionally, many colleges offer a variety of online courses or massive open online courses (MOOCs) that enable students to take courses while maintaining their employment or family responsibilities. This eLearning industry opens up new opportunities for teachers to create content and for students to access eLearning resources. The demand for ongoing education has only grown due to technological advancements and automation. For instance, it is predicted that automation will result in the loss of ten million US jobs during the following 5 years. Professionals need to engage in this type of constant learning now more than ever, and AI can make it possible in a manner that conventional training just cannot. Users are more likely to remember material in a mobile learning environment by offering a more customized learning path based on a learner's abilities or industry-specific information they may require access to at any time.
- *Chatbots/messenger:* Without constantly needing a human instructor, chatbots enable students to ask questions or request explanations in natural language. This has considerable advantages regarding cost-effectiveness and gives companies access to markets worldwide that frequently cannot afford to hire a full-time trainer. There are several ways to include chatbots in eLearning programs. They can send brief messages from the company group chat about a particular subject of interest to a learner or instantly respond to frequently asked inquiries for learners. In addition, they can offer a "genuine" experience by having a live discussion on the website where the eLearning software is installed. Chatbots can also be used as a tool for evaluation. AI can swiftly determine whether a student's written responses are valid or incorrect, allowing instructors and mentors to offer feedback before the learner continues with this new information or skill set. This allows for significant time savings and guarantees that students will always have access to the required materials.
- *Virtual assistants (VAs):* Learners can also communicate with a virtual assistant, mentor, or trainer using artificial intelligence. A virtual assistant can support educators and students by responding to inquiries often directed to a professor. These are similar to chatbots, but there is still some differentiation. They can aid in planning and explaining how the course materials function within a particular subject. This is more common in the corporate sector than in academia or educa-

8.7 Different Ways That AI Is Being Used in eLearning

tion, but as advances in machine learning and natural language processing advance, we will see its application transition from business-oriented to educational. Digital technologies are evolving, so they can now automatically grade tests. This saves time, resources, and money for educators/trainers, students, and businesses. They can assist students in navigating the course material and serve as a motivating mentor for them when they encounter difficulties. Although most are still in the beta stages, virtual tutors are also available.

- *Personalization in learning:* One of the fascinating aspects of AI is that as they acquire data and improve their efficiency through machine learning, they learn how to react to user interactions. Based on the users' preferences and preferred learning techniques, artificial intelligence in eLearning develops customized courses for each user. These courses can constantly modify depending on how a student responds to the material, providing extra assistance where needed and omitting anything that would not be considered "relevant content." This is known as adaptive learning, accomplished by employing machine learning algorithms. Adaptive learning, sometimes called adaptive teaching, is a teaching strategy that combines artificial intelligence and computer algorithms to manage interactions with students and deliver resources and learning activities specifically tailored to meet their individual needs. Individuals may "test out" some training during professional development or corporate training to ensure they are interested in innovative material. Then, taking into account the student's responses to the questions, tasks, and experiences, the learning management system adjusts the display of the online learning material. The goal of adaptive learning systems is to change the learner's role from that of a passive receiver of knowledge to that of a participant in the educational process. While business training for corporations is another common application of adaptive learning systems, education is their primary field.
- *Grading and exams/assessments:* Reading and grading several examinations and evaluations is a professor's or teacher's most essential and time-consuming job. To ensure the student has complete comprehension, teachers must analyze the quality and the content. AIs have stepped up to the plate in this situation and have developed into quite effective graders of longer, more challenging exams. Google's neural matching program is now a leading illustration of how computers can decipher the questions and solutions hidden in written exam assessments. In the ensuing years, this will only get more honed.
- *Detection for cheating:* Contrary to other forms of cheating, many plagiarism detection methods and programs do not require artificial intelligence. An illustration of this is when AI can extrapolate from a dataset of submitted assignments to determine whether a particular student or another person completed an assignment by comparing similarities in a sample of a student's writing to those in other submissions.

8.8 Types of AI in Online Education

The education system underwent significant modifications as a result of the Industrial Revolution. As factory occupations displaced agrarian jobs, math and reading abilities became more crucial. The focus of public education changed to a factory model, where students would acquire the skills necessary to work in those factories. A comparable seismic shift in how we teach and learn might be brought about by the upcoming artificial intelligence (AI) revolution.

Education has centered on specialization—learning more about less—since the middle of the twentieth century. That particular knowledge, however, becomes obsolete more quickly in a world where automation is on the rise. Students will come from a broader range of backgrounds and age groups as time passes. They must pick up new talents and revise old ones throughout various occupations. Online education will eventually be accessible to anyone, and AI may help make that happen.

Online education has dramatically benefited from AI, even if just indirectly. The nation's leading AI labs gave rise to well-known online learning platforms like Udacity, edX, and Coursera. As AI-powered modules are now becoming available in every field of education, that association might develop into a strong bond.

Online course delivery (Garrett 2018) has already increased graduation rates, decreased costs, and decreased inequality. Due to the AI revolution, online learning could become even more innovative, quicker, and less expensive. It has already begun.

The following are the three primary types of AI used in online education (OnlineEducation 2022):

1. *Adaptive Learning:* Adaptive learning is learning software tailored to each student separately. As a result, concepts are presented in the sequence that each student finds to be the most understandable and may be finished at their own pace. They might be introduced in a much more detailed manner as they progress. Currently, adaptive learning models work best when a sizable group of students must study the same content, allowing for the simultaneous collection of comparable data. With artificial intelligence, apps like Cram101 from Content Technologies can distill a textbook into a study guide that includes chapter summaries, practice exams, and flashcards. A portion of the high school curriculum is already being distributed simultaneously to thousands of schools through the Brazilian adaptive learning firm Geekie. Overall, adaptive learning tools will continue to improve learning by making it more efficient, intelligent, and personalized.

2. *Intelligent Tutoring Systems:* AI-powered solutions specifically designed for each student's needs and talents are intelligent tutoring systems. The Carnegie Learning product MATHiaU simulates a human coach's capacity to give feedback, rephrase inquiries, and thoroughly assess a student's progress. MATHiaU focuses on remedial math classes for college students, which, when pursued conventionally, cost $6.7 billion with only a 33% success rate. Intelligent tutoring systems can significantly reduce that expense while also increasing success rates. The writing tool Bartleby, created by Barnes & Noble Education, has an

AI-powered writing module that checks papers for plagiarism, corrects grammar, spelling, and punctuation, and even assigns a rough score. When implemented correctly, these solutions reposition teachers more toward a mentoring position rather than replacing them.

3. *Virtual Facilitators:* Imagine if chatbots and video games had a child, but the objective was to progress a user's education rather than to achieve a high score or to solve a customer service issue. Virtual facilitators will soon become a reality in this manner. USC's Institute gives a head start for Creative Technologies. They have already produced prototypes for virtual counseling for the US Army and are skilled at building AI-powered 3D settings and lifelike virtual personalities. Captivating Virtual Instruction for Training (CVIT) is a project that combines virtual tutors, augmented reality, and live classrooms. In the meantime, Jill Watson serves as a virtual teaching assistant for IBM's Watson. Jill was first introduced at Georgia Tech in a course named "Knowledge-Based Artificial Intelligence." She participates in an online discussion forum with other human teaching assistants to respond to student inquiries. By responding more swiftly, she frequently does better than her human colleagues. Students at Georgia Tech in 2016 could not identify which teaching assistants were AI programs.

8.9 How Is AI Revolutionizing the eLearning Industry?

Businesses are becoming increasingly aware of the possibility of adopting AI for learning and development. Here are the ways artificial intelligence is changing the eLearning sector (SHIFTelearning 2022):

Provide the appropriate information to the individual at the appropriate time through personalized learning paths. The modern workforce expects personalization; it is no longer merely a desire. Your employees want material where they play the main character in a tailored experience.

Rather than using a one-size-fits-all approach, eLearning solutions based on artificial intelligence can customize the material for each learner.

"Personalized" or "adaptive" learning is a data-driven strategy that continuously monitors each student's performance. It is more time efficient and motivates students to learn when each student has a customized learning path with pertinent topics. Machine learning algorithms forecast outcomes and modify information to each student's skills and preferences. As a result, until a student has thoroughly learned the subject, the platform will continue to adjust the content and difficulty levels based on their progress.

For instance, the employee requires a variety of viewpoints on the subject being studied to understand it, especially for complex subjects.

To build an internal combustion engine in mechanical engineering, a student must comprehend how the engine functions and its components interact. They must examine many models in order to gain a thorough understanding of how each one differs from the others while adhering to the same rules and serving the same purposes.

This procedure is not sequential and differs for every student. One student might learn something more quickly by seeing a video and putting it into practice, another would find it simpler to see a visual blueprint, and another might comprehend it by thoroughly explaining how it operates.

Similar principles apply to learning other subjects: it takes more than one approach to understand a concept correctly, and each student will require a distinctive combination of approaches depending on their learning style.

The content is general and not tailored to each student's interests when using traditional training. There is just one learning path, and the teacher or course author determines the same arrangement of content for all students.

Integrating eLearning platforms and onboarding artificial intelligence can make corporate development systems more effective. Content is modified, and individual learners receive personalized learning paths and recommendations based on their roles, interests, and past actions on eLearning platforms.

The result is a dynamic, adaptable, personalized, and successful training strategy that helps each employee become the director of their learning and adjust as a living organism to their needs.

Advanced Analytics for Better Decision-Making Instructors and/or training leaders frequently run into two issues while evaluating the performance of their learners: they take a long time, and the data is not sufficiently detailed.

It is feasible to swiftly analyze enormous volumes of data and uncover patterns and trends to enhance and continually improve learning experiences by utilizing an artificial intelligence-based eLearning platform.

Content analytics primarily refers to eLearning platforms that use machine learning and AI to enhance learning modules. This allows corporate leaders to manage and produce eLearning content using sophisticated data analytics to gather crucial information about student progress and comprehension.

Using artificial intelligence, instructors and L&D leaders can get comprehensive data about each student's performance, areas of strength, areas of weakness, and attendance issues. This simplifies deciding, optimizing, and taking action before the learner loses interest and abandons the course.

Faster eLearning Course Creation Creating courses has historically been one of the most time-consuming chores for subject matter experts and instructional design specialists. Fortunately, using AI to eLearning helps create courses that are considerably easier to create, quicker to develop, and more agile without compromising quality.

A fantastic example of how artificial intelligence improves eLearning production is the automatic translation and localization feature, which offers more speed and efficiency.

It is not easy to translate eLearning content while utilizing conventional development techniques. Making the same information accessible in several languages becomes considerably more time-consuming and expensive when considering the content that must be developed!

However, with AI, it is now possible to create multilingual content for multinational corporations facing the challenge of developing helpful content for branches in multiple countries or for the situation where companies work with remote teams that speak different languages, which is becoming more common.

By using an authoring tool like SHIFT, businesses may speed up the development of projects that call for material in many languages by cutting the time required for translation services of an eLearning program from months to only days.

Chatbots and virtual tutors to support learners as part of increased engagement. Assessments can be completed quickly, and questions from staff or students are handled in real time through artificial intelligence, which speeds up and customizes the learning experience.

It can be portrayed as a clever chatbot that reads and replies to the employees' conversational text messages and inquiries. An illustration would be a chatbot that "decides" what questions to ask a student depending on the student's initial responses, such as adding questions in areas where the student has given the most inaccurate answers or moving up a level when the student consistently inputs the correct answers. Another frequent usage is to provide straightforward answers: the AI algorithm may be provided with the fundamental knowledge that, for instance, a new contributor may need.

Virtual assistants, like chatbots, can support both students and teachers by responding to inquiries that might otherwise be directed to the teacher or by guiding students through course content in a more approachable manner.

Additionally, chatbot-enabled eLearning platforms act as a "guide" for students, assisting them at every step of the process. For instance, they might propose different learning resources based on a user's profile and areas of interest, saving the time and effort required to find these resources manually.

8.10 AI's Impact on eLearning

An overview of how AI interacts with and affects eLearning (Lawton 2020) (Hogle 2022) is given in this section.

Off-the-Shelf AI Technology Some eLearning authoring tools and platforms come with built-in AI-based technologies, which can be licensed within a software platform. AI tools based on Amazon (AWS), Google (GCP), IBM (Watson), and Microsoft (Azure) are widely used in eLearning and other online tools. L&D professionals do not need to build AI-based solutions if they use or develop eLearning platforms and authoring tools.

Where AI Shows Up in eLearning AI-based tools alter how people use technology, go about their daily lives, go shopping, discover information, and study. The tools and methods used by L&D professionals to produce and deliver eLearning content are also altered. A few crucial areas where AI is having an impact are (Hogle 2022):

- *Content creation and improvement:* The creation of information for multilingual learner groups is made simpler, quicker, and more affordable through automated translation. Grammar and spelling checkers may make information easier to read. AI-based systems may provide transcripts, closed captions, and alt text for video footage.
- *Getting the right content to learners:* According to learners' interests, performance, job roles, or past training, AI-based systems may automatically tag information and power recommendation engines. In adaptive training, tailored content is sent to each student based on performance and mastery objectives.
- *Gathering and analyzing data:* The effectiveness and quality of training can be enhanced by L&D teams using predictive analytics that analyzes learner data. Data on training history and performance could be mapped to job performance data to identify skill or knowledge deficiencies. Alternatively, it may analyze staff and customer communications to find common points of confusion and develop or enhance training in those areas.

How AI Supports L&D Teams Pattern recognition is a specialty of AI. Massive amounts of data may be analyzed swiftly by an AI tool, which can then spot patterns and connections that human analysts would probably miss or be unable to uncover due to the sheer volume of data they must process.

Routine chores can be automated by AI tools, freeing up human L&D professionals to concentrate on their more creative work. The L&D staff can concentrate on creating content or reviewing the results to identify which assessment questions want improvement and which subjects require more or better information. It is possible to automate these operations to generate daily or weekly reports rather than spending hours each week registering learners, reminding them to finish training, and determining who is and is not making progress.

8.11 How AI Is Transforming eLearning?

AI is revolutionizing education and opening up new opportunities. By 2025, the AI market is expected to be worth $190.61 billion, altering a variety of sectors, including e-learning (Ivanov 2020). We may utilize e-learning systems (LMSs, LXPs, LAPs, etc.) to a greater extent by integrating AI technology. In other ways (Ivanov 2020), AI fundamentally alters the e-learning sector.

Define Learner's Pathways Each time a person interacts with the technology, AI can collect and evaluate personal data about them. Thus, the learner's courses through the educational process may be more effectively defined. In response to the queries asked by the user, AI technology can:

- Identify the learner's next degree of achievement.
- Get him or her to that stage by giving them or the relevant content.
- Use the information to trigger the relevant course materials, making the education process more tailored to the individual.

8.11 How AI Is Transforming eLearning?

Personalized Tutoring Session There is no denying that no one learning method works for everyone. Each learner has a different learning style, speed, and set of skills. Why not customize education when we can now obtain individualized entertainment and shopping?

AI technology can tailor tutoring sessions to the learners' needs, much like Amazon or Netflix, and tailor content, recommendations, and adverts based on the user's choices, likes, and previously purchased or viewed movies. As a result, AI integrated into an e-learning solution can:

- Keep track of the student's prior performance
- Determine where each learner's proficiency is lacking
- Utilize the information to customize learning by alerting the instructional materials accordingly

Content Analytics Online education entails a vast library of unavailable materials, including texts, papers, media, audio, photos, etc. Most data is typically unstructured, making it difficult for teachers and administrators to handle it effectively. Teachers and students can benefit from the course materials because of AI's ability to handle and analyze big datasets rapidly and effectively.

Thus, the technology can identify patterns and trends, gather information about the learner's unique learning preferences, pace, and gaps, and then highlight those to the user for further interpretation and decision-making.

More Targeted Marketing Many companies gather more user data than necessary and know how to exploit it. Big data can be burdensome for businesses because it needs to be maintained securely. Additionally, businesses cannot provide focused marketing since they cannot adequately handle all the collected data.

First and foremost, AI can determine which data points are essential and pertinent and stop collecting extraneous user data. In addition, technology can evaluate data more quickly to offer marketing collateral and, more precisely, targeted advertising. Thus, the audience most interested in your online course will see your adverts.

AI-Based Virtual Assistance Virtual assistants are now widely used in both our personal and professional lives. They support us, provide information, offer advice on various topics, etc. As a result, AI-based chatbots are quick, efficient, and accurate helpers in various industries like retail, healthcare, etc. They can also be applied to education to offer real-time assistance.

Along with offering round-the-clock guidance, AI-based assistants may converse with users by comprehending human language via machine learning (ML) and natural language processing (NLP). Because of NLP, virtual assistants may track user behavior, offer extra learning resources, impart information from subject matter experts, provide feedback and assistance that is specifically customized to the user, and more. Thus, technology increases users' productivity and engagement.

Deeper Engagement with Virtual Reality (VR) Online education can advance thanks to a mix of VR and AI technology. You can build online training simulations and give consumers in-depth, real-life scenarios by combining different solutions. In this way, students can get fully immersed in a learning environment, study a subject in greater depth, practice, assess their comprehension of a subject, etc. Additionally, such interactivity can improve engagement and the user experience.

Automatic Grading Along with utilizing AI technology, the solution integration can also take advantage of solid automation features that simplify grading. It gives teachers more time to communicate with students, create materials for online classes, and other things. The solution's integration can speed up reviewing and grading the students' written work in many languages.

Real-Time Questioning AI responds to requests in a quick, precise, and effective manner. Sometimes it is critical to have answers right away without having to go to the teacher or look them up online, which would disrupt the learning process. AI-based systems can process user inquiries and provide real-time responses, including all necessary justifications and explanations. The resources are also revealed, learning assets are suggested, and the time and effort required to perform all that manually is eliminated when AI is integrated into eLearning courses.

8.12 Ways Artificial Intelligence Is Transformed eLearning

A crucial symbolic development in computing technology occurred in May 1997 when IBM's Deep Blue artificial intelligence defeated global chess champion Garry Kasparov (Greenemeier 2017). Using a brute force technique, Deep Blue could compute hundreds of potential moves quickly and select the ones that would most likely result in victory.

The ancient Chinese strategy game Go has recently been cracked by artificial intelligence. In contrast to the more structured game of Chess, Go is an open-ended game with few rules and a broad scope of play. After finding that brute-force algorithms were ineffective, the developers of AlphaGo turned to neural networks to enable the AI to learn strategy by playing millions of games against itself. In March 2016, AlphaGo bested the 18-time world champion Lee Sedol (Mozur 2017).

Grandmasters have been defeated in some of the oldest and most challenging games known to mankind, elevating the status of AI, but it has also been used for more valuable tasks. Artificial intelligence can identify some diseases earlier and more accurately than medical professionals (Kay 2017). While this was happening, a pair of chatbots that Facebook developed to conduct speedy negotiations developed a puzzling code language (LaFrance 2017) to communicate.

It is evident that because AI is a new technology, its full potential has not yet been realized. It is also evident that they will have numerous applications for online education as they advance and become more widely available. Here are a few examples (LearnDash Collaborator 2019a).

8.12 Ways Artificial Intelligence Is Transformed eLearning

Artificial intelligence (AI) will assist educators in developing new, immersive environments for scenario-based learning. The complexity and number of alternatives rise exponentially as the scenario develops is currently one of the main obstacles to using branching scenarios in e-learning (LearnDash Collaborator 2018). Although students gain a lot from these circumstances, it can be challenging for teachers to create them.

However, AI might help educators by producing spontaneous responses to a scenario. It could consider more things and produce a more realistic atmosphere than following a pre-planned script. For instance, the scenario's conditions might alter if a learner responds slowly or if a particular scenario path leads back to a previous option; the scenario may remember the learner's responses and alter potential future choices.

With the advent of online education, teachers now have a significant advantage in producing lessons that can be distributed throughout tens of thousands of online courses. As a result, the instructor has more time to develop new course materials, promote their curriculum, or interact with students. Students will benefit from individualized tutoring sessions.

However, though automatically distributing content to many students simultaneously provides clear advantages for operating an online business, it can also leave students behind (LearnDash Collaborator 2019b). There are restrictions on how much one-on-one time a teacher can spend with each student, and as a course gets bigger, those restrictions are quickly reached.

Soon, artificial intelligence will not be able to take the job of an instructor, but it can ease the burden. For instance, if an AI can recognize early sickness symptoms, it may also recognize students ready to lag in their studies and choose the best method to support them. Or why not develop advanced chatbots to assist with language training because we are currently designing them to handle customer service calls?

Intelligent Automation Is on the Way We strive for more effective techniques to automate routine operations (Ferriman 2016). Multiple-choice tests and pre-programmed workflows already manage repetitive tasks like sending email reminders and grading them effectively. Some automation, meanwhile, is too complicated and has too many variables and circumstances for most people to design properly, and we have not yet created an AI that can grade term papers.

Even though it may sound unusual, the time may come when AIs can evaluate brief or lengthy responses to a quiz and compare them to crowdsourced data collected from the Internet to check for accuracy. This would enable professors to design more in-depth tests without being overburdened with grading tasks.

Less Invasive and More Targeted Marketing Many big data-focused businesses collect more data than they can use. They are more likely to regress to the mean and broadcast messages that appeal to the audience's lowest common denominator since they cannot make sense of this enormous amount of unsorted data. The idea that a more sophisticated AI could give better-targeted marketing and advertising materials without requiring much client personal information may seem counterintuitive, but it is accurate.

A more advanced AI could determine crucial information and stop gathering irrelevant data (LearnDash Collaborator 2019a). Perhaps it does not require access to my Facebook account (along with my complete friend list, their friend list, etc.) to understand that I would be interested in an online language lesson. YouTube might stop showing me adverts for drugs to treat rheumatoid arthritis if businesses knew how to tailor their advertising correctly. Although it may at first seem unsettling, this is a positive step.

8.13 Examples of AI Being Used in eLearning

Because we are accustomed to thinking of AI as potentially evil or terrifying, it can be challenging to write about it in the context of e-learning without feeling like you are participating in speculation, a task typically reserved for science fiction writers. However, whether we realize it or not, AI is becoming commonplace daily.

Because the current AI differs from the self-aware, human-passing androids that novelists like Isaac Asimov, Philip K. Dick, or Arthur C. Clarke led us to expect, this disconnect affects many of us more than it should. Instead, we now have powerful software tools that are excellent at identifying patterns and then modifying behavior in response to those patterns to produce a relatively constrained set of outcomes (LearnDash Collaborator 2020).

That may not sound as thrilling (or terrifying) as your average sci-fi book, but it does provide some intriguing use cases that can be used in online learning today.

Let us examine some companies (LearnDash Collaborator 2020) already utilizing them.

Duolingo The most well-known application of AI in education right now is undoubtedly Duolingo. They have been quite open about the research that went into developing their language learning software, to the point that their branding now incorporates the strides they have achieved in using machine learning to teach languages. Even a section of their website is devoted to their studies.

How do they use this research in their lessons? First, Duolingo's AI customizes lessons by tailoring them to the preferences and strengths of each learner. It will consider the vocabulary the students already know, the grammar concepts they struggle with, and the subjects they appear interested in.

The artificial intelligence (AI) behind Duolingo also uses natural language processing to provide chatbot experiences that let users practice communication in real time. It enables language students to develop their abilities and confidence before speaking in front of a live audience.

Thinkster Thinkster offers K–8 students individualized math tutoring using AI, similar to Duolingo. After the learners complete an evaluation test, the AI can tailor the questions depending on their prior knowledge and how they interact with the material.

The unique aspect of Thinkster's strategy is how it mixes artificial intelligence with instruction from qualified math tutors. As a result, teachers spend more time concentrating on the content that students need. This indicates that personalization is taking place for more than just the students; it is also assisting in preparing tutors to provide more focused lesson feedback.

Querium Querium takes a different approach than the popular trend of using personalization in AI learning. This online tutoring program evaluates students' steps to solve a STEM problem and gives them immediate feedback on what they are doing correctly or incorrectly. This safeguards the education of the students by protecting them from being exposed to the incorrect solution and relieves the burden of grading on the educators.

AI, in this context, is unique because it must comprehend learner input data that may not always take the same shape to deliver the appropriate feedback. This is a lot more difficult than just selecting a structured answer from a pre-made list and giving feedback, but it also enables more precise training.

Alta by Knewton Using high-quality learning resources chosen from its databases, Alta, a new product from Knewton, a name synonymous with higher education, employs adaptive learning to spot learner knowledge gaps.

In this case, the program functions as a study aid, spotting and filling knowledge gaps. When used differently, it can also assist companies in maintaining staff training to keep up with new skills or legal requirements.

In summary, there are four different kinds of AI in use today. Although there are more instances of online instructors using AI, they almost all fit into the categories (LearnDash Collaborator 2020) stated below:

- *Natural language processing:* used for both significant accessibility applications as well as language instruction. It tends to be flawed around young children or multilingual persons.
- *E-learning personalization:* modifying the curriculum to suit the needs and preferences of the learners.
- *Virtual tutoring:* Grading assistance to spot and fix student mistakes.
- *Adaptive learning:* actively locating and filling up knowledge gaps for learners.

A more prosperous learning environment powered by AI can be created by combining many of these. The more software can link these different sorts, the more they can do with them, even if AIs frequently need the training to reach a position where they can act intelligently.

8.14 The Future of eLearning

The training and development sector has seen a 47.5% growth in this technology over the last 4 years, and by 2025, it is anticipated that investments in artificial intelligence will total $190.61 billion (SHIFTelearning 2022).

In the future, artificial intelligence will likely control many functions humans perform (SHIFTelearning 2022). However, this should not cause fear because it will improve human training and enable them to handle more challenging jobs.

In order to save instructors' and employees' time and free them up to work on more essential duties, companies can deliver individualized learning at scale by utilizing the power of artificial intelligence. Additionally, because of the advantages like adaptive learning, advanced analytics, and time optimization during the creation process, employees will be more engaged and motivated in learning, leading to better outcomes and higher productivity.

8.15 Where Do You See the Future of AI in eLearning?

There are still issues to be solved, even though many educational institutions plan to or have already implemented AI in various activities. It is crucial to convey to students how AI will automate and carry out monotonous jobs. Preparing the students for this change is the most important.

However, roles always call for creative, cognitive, and emotional intelligence. AI and human skills should be combined for the most significant outcomes.

AI-based learning systems, for instance, might be very effective teaching tools for arithmetic and foreign languages (ColorWhistle 2023). An instructor would still be required to help students with concepts they did not fully grasp, such as subtleties and exceptions to rules.

While AI has much exciting potential to advance eLearning, its application is still in its infancy (ColorWhistle 2023). For implementation to be successful, more testing and investigation are needed.

We advise e-learning administrators and leaders to take the initiative and launch pilot projects to test AI in diverse contexts. Inform the students about using their data if you test it in real-time.

8.16 Potential Applications of AI in Remote Education

Self-improvement is ingrained in the process of AI-powered online education, which is still in its infancy (OnlineEducation 2022). Compared to human teachers, AI systems are more visible, making it simpler to audit and follow the thought processes that led to a teaching moment.

AI systems will have access to more data as more are implemented, but that data must be gathered ethically, securely, and openly. These tools will improve fluidity, naturalness, and efficiency over time. Students will learn more quickly than ever before and will increasingly be able to gain skills that will be useful to them in an automated future thanks to improved AI-enabled online education.

However, there are still pitfalls. All 109 public schools in Washington, DC, that are part of the IMPACT program implemented AI and machine learning techniques in 2009 (OnlineEducation 2022). The goal was to evaluate teachers' effectiveness, offer thoughtful feedback, and raise the bar for education. It did not work out well. Many teachers voiced opposition. For better grades, some people manipulated the system. Due to flaws in the system, the results of roughly four dozen teachers were mistakenly downgraded. It was called a scandal by *The Washington Post*.

Future developments in AI education must put the demands of the users—teachers and students—first and foremost. Only 38% of instructors who participated in an Economist Intelligence Unit survey believed their training had prepared them to use digital technologies for instruction (OnlineEducation 2022). Additionally, more progress must be made to incorporate these advances into the current system.

Teachers, students, and AI developers still have much to learn about the future of AI-enabled education.

8.17 What Is AIaaS in eLearning?

It makes sense to question where you may get AI tools to save time and money by forgoing the need to create your own. Do not be alarmed by the advertisement for "AI as a Service" or "AIaaS"; even small educational institutions or learning and development professionals can get a license for AI tools and components (ColorWhistle 2023).

Although such tools may not be appropriate for every e-learning ecosystem, they may have alluring advantages, such as expanding your toolkit with common AI tasks (logic, decision-making).

Here are some of the popular tech companies' AIaaS tools and platforms (ColorWhistle 2023), most of which are cloud-based.

- *Microsoft Azure:* Building and managing AI applications like bot-based apps or image recognition can be done using cloud-based AI services.
- *IBM's Watson:* Services for managing and storing your data in the cloud and can be linked to your apps.
- *Google's TensorFlow:* An open-source, full-featured machine learning platform.
- *Amazon Web Services:* Provides a large selection of products and services on Amazon's cloud.

Other AIaaS platforms, such as DataRobot, Petuum, and H2O, demonstrate the industry's growth.

8.18 Conclusion

Many industries, including eLearning, are changing due to rising technology like AI. eLearning with AI benefits students, teachers, parents, and schools. It makes high-quality education more widely available and allows students to learn at their own pace. AI-driven tools can assess essays, provide personalized resource recommendations, and respond to questions from students. Knowing when a student will leave school will enable institutions to provide them with the additional support they require. The use of AI in eLearning solutions benefits: make personalized learning pathways, personalize the online classes by distributing the proper materials to the right students, analyze the information to raise student interest, and automate and streamline the grading and learning processes.

References

ColorWhistle. (2023). *Impact of AI in E-Learning Industry*. ColorWhistle. https://colorwhistle.com/impact-of-ai-in-elearning-industry/

Denton, M. (2022). *How is AI being used in eLearning in 2022?* Archy Learning. https://archylearning.com/blog/how-is-ai-being-used-in-elearning-in-2022/

Ferriman, J. (2016). *Automation in LearnDash Courses*. LearnDash. https://www.learndash.com/automation-in-learndash-courses/

Garrett, R. (2018). *Does Online Higher Education Reduce Inequality?* (pp. 1–27). EV SUMMIT 2018.

Greenemeier, L. (2017). *20 Years after Deep Blue: How AI Has Advanced Since Conquering Chess*. Scientific American. https://www.scientificamerican.com/article/20-years-after-deep-blue-how-ai-has-advanced-since-conquering-chess/

Hogle, P. S. (2022). *What Is AI's Impact on eLearning?* Neovation. https://www.neovation.com/blog/16-what-is-artificial-intelligence-impact-on-elearning

Ivanov, B. (2020). *The Role of Artificial Intelligence in E-learning*. Becoming Human. https://becominghuman.ai/the-role-of-artificial-intelligence-in-e-learning-41ac88ee3e8d

Kay, J. (2017). *Computers are already better than doctors at diagnosing some diseases*. MaRS. https://www.marsdd.com/magazine/computers-are-already-better-than-doctors-at-diagnosing-some-diseases/

Kurkina, I. (2022). *AI/ML IN ELEARNING*. Academy SMART. https://academysmart.com/ai-ml-in-elearning/

LaFrance, A. (2017). *An Artificial Intelligence Developed Its Own Non-Human Language*. The Atlantic. https://www.theatlantic.com/technology/archive/2017/06/artificial-intelligence-develops-its-own-non-human-language/530436/

Lawton, D. (2020). *AI Is Molding The Future Of eLearning: How Will It Impact*. ELearning Industry. https://elearningindustry.com/artificial-intelligences-impact-on-elearning-2020

LearnDash Collaborator. (2018). *How to Use Branching Scenarios in E-Learning*. LearnDash. https://www.learndash.com/how-to-use-branching-scenarios-in-e-learning/

LearnDash Collaborator. (2019a). *4 Ways Artificial Intelligence Will Transform E-Learning*. LearnDash. https://www.learndash.com/4-ways-artificial-intelligence-will-transform-e-learning/

LearnDash Collaborator. (2019b). *How to Avoid Alienating Learners in your Online Course*. LearnDash. https://www.learndash.com/how-to-avoid-alienating-learners-in-your-online-course/

LearnDash Collaborator. (2020). *4 Examples of AI Being Used in E-Learning*. LearnDash. https://www.learndash.com/4-examples-of-ai-being-used-in-e-learning/

Mozur, P. (2017). *Google's AlphaGo Defeats Chinese Go Master in Win for AI*. The New York Times. https://www.nytimes.com/2017/05/23/business/google-deepmind-alphago-go-champion-defeat.html

References

Neelakandan, N. (2019). *Artificial Intelligence-Based eLearning Platform: Its Impact on the Future of eLearning.* ELearning Industry. https://elearningindustry.com/artificial-intelligence-based-platform-impact-future-elearning

OnlineEducation. (2022). *Artificial Intelligence Innovations in Online Learning.* OnlineEducation. https://www.onlineeducation.com/features/ai-in-distance-learning

Ray, T. (2019). *How Machine Learning and AI are Making Online Learning More Beneficial.* Stoodnt. https://www.stoodnt.com/blog/machine-learning-ai-online-learning/

SHIFTelearning. (2022). *How Artificial Intelligence is Transforming the eLearning Industry.* SHIFTelearning. https://www.shiftelearning.com/blog/artificial-intelligence-elearning

Chapter 9
AI-Enabled Smart Learning

9.1 What Is Smart Education?

Smart education is "a form of learning tailored to new generations of digital natives" (morningfuture.com 2018). In contrast to conventional classroom teaching methods, smart education is an interactive, collaborative, and visual paradigm that enables teachers to adjust to their student's talents, interests, and learning preferences while increasing student engagement (Glasco 2019).

Professor Byeong Guk Ku, a teacher in South Korea and pioneer of smart education, says that in the past, "what students could see, hear and feel was bounded by the walls of the classroom." According to Professor Ku, one of the most significant benefits of innovation in education is that new technology allows students to relate to the outside world. Professor Byeong Guk Ku created an interactive learning model with social networking and cloud-based capabilities (Glasco 2019).

Unfortunately, the uptake and efficacy of educational technology (Deloitte 2016) trailed behind other societal changes, such as consumers' quick uptake of digital products and services. The learning method is expanding due to students', instructors', and parents' "increasingly digital and tech-centric behaviors."

As one might anticipate, younger teachers, especially "digital natives," strongly believe in the educational benefits of using technology in the classroom. More than 80% of educators with 10 or fewer years of experience "think educational technology at school makes a 'huge' or 'very substantial positive influence' on students' learning," according to a Deloitte survey on digital education (Glasco 2019).

Many children need to relate to knowledge differently for it to be meaningful, according to Sean Arnold, a special educator, STEM coach, and teacher in New York City's District 75 special needs program (Arnold 2018). Arnold adds that teachers must use innovative presentation strategies "to engage students who learn best visually, aurally, kinesthetically, and tactilely."

9.2 Smart Education vs. Traditional

Let us evaluate the two educational systems and decide which is best for you (MyEdu 2021).

- *Communication:* Other forms of effective communication cannot replace in-person interaction. However, utilizing technology can improve communication significantly. Thanks to the smart school administration system, it is simpler to update parents with important school news, such as PTM. The student, instructors, and parents were previously manually alerted of the school's modification.
- *Administrative Task:* Keeping records was a major hassle in the traditional educational system. It takes a lot of time and effort to manually handle the record, as requested by the employees. Such labor significantly decreased output. On the other hand, the school management system has completely replaced all manual record-keeping by automating processes. The administrative staff is relieved of the burden of monitoring numerous records and devoting additional time to record verification.
- *Affordability:* Because human record-keeping and data entry require much time and are more prone to error, they are more expensive. Instead, the automated software makes it easier to manage data quickly and accurately, which saves time and money.
- *Flexibility:* In a traditional educational system, students are under constant pressure to perform at a speed they might not feel comfortable with to stay up with other students. On the other hand, a smart educational system is characterized by the flexibility that allows students to learn at their rate and dispels teachers' concerns.
- *Learning Material:* The only way to learn the subjects in a traditional classroom is through books and printed materials. Students can explore learning resources in various forms in the modern educational system, including e-books, PDF papers, audio/video lectures, and many more.

The traditional education system provides a better social learning environment than the smart education system. Skills like leadership and teamwork can be successfully exhibited in the conventional classroom setting. Additionally, various extracurricular activities are available for students to engage in.

A smart education system, however, provides more benefits than a conventional one. Through the automated system, it offers streamlined operations with swift school management.

9.3 Why Should You Choose a Smart Education System?

Depending on the criteria employed, you can choose between a traditional education system and one that uses technology. Both educational institutions undoubtedly have benefits and drawbacks. However, given the numerous ways technology has

9.3 Why Should You Choose a Smart Education System?

advanced, parents and students are prepared for digitalization in educational institutions.

A smart educational system increases operational effectiveness while allocating more time to high-quality education. The school management software includes valuable features, including updating exam results, managing schedules, and tracking attendance.

This functionality allows administrative staff and teachers to increase productivity and focus on their primary duties. For instance, when you allow your teachers to attend management automatically, you may spend more time providing the students with high-quality instruction.

Check out the main advantages (see Fig. 9.1) of the smart education system as well (MyEdu 2021):

- Effective communication between parents, instructors, students, and the administration of the school
- Enhancing interactions between students and teachers
- Enhances operational effectiveness
- Send updates, alerts, and notifications immediately
- Online fee administration (secured and safe)

A smart education system must be chosen because the next generation needs creative learning methods. The contemporary educational approach not only makes teaching a pleasurable experience but also encourages higher production.

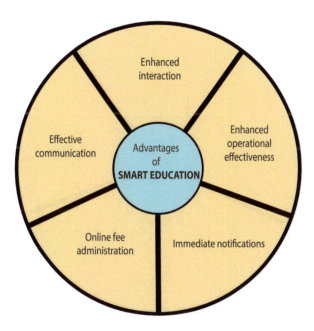

Fig. 9.1 Advantages of smart education

9.4 What Is Smart Learning?

The term "smart learning" refers to any method of education that improves upon traditional methods. This education helps students quickly and conveniently consume knowledge and information. Imagine spending hours on challenging, in-depth research only to comprehend one straightforward idea. Imagine, however, that you could understand the same notion with a brief video clip or a well-written essay; this would save you time and make it simpler for learners to understand the concept. Smart learning makes accessing online content easier and enhances the learning process. Learning can benefit significantly from technology tools. Teachers can transform lengthy paragraphs or words into images, graphs, flowcharts, and animated films to help students understand a concept better. Images, rather than words, have been shown to aid information retention. Children benefit from its help in long-term memory retention.

The following (see Fig. 9.2) are some advantages of smart learning (teachmint@wp 2021):

- This method of instruction is smart and efficient.
- These lessons guarantee that the students will remain motivated.
- For the students, it makes the teaching and learning process simpler.
- It is a cost-effective method of learning.
- Because so much paper is saved, it benefits the environment.

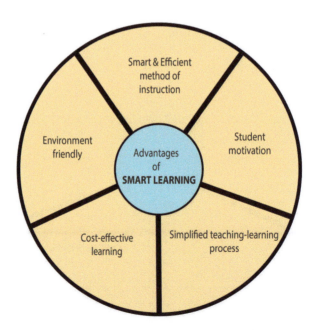

Fig. 9.2 Advantages of smart learning

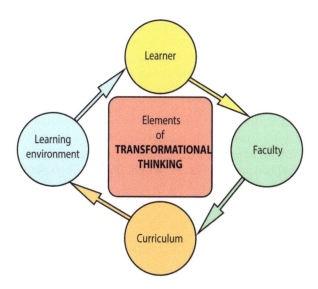

Fig. 9.3 Elements of transformational thinking

Many individuals still have trouble understanding the concept of smart learning, even though it represents a significant paradigm shift in contemporary education. It is best understood from the Three T's, or Total Transformational Thinking, point of view.

The learner, faculty, curriculum, and learning environment are the four components (see Fig. 9.3) that make up total transformational thinking (Awar 2022).

- *Learner:* The student transforms from a passive follower of the educational process to a proactive leader.
- *Faculty:* Instead of only teaching, faculty members increasingly emphasize mentoring and coaching, which calls for effective training to transfer information within a learner-centric framework.
- *Curriculum:* The curriculum has been updated to reflect how knowledge is delivered and presented.
- *Learning environment:* Finally, the learning environment is broadened to consider contemporary realities, such as the prevalence of mobility, which has created many chances for mobile learning.

9.5 Smart Learning: The Wave of Higher Education in the Future

The future of higher education can be secured most effectively through smart learning (Awar 2022). In the coming years, colleges and universities will keep using more nontraditional ways to bring in new students.

Exciting new technologies blur the lines between the physical, the digital, and the biological. For the education community worldwide, this new era is giving us the tools, techniques, and beginnings of an infrastructure we need to reach our ultimate goal of educating everyone. The dream goes beyond the typical classroom because it reaches out to people who want to learn but cannot because of their situation.

The mind is like a parachutist; it will not work without opening it. All of us who have the will and resources to help students successfully navigate the smart new world must collaborate to realize the full promise of smart learning.

The educational community, like the Wright brothers, who dared to take flight and transform the world, should extend its wings boldly and strategically to bring about a brighter future for all people.

9.6 Pillars of Smart Learning

Accessibility, flexibility, and affordability are the three pillars (see Fig. 9.4) on which a smart learning service or provider is built (Awar 2022).

1. *Accessibility:* Awar (2022) proposed the adoption of a lifelong learning model (4 C's Model) to classify learners as Casual, Committed, Concentrated, and Continuing Learning and to use context-specific learning strategies accordingly.
2. *Flexibility:* Regardless of gender, physical limitations, age, religion, or other categories, smart learning should be adaptable for everyone.
3. *Affordability:* In traditional education, affordability is a recurring problem because of institutions' ongoing struggles with space constraints, high tuition costs, and other factors. While many people lament the cost of education, the

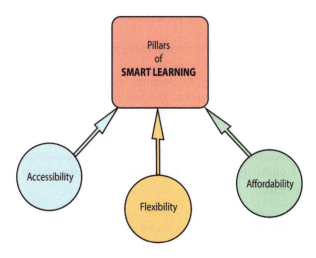

Fig. 9.4 Pillars of smart learning

truth is that ignorance is more expensive. Smart learning lowers transportation costs and classroom requirements, giving students the more financial freedom to complete their education and positively contribute to society.

9.7 The Challenges and Barriers to Smart Learning

Typically, society is reluctant to change. The scientific community, for instance, mocked the Wright Brothers for thinking that human-crewed air flight would revolutionize transportation. Today, it is impossible to envision a world without airplanes.

Smart learning encounters several obstacles because it is still in its early phases. The fundamental difficulty is that smart learning goes against traditional education's rigid structure. Instead of concentrating on managing to learn, institutions nowadays are more concerned with managing employees, buildings, and finances (Awar 2022).

Smart learning solves many issues that the public and the academic community should accept (Awar 2022). For this approach to work, we must adopt a new educational perspective and acknowledge that traditional schooling cannot keep up with the changing world. To make higher education more useful for today's learners, we must overhaul the entire system's operations.

9.8 AI Is the Next Step of Smart Learning

While there may be disagreements over AI and its relationship to smart learning, one thing is for sure: AI can improve it (Smyth 2019).

It Keeps Getting Better Let us start with machine learning, which is where it all began. As the name suggests, machine learning is how electronically programmed devices and software adapt their operations to each input.

Let us look at it this way. Three subjects (X, Y, and Z, specifically) are tested as part of an eLearning course (http://firstclasseducation.org/online-courses/a--definitive-guide.php), and two students participate in the first round of testing. One of the students excels in subjects X and Y while struggling in Z. The other one succeeds in tests Y and Z but fails exam X. Results are revealed.

As a result, the first student must pay closer attention to topic Z, and the second must put much effort into subject X. An eLearning course using AI can provide tailored advice, recommendations, or course assistance according to the subject(s) in which each student is poor. Moreover, that is not all, either. A smart learning course can meet several other needs with AI integration (Smyth 2019).

It Can Find Areas Where the Course Needs to Improve The ability of machine learning and AI to assist teachers in raising the caliber of a particular course is another fantastic benefit for the education sector (Smyth 2019).

How? Have you read about its capacity to use students' test results to provide them with more appropriate advice and suggestions? The findings advise professors to improve course quality or remind students of a missed topic.

For instance, if many students respond incorrectly to questions about a specific topic, the topic may be unclear. Alternatively, it might have even gone unnoticed. AI can be employed to alert instructors and course designers to the same.

It Can Provide Students and Educators with Helpful Feedback Feedback is crucial to every instructional program (Smyth 2019). If your teachers cease pointing out your weaknesses, you might never achieve success.

AI can ensure that this does not occur. A smart learning platform or AI-powered course would offer professors and students pertinent, helpful feedback on each student's performance. Teachers and students can use this feedback to improve their weak areas.

It Might Change the Experience of Online Education. Entirely! ELearning is already changing how education is delivered (Smyth 2019). The addition of AI to smart learning will therefore cause several new modifications in the educational system. AI is constantly growing and learning. As a result, employing an AI-driven learning platform will make it extremely intelligent, enabling it to improve its reactions to every user action.

An AI system can become skilled at serving that specific audience in this way (students and teachers for a particular course or subject here). Additionally, it may compile comparable information from each and every other user. This would undoubtedly improve the educational experience for both students and teachers and make it simpler for them.

AI Can Make Trial-and-Error Learning More Comfortable Anyone who attended a traditional school will be familiar with the humiliation of failing and feeling disrespected in front of peers or teachers. eLearning eliminates this suffering. Furthermore, it improves significantly when combined with AI.

Not getting it? Keep following along. Even while trial-and-error learning is beneficial, school students are typically reluctant to make errors that could be seen as embarrassing. Students will find it less intimidating with an online course.

After that, AI will continue to use inputs to improve its recommendations to students about their trials and how they should construct them. The idea is to allow children to attempt new things without worrying about failure or criticism.

Reason? An AI environment is ideal for learning through trial and error. AI itself learns through successes and failures.

It Can Help Ease the Transition Between High School and College Transition is one of the main issues that several students occasionally encounter (Smyth 2019).

You learn in a grade and discover that everything is pretty simple there. The next one after that draws you into a headache.

Many of us have, at some point, encountered this particular issue. This can be prevented by taking a decent AI-driven smart learning course. The AI system can let students know what subjects will be covered in the following grade, easing the transition. They will be better briefed, as a result, making it simpler to advance to the subsequent learning stage.

AI Can Help Create Smart Learning Content After discussing how AI and machine learning works together, it is clear that everything is data-driven—data provided by users (in this case, students).

In addition to providing feedback and a variety of other services, this data is used by AI-driven educational platforms to assist in producing content that will pique students' interests and meet their educational goals.

All of this is also simple to complete. All you have to do is prepare your eLearning course and inform an LMS consultancy of your requirements. Once they have provided you with an LMS quote, you can finalize the sale if satisfied.

Your eLearning course will be simple to prepare with its assistance. You can integrate AI with the aid of proper consulting.

9.9 Applying Artificial Intelligence to Smart Learning

Responding to each learner's particular needs and learning path was, until recently, a nearly impossible task (Hopp 2018). Technology based on artificial intelligence (AI) has altered that. Artificial intelligence software and smart learning systems are used to predict what would pique each person's attention and keep them engaged. Intelligent software examines how people respond to learning, how quickly they pick things up, and how well they assimilate new ideas. Based on that analysis, algorithms will adjust learning delivery to each person's preferences, substituting engaging active learning experiences for passively consuming learning modules.

This strategy frequently referred to as "the user-centric approach," is especially effective for teaching foreign languages (Hopp 2018). Based on their mother tongue and prior language acquisition experiences, people acquire languages in diverse ways and at varying rates for hearing, reading, speaking, and writing. Language acquisition requirements usually supplement a learner's basic skill sets. A learner may need to scrounge up much extra time and drive to study a language in addition to regular work.

To address this, intelligent learning technologies use AI-driven algorithms to match each learner with the most fascinating and pertinent information, such as industry-specific knowledge, enabling them to use newly acquired language skills on the job right away (Hopp 2018). As a result, productivity and learner happiness should all see measurable benefits. If not, learning experts can use analytics to track how the learner interacts with the system to create future programs that are more successful.

Design thinking principles considerably maximize cloud-based learning delivery for skill development (Hopp 2018). Individual learning experiences that accomplish the intended results and fulfill academic goals will be driven by the user-centric design thinking approach, which starts with profound empathy with each learner, their requirements, and their pain spots.

9.10 AI-Enabled Smart Learning Examples

Artificial intelligence (AI), the theory and practice of creating computer systems that can carry out tasks that traditionally require human intelligence, is relevant in this situation; for example, see the list below (Bose and Khan 2020):

- *Classcraft:* Classcraft, a teacher-friendly gamification tool introduced in 2015, is currently being utilized in over 50,000 classrooms across 75 countries and 11 languages. The Quebec- and New York City-based education technology startup addresses student motivation using gaming ideas. It uses gaming principles to promote social-emotional growth and individualized learning, allowing teachers to modify curricula and teaching methods to suit the needs of individual students. This ground-breaking teaching strategy is adaptable, can be applied to any subject, and has been highly effective at raising student motivation, raising engagement, and fostering secure team building to create a positive classroom community.
- *Alta:* Knewton, an adaptive learning firm headquartered in New York, created Alta, a software application based on a personalized learning engine for students pursuing higher education. Knewton released Alta in January 2018 following 10 years of working with publishers. It is supported with high-quality internal content that industry veterans have carefully selected. Universities and institutes can use the software as a comprehensive tool for all of their students, and students can access it as a standalone package. The product includes lessons in statistics, economics, chemistry, and math. Textual, graphical, and visual information are all included in courses. Students can purchase the software in a stand-alone edition. Every student can now use the mobile software of Alta. The most remarkable aspect of Alta is that students are not only left to fend for themselves with the program; there is 24-h online chat help for student questions.
- *Squirrel AI Learning:* After Derek Li Haoyang left his position as CEO of his previous education company, which had an IPO, he created Squirrel AI in 2014. With approximately 2000 classrooms around China, Squirrel AI is a Shanghai-based after-school tutoring company. Students study their lessons in a classroom under the guidance of a subject-area teacher while using a laptop computer with the company's software installed.

- The primary goals of Squirrel AI were to address the issues with the educational system, including the lack of individualized attention in classrooms and the unfair distribution of educational possibilities. The inflexible, ineffective educational system has reduced students' interest in studying, which inspired Derek Li to create China's most comprehensive AI-powered education product. The extent and reach of Squirrel AI are excellent. However, the idea behind systems like Squirrel AI and others that support adaptive learning will not soon render teachers redundant. Instead of teaching the "nuts and bolts" of each subject, Squirrel AI is intended to support and supplement teachers' work (Building Personalized Education With AI Adaptive Learning—AI Business, 2019).

9.11 Conclusion

Implementing AI in education places a premium on improving upon established instructional approaches and creatively using readily available digital tools for education. AI-enabled smart learning is the next natural phase in integrating technology into classrooms and educational establishments.

However, it is not as simple as picking out a piece of equipment; technology is (whether we like it or not) an integral element of any sector, and children would be well to start learning about it as early as possible due to the rapid pace at which it evolves. Even more importantly, a tried-and-true strategy must be implemented to help students grow and improve their abilities gradually, naturally, and efficiently. Therefore, we keep in mind that the purpose of technological and pedagogical advancements is not to replace the established methods of learning and education but rather to offer a comprehensive spectrum of additional tools to help smart learning and education realize its full potential.

References

Arnold, S. (2018). *8 Tools for Visual Learners (and others too)*. Braveintheattempt.Com. https://braveintheattempt.com/2018/02/07/8-tools-for-visual-learners-and-others-too/

Awar, M. Al. (2022). *Pioneering smart learning*. Ellucian. https://www.ellucian.com/emea-ap/blog/pioneering-smart-learning#:~:text=Smart learning is a broad,more effectively%2C efficiently and conveniently

Bose, D., & Khan, P. F. (2020). Artificial Intelligence enabled Smart Learning. *ICED 2020, 2*(2), 153–156.

Deloitte. (2016). *2016 Digital Education Survey*. https://www2.deloitte.com/cn/en/pages/technology-media-and-telecommunications/articles/2016-digital-education-survey.html

Glasco, J. (2019). *Smart Education for Smart Cities: Visual, Collaborative & Interactive*. Bee Smart City. https://www.beesmart.city/en/solutions/smart-people/smart-education/viewsonic-smart-education-for-smart-cities

Hopp, A. (2018). *Applying Artificial Intelligence to Smart Learning*. LinkedIn. https://www.linkedin.com/pulse/applying-artificial-intelligence-smart-learning-armin-hopp/

morningfuture.com. (2018). *Smart Education, the old professor goes to the attic*. Morningfuture. Com. https://www.morningfuture.com/it/2018/02/09/smart-education-andrea-cioffi/

MyEdu. (2021). *Smart Education Vs Traditional Education System – Which is Best?* https://www.myeducomm.com/. https://www.myeducomm.com/blog/smart-education-vs-traditional-education-system-which-is-the-best/

Smyth, D. (2019). *Is artificial intelligence (AI) the next step of smart learning? Author AI the next step of smart learning. Really? How?* Crayon. https://www.crayondata.com/is-artificial-intelligence-ai-the-next-step-of-smart-learning/

teachmint@wp. (2021). *Smart Learning*. Teachmint. https://www.teachmint.com/glossary/s/smart-learning/

Chapter 10
Chatbots for Education

10.1 What Is Chatbot?

A chatbot is an AI-powered interactive interface that allows users to communicate their needs, concerns, and inquiries using text, speech, or a combination of the two (Docken 2023). A human operator may be present to assist a chatbot in certain circumstances, but in the vast majority of cases, the chatbot may handle the entire discussion with the customer, provided the latter's inquiries and responses are structured according to a set of guidelines. Chatbots, in a nutshell, are computer programs that can take human input and reply with a standard set of responses.

Some of the biggest names in technology are touting chatbots (also called conversational agents, automated chatbots, and virtual assistants) as the future of customer service (Docken 2023). Big tech companies like IBM, Amazon, Facebook, Google, and Microsoft are touting the benefits of chatbots and how they can change how we engage with students in higher education.

10.2 Chatbots Also Participate in Education

Education and technology need to work together in today's rapidly evolving environment. The use of chatbots in educational institutions has already shown promising outcomes. Artificial intelligence and bots are altering how students are served. This means that chatbots can now be found in the classroom.

What Do Students Think? Digital learning tools (DLTs) are great for automating queries and maximizing efficiency.

Statista found that over 79% percent of college students agree that digital learning technologies (DLTs) make lecturers and teaching assistants more efficient and thriving in the classroom. However, 78% believe these tools facilitate harmony

© The Author(s), under exclusive license to Springer Nature Switzerland AG 2023
M. Kurni et al., *A Beginner's Guide to Introduce Artificial Intelligence in Teaching and Learning*, https://doi.org/10.1007/978-3-031-32653-0_10

between academic and personal pursuits. In conclusion, 81% affirm that technological aids aid academic performance (Aivo 2019).

Given these numbers, it is clear that integrating automated Student Service into students' daily life is essential. A good model in this regard is Siglo 21 University (Aivo 2021). They have over 50,000 students and realize that chatbots are the only way to give each one of them the attention they deserve.

Students will be more motivated to continue their education after a positive first school experience. Their careers can get off to a good start in this way.

Will Chatbots Be the New Tutors? Unfortunately, we were unable to verify that. Perhaps in the not-too-distant future, we will turn to robots as our new online educators. So, it is safe to conclude that soon, intelligent chatbots will be the most sought-after resource by both students and universities.

People expect instant responses to inquiries. Why? This is because millennials make up the largest segment among those registered. They constantly interact with one another, and their conduct is influenced by technology because of how they live.

So, why are chatbots so well-suited to carry it out (Aivo 2019)?

Chatbots are available whenever students have questions, whether during a marathon study session or a little break between courses. They adapt to students' lifestyles. This new generation has outgrown the communication preferences of previous generations. It is as far away as writing a letter to dial a phone.

Their preferences are more in line with automation and self-service. As a result, they will not waste time waiting in line at the administrative office and may instead focus on their studies. Because of them, the data will be at their disposal whenever required.

They answer a wide range of questions. Information such as course offerings, exam registration dates, financial aid opportunities, accepted payment types, online platform support, and student contact information are all readily available to students. They will know everything they need to know to maximize their schooling opportunities.

Students who like to study from a distance will enjoy engaging with chatbots. They are helpful for traditional and online education! They will not need to constantly make phone calls or send emails whenever they have issues with the online learning environment. Though this may seem obvious, it is worth restating for clarity's sake.

Faster and more effective communication is possible with the help of a chatbot. Additionally, they provide enhanced solutions with visual resources like images and videos to aid problem-solving.

They work on digital channels everyone knows. Chatbots are compatible with mobile devices and desktop computers used by millennials. They provide the same service regardless of the communication channel: Facebook Messenger, text message, or web chat. Instead of trying to get them to switch to another app, why not just help them with the one they use daily? That is what we call an omnichannel approach!

Reduce costs and optimize resources. Not only do the students benefit, but so do the teachers and administrators. The Bedelia division spends less time on mundane activities thanks to chatbots.

Frustration caused by lengthy processes and pointless labor is history. The support team may now give more attention to counseling and mentoring pupils. Bots will complete the remaining tasks.

10.3 To What End Are AI Chatbots Being Adopted by the Education Sector?

Implementing AI in schools has been eclipsed by its use in other fields. However, schools and educators are increasingly seeing the benefits of this low-cost strategy for maintaining students' interest and facilitating more effective, anywhere-accessible learning. Their myriad advantages are a compelling argument for their widespread popularity. So, let us talk about why it is functional (BotPenguin 2023; Khan 2020; Verma 2021).

- *Better student engagement:* Student life does not appear attractive because learning may be dull. Even the most diligent and brilliant student can struggle with reading material that must be memorized. Therefore, students prefer getting answers quickly through various channels (videos, search engines, etc.). In addition, students are accustomed to rapid gratification, making it difficult to wait for anything. For this reason, chatbots can be helpful in the classroom by providing instantaneous support, boosting student engagement, and streamlining the learning process. A learning bot can use decision trees to lead students through any topic, question, or answer. Let us say you have some creative tutorials or videos you want to make interactive for your audience. If so, a teacher bot may use your website or library to pull in study materials that would be most helpful to students. Finally, excess to schools or institutions becomes limited in the current situation of the Covid-19 epidemic or any other natural calamity. A chatbot can be a more effective learning tool for students worldwide than relying solely on textbooks and human teachers.
- *Efficient teaching assistants:* Chatbots used in the classroom and other technological advancements have allowed students to obtain information quickly and easily. They have instantaneous access to knowledge in the universe, and their appetite for it is ever-growing. Therefore, to capture this fast-moving generation's attention, educational institutions must stay up and speed up their student communication process. Intelligent tutoring systems are one of the more well-known uses of AI because of the individualized learning environment they create for pupils based on their responses and progress through the material. Artificial intelligence (AI) bots can be similarly used in the classroom by translating a lecture into a string of text messages that can then be used to create a more uniform chat interface. The level of comprehension can be evaluated, and the next

section of the lesson can be planned accordingly. Educators will have a much simpler time keeping tabs on progress. They can save time for teachers and address any concerns or questions students may have about their assignments.
- *Instant assistance:* The effectiveness and efficiency of a chatbot in the classroom are its primary selling points. A chatbot can replace human interaction in the classroom by providing immediate answers to frequently asked topics. Teachers would be able to have open lines of communication with their students at all times. They are flexible regarding working hours and can do so around the clock. After midnight or before sunrise, you can assist them with their homework. Many prospective students contact the school's administrative offices to learn more about the application procedure, financial aid, course selection, etc.
- *Student support:* Where digital education is lacking, it provides excellent teachers and modern laboratories. If we take the time to discuss the industry's genuine demands, chatbots have the potential to be of excellent service in education. The education chatbot is a quick and simple way to relay suggestions like dormitory amenities, room assignments, library membership procedures, scholarship applications, and more. Assist students upon arrival, on-campus visits, and throughout their time at the university. They can help students with the application process and give them details about the departments and instructors teaching each area.
- *Quick accessibility to institutional information:* Artificial intelligence chatbots are a fantastic medium for disseminating knowledge and establishing a solid web footing. Using push alerts, you can keep them up-to-date on current events, future contests, college or school-related activities, lecture schedules and times, and much more. A student's questions and concerns about your school can be answered by visiting the website and chatting with the education chatbot there rather than having to make an appointment with an administrator. A wider audience can be reached, and reminders, updates, and other information can be disseminated more effectively. That is why they are great for enhancing efficiency and communication within and beyond your organization.
- *Proactive assistance:* In education, chatbots could be adequately trained to deliver answers to students before they enquire. A direct line of communication between students and institutes may be established when schools provide personalized messages like "Bring your water bottles; there is an issue with the school water tank" or "due to the storm, the school will be closed today." Proactive measures to improve the student experience may include aid with payments, adding a new module to the curriculum, or meeting a deadline.
- *Obtaining feedback:* Input collection is a regular necessity for any organization. The educational sector has a large quantity of data collection needs. It is now possible for schools to collect data on everything from their teachers and curricula to their admissions processes and the quality of their facilities. An educational chatbot's post-discussion or -procedure feedback collection capabilities are a huge boon to the field. It can help schools gather crucial information and identify the root causes of poor performance.
- *Evaluation and assessment:* Both students and educational institutes should be evaluated. Various techniques can quickly analyze multiple-choice questions and

single-word replies, but more nuanced or complex responses require human review. AI and machine learning may automatically examine and score student responses. Teachers may use technology to fill in students' grade books using data from artificial intelligence chatbots. It was discovered that chatbots used in educational settings could supply students with further reading and access to relevant resources when identifying problem areas. Thanks to this development, educators will have more time with their students because they will not have to worry about giving and grading tests.

- *Repository of data:* Chatbots are used for information gathering and dissemination in education. Teachers can use them to communicate with all their students simultaneously, sending them lessons and other important information. There is a space for students to submit their details and data and then view their generated results. When data collection and distribution are automated, errors are less likely to occur, and the process can run around the clock. Having all an organization's data in one location can improve its ability to make decisions, address issues, and draw meaningful conclusions.

- *Technology in education on a global scale:* Regarding instructional materials and media for students, Brazil ranks high globally. Several pieces of software and hardware were created in Brazil with the express purpose of assisting the ed-tech industry. Some of the better examples of such a blended learning platform are Bedu and Digital House, which provide business training alongside technical courses in areas such as mobile and web development, data science, and more—in addition, combining the use of artificial intelligence (AI), chatbots (Chatbots) for education, and augmented reality (AR) to create a platform that aids in the development of various bits of intelligence in young children. Finally, the USA saw a surge in interest in using chatbots from the artificial intelligence and education sectors in classrooms. Chatbots for education are becoming increasingly popular in K-12 and higher education settings. Bots use machine learning, artificial intelligence, and deep learning to facilitate student-to-student interaction in data collection, storage, and analysis. Recent market study by Technavio projects a CAGR of over 48% for the artificial intelligence market in the education sector in the USA from 2018 to 2022.

10.4 How Do Chatbots Transform the Traditional Education Process?

There are many possibilities as AI spreads throughout the industry. AI-based chatbots have played a significant role in revealing their potential to complement human talents across various applications.

AI-powered chatbots are already having a far-reaching impact on the field of education. Chatbots powered by artificial intelligence are increasingly used in the classroom to improve communication between educators, students, and administration. With only a few keystrokes, chatbots can open up a world of possibilities.

Chatbots can serve as an alternate helper in educational institutions such as universities and colleges by providing instantaneous advice and direction. Students today can comprehend the technological revolution and demonstrate an interest in integrating new methods into conventional education.

Many students spend significant time using mobile social networking and entertainment apps today. That is why it might work well for teachers and students if they could use educational chatbots in the learning environment.

Examine how AI chatbots can improve the value of information exchange. Learn why implementing a chatbot into the education industry is a win-win situation. The application of AI chatbots in institutions will also be investigated.

Chatbot Benefits for the Education Industry Educators can relieve some of the burdens of their daily responsibilities and improve the quality of their instruction with the help of chatbots. Before we go any further, however, you must understand the primary advantages of chatbots in education (Das 2021).

- *Impact of chatbots on the education industry:* The inability of teachers to devote sufficient time to each student and thoroughly answer their questions is a common reason why students seek out alternative ways to further their education. Regarding education, chatbots can answer various questions quickly, including school news, assignment help, professor availability, and course materials. Teachers will have more time to focus on enhancing instruction, fostering student growth, and addressing skill gaps when routine activities and redos do not bog them down.
- *Chatbot benefits for students:* Nowadays, students choose a more individualized and interactive teaching method. Chatbots and other intelligent virtual assistants driven by AI give students access to this learning experience.
- *Secure and smart feedback:* The education process can only advance with the help of teacher and student feedback. Most classroom comments are now made digitally rather than on printed materials. Teachers can improve their lessons by listening to student comments and identifying where they fall short. The students can see where their teachers feel they need more practice by reading their responses. Teachers can quickly react to students with examinations, quizzes, and homework. AI-powered chatbots are the key to bringing about this paradigm shift. However, chatbots can make this process feel more natural and exciting. The bot communicates with students by asking them how questions can be answered, what should be changed, what is going well, and what is not. After analyzing the responses, the bot compiles the most popular suggestions from the students and sends them to the instructors. To elaborate, students can use this feature.
- *How do you begin with chatbots?* In order to keep students interested, answer their questions, provide them with resources, and help them finish their projects on time, a wide variety of chatbot platforms are now available. Students love using chatbots for their education because it makes learning more engaging and

allows them to get their questions answered quickly and on their chosen device. This chatbot can be accessed from Facebook Messenger, WhatsApp, and other apps and websites. Finding solutions does not require switching between different services. Chatbots powered by artificial intelligence make it possible to read lengthy chapters rich with visuals, audio, and video that keep students engaged and interested in their studies. Ensure that the student's time spent studying is productive and stress-free.
- *Future of education chatbot:* The world is advancing swiftly toward advanced technology. Chatbots are being used in the education system by many educational institutions. Chatbots have provided educators with novel entry points for imparting information. Chatbot solutions in education create a unique experience for students and urge them to participate more in academics.

10.5 How Can We Best Put Chatbots to Use for Education and Learning?

Artificial intelligence has many potentials, and chatbots are just one of them. They were envisioned as a novel user interface that may supplant or supplement traditional methods of accessing online services, such as downloading an app or visiting a website.

How Do They Work? These automated systems, sometimes called "bots," can understand human speech and provide automated responses to questions.

These responses, however, are not always found in the form of text but might take the form of tangible activities like playing a video in response to a user request, displaying a photo, completing a transaction, setting up a meeting, and so on.

As a result, this technology is being used by various industries since it allows customers and clients to interact with machines as effortlessly as they would with a live person, i.e., as effortlessly as if they were conversing.

The development of this technology has progressed to the point that social media giants like Facebook have introduced application programming interfaces (APIs) that enable brands to adopt and employ bots in their messenger to engage with customers (ChatCompose 2022). However, education is another promising field for chatbots to enter.

Chatbots in Education We have been teaching for decades and have always known that no two students are the same, even if they share a classroom. Therefore, everyone can benefit from working with an expert tutor.

Even the most expensive schools worldwide do not provide this service, which is disappointing.

Is there a more reasonable and economical way to fix this? Chatbots for education.

Chatbots can often give introductory courses. In other words, they modify their approach to learning accordingly. The hope is that chatbots can replace human tutors by learning a student's strengths and weaknesses (ChatCompose 2022).

However, the newest plans call for chatbots to engage in a two-way conversation with each student, functioning as vertical instructors. In this way, they can meet them and find where they need assistance.

Advantages of Using a Chatbot Chatbots' primary role is to understand the user's intent. The chatbot then uses this identifier to parse the request for the appropriate information. However, you cannot help the user if you misunderstand their question.

The chatbot's next step, after understanding the user's intention, is to give them the best possible answer, which can be (ChatCompose 2022):

- A standard, predetermined answer in text format.
- Information provided by the user to create a context.
- Records kept in databases.
- A particular action (the chatbot interacts with one or more applications).

Applications for Chatbots in Education Students of all ages and levels use message services to communicate with one another and, occasionally, with their instructors. These are commonplace in online learning environments like Google Classroom and allow for a two-way conversation whose goal is to further student's education outside of formal classroom settings.

The ability to engage in critical debates about the material being studied has also been shown to help students get a deeper comprehension of the material and hence aid in their education. Further, several studies have found that students learn best when they can engage in critical discussions about the material they are studying (ChatCompose 2022).

This might be scaled up with the help of chatbots, providing students with channels to have in-depth conversations with "experts" on any subject, ask pertinent questions, and arrive at insightful conclusions that deepen their knowledge of the material.

According to an interview with *The Verge* published on April 25, 2016 (Casey 2016), Bill Gates explains the potential benefits of such systems for tailoring instruction and improving outcomes.

Microsoft's founder claims he learned the most throughout his life by identifying individuals more knowledgeable than himself on a given subject and corresponding with them to get insight into the topic or confirm their opinions.

He went on to say that with the help of chatbots, this method of absorbing information would be available to anybody. Furthermore, in his opinion, they can become virtual experts in various topics and act as mentors and study partners of students of varying levels, guiding them to comprehend and grow within each topic at their own pace, asking pertinent questions, and fostering constructive exchange spaces that encourage students to share more of their knowledge.

Some of how chatbots can revolutionize virtual education are as follows (ChatCompose 2022):

- When the chatbots can identify a student's emotional state, they can tailor their responses to that state, whether using different language or cracking a joke.

- Allows for personalized learning tailored to each student's pace and individual needs. Communicating with other people about a course or responding to questions about a course facilitates more direct communication.
- Chatbots can answer students' frequently asked questions in seconds, saving teachers valuable preparation and administration time. The time you save can be spent supervising and inspiring your group, doing course-related research, or completing outstanding assignments.
- Accurately record and examine information concerning student performance and development. This is possible due to the incorporation of AI, which aids students in efficiently and quickly allocating their time and assigning work to their goals.
- Enhances students' opportunities to learn. The automatic learning tool prioritizes formation and interaction over a resource, language, and geographical factors. It is possible to think of it as the "democratization of learning."

10.6 How Can Chatbots Be Utilized in Higher Education?

At some point or another, the inboxes of every university office become flooded with messages, and when ordinary higher ed. staff members there may begin to feel like call center agents attempting to keep up with the overwhelming demand for information. New students, faculty, and parents often have questions about course enrollment or need clarification.

"AI-enabled chatbots, in particular, are being used to boost student engagement while also serving as a teacher's virtual assistant" (CB Insights Research 2021).

Top Higher Education Applications for Chatbots There are many advantages to using a chatbot in higher education. Some vital applications of chatbots in higher education are as follows (Docken 2023):

- *Centralized Information:* By providing instantaneous responses to frequently asked questions through instant messaging, chatbots help keep teachers, parents, and students on the same page.
- *Swift Communication:* Students' ability to convey information clearly and concisely may affect their judgments here and now.
- *Day or Night:* The university administration is available 24/7 for student inquiries.
- *Expedited Enrollment:* A chatbot can be used on instant messaging platforms or via text message to answer fundamental enrollment issues such as class size, residence availability, and costs.
- *Access to Information:* Students' chances of succeeding can be increased with the help of chatbots because they facilitate access to university documents and other forms.
- *Team Focus:* Chatbots may respond to hundreds or even thousands of queries simultaneously, so your staff will not have to spend all day fielding routine calls or writing boilerplate responses to frequently asked topics.

- *Document Questions & Processing:* University paperwork, from the Free Application for Federal Student Aid (FAFSA) to enrollment forms and financial aid applications, can be navigated with the help of a chatbot.

10.7 Best Chatbots for Higher Education

The greatest chatbot for your university's admissions office uses algorithms and is smart enough that students and professors will not need to call or email the support desk. Instead of learning a new virtual assistant, higher education institutions may find it more beneficial to implement a chatbot like Drift's Mongoose Harmony, tailored explicitly to university employees' needs (Docken 2023). All four bots listed below (Docken 2023) were created with faculty and students in mind to enhance the educational experience at universities.

Mongoose Harmony by Drift

- Harmony is a chatbot and virtual assistant developed by Mongoose, especially for use in higher education to address the rising need for student participation and convenience.
- Drift's chatbot can efficiently direct website visitors to the necessary personnel and relevant content, helping educational institutions adapt to the needs of today's digital natives.
- Drift can assist in transforming a website into an easy-to-use hub of answers and facts if you are weary of using call center staff to answer the same issue repeatedly.

Amazon's QnABot

- Students can use the conversational platform provided by Amazon's artificial intelligence bot, pronounced "Q and A bot," to ask questions and quickly categorize information using Amazon Alexa and Amazon Lex.
- QnABot, a service offered by Amazon, is built on the premise that students should have easy access to valuable answers provided by their institutions.
- Amazon's QnABot, like many other AI chatbots, facilitates the addition of features and functionality for educational institutions and provides a forum for students to submit feedback.

IBM's Watson

- IBM's Watson has been trained by academic institutions across the globe—in the UK, Europe, and the USA—to function as an interactive chatbot.
- Watson Conversation Service (https://www.ibm.com/watson/products-services) is a technology used by IBM Watson that helps students respond quickly, download and give materials as requested, and get answers to topic-specific queries.
- IBM's Watson recognizes the usefulness of a virtual assistant and has developed a practical method of adapting the system to higher learning needs.
- Together, IBM's Cognitive Platform and Watson Conversation Service simplify the creation of a chatbot for every user.

HubBot by HubSpot

- Like IBM's Watson and Amazon's QnABot, HubBot is an AI chat service.
- HubBot can also book meetings, interact with HubSpot CRM, and track conversations in an easily filterable manner, in addition to answering simple inquiries according to a pre-loaded script.
- HubSpot's HubBot is designed to appear natural in automated discussions as if the replies came from a natural person.
- HubSpot has made a significant effort to ensure that HubBot is as simple as possible. Both students and teachers will appreciate how easy the procedure can be.

10.8 Various Ways in Which AI and Chatbots Influence the Education

More than we may think, chatbots and artificial intelligence (AI) are revolutionizing society. Artificial intelligence (AI) and chatbots are becoming commonplace daily, completing various activities. Numerous industries, like education and online tutoring, have significantly benefited from technology.

AI-driven technologies change the game in the advanced edtech industry by enhancing student connection and cooperation. Educators and educational institutions have provided students with a personalized learning environment through artificial intelligence. Here are five ways (Gill 2019) chatbots and artificial intelligence affect and transform education.

Personalized Learning According to each learner's interests, AI aids in optimizing the teaching style and pace of educational programs. AI constantly completes progressively challenging tasks to quicken learning by adjusting to an individual's learning rate. As a result, slow and quick learners can continue learning at their own pace.

Through AI, students can receive individualized online tutoring outside the classroom. When students begin an assignment and need to refresh their knowledge or master new concepts, AI gives them the extra resources they need to succeed.

Automatic Grading and Performance Assessment
Teachers now have all the assistance they need for grading, thanks to AI. In actuality, the grader's job is transferred thanks to this technology. With today's AI technology, multiple-choice questions can be graded automatically. However, it is anticipated that as AI advances, it will be able to grade more types of exams than only standardized ones.

Proctoring
The online proctoring industry is one of the sectors where AI has grown in importance. By prohibiting test-takers from using a proctor to cheat on the exam, proctoring is a technique to assure the validity of the results. Currently, this virtual field is being strengthened with the aid of AI technologies.

Remote exams are part of distance learning. During these exams, minimizing students' chances of cheating is crucial. The AI-powered proctoring systems step into the rescue at this point.

Feedback Sessions

Feedback is essential for enhancing both students' and teachers' learning. Feedback on students enables teachers to find areas for improvement in their instruction. On the other hand, teachers' feedback helps pupils identify areas where they need to exert more effort. Teachers may easily give students feedback in addition to assignments, quizzes, and assessments. Additionally, educational institutions use printed and online forms to give students feedback.

It is now simpler for students to express themselves freely, thanks to the many artificial intelligence-driven chatbots already available. The bot aggregates the critical points most students cited in response to the questions and feedback it received, sends it to the teachers, and then summarizes it based on those points. With AI and chatbots, this feedback-sharing process becomes very real and exciting.

A few AI-powered platforms provide feedback sessions inside classrooms to speed up the learning process and student-focused curriculum activities.

Instance Assistance to Educators and Learners

The use of technology allows students in the modern era to access everything instantaneously. Sending emails and sharing photographs are as easy as a few clicks away. Teachers, online tutors, and educational institutions must improve student communication in this fast-paced environment, particularly during admission.

When students visit college websites or offices to learn more about the admissions process and related information, AI and chatbots offer immediate assistance. The technology makes the laborious process of personally responding to each inquiry into an instantaneous automatic one. Students' time is saved, and the strain on institutions to manually answer questions is lessened.

At Deakin University in Victoria, Australia, the Genie Chatbot is one illustration. The chatbot responds to all inquiries on everything a student might have about their needs on campus. William Confalonieri, CIO at Deakins University, conceptualized the initiative.

Confalonieri said, "The most promising opportunity to use this technology is to support a much more personalized approach to on-campus services that still appeals to a large crowd. The system will also help lower the burden on stressed-out faculty, as they no longer have to explain the same things repeatedly to different students."

AI helps teachers in a variety of ways. AI assists teachers in managing everyday chores effectively and assisting them with grading.

10.9 Advantages of AI-based Chatbots in Education

There are numerous obvious advantages of an AI-based chatbot for educational institutions (Marc. 2020):

- *Support for employees:* To streamline communication with website visitors, chatbots can be the initial point of contact; human staff members can be notified for more sophisticated questions.
- *Shorter waiting times:* With the chatbot's ability to serve several users at once, waiting times for visitors are reduced while they obtain the information they seek in real-time.
- *24/7 service:* Chatbots provide around-the-clock support to their users.
- *Precise information:* Instead of relying on student-to-student interactions for knowledge, which can be fraught with ambiguity, schools can provide students with information on demand.
- *Documentation of customer inquiries:* With the use of analytics, you may learn what queries and problems matter most to your target audience by looking at the chat logs generated by your chatbot.

10.10 Benefits of Using AI Chatbots in the Education Sector

Education institutions have traditionally struggled with how each student learns and processes information. While juggling the demands of students, parents, and teachers, the education sector has been making compromises regarding considering students' learning experiences carefully.

Analyzing technology advancements in various industrial sectors, particularly as the "digitalization" trend spreads and aims to achieve easier and faster workflows. As this tendency continues to grow, chatbots are among the most widely used applications in the education industry.

A chatbot benefits the education sector, according to research.ai, to a degree of 14% (Marc. 2020). By making learning experiences more engaging and participatory, chatbots for education enhance learning and boost student interest. Including chatbots in educational websites or applications is unquestionably beneficial for students seeking immediate information.

Let us examine the advantages of chatbots in the educational space by first considering the difficulties (Marc. 2020):

1. *Increases Student Interactions:* Nowadays, the Internet serves as students' primary source of information, making applications that provide comprehensive answers common and valuable. Due to their intuitiveness and enjoyable user interface, these educational applications are much more popular than traditional textbooks. A chatbot simulates classroom interactions for students by simulating the real-time exchange of questions and answers. Additionally, information on any subject of study is constantly accessible.
2. *Act as a Teaching Assistant:* We typically ask a teacher for help when a subject is challenging to comprehend. However, thanks to the utilization of pertinent study material readily available online, a chatbot make learning anything possible without a teacher's aid. Other than this, a chatbot can:

(a) Allocating work, ranking exams, and tracking project assignments are all made easier.
   (b) Answer questions regarding the course modules, assignments, and deadlines.
   (c) For a better learning experience, assist teachers in providing specifically targeted information.
   (d) To improve learning, assist teachers in providing messages specifically targeted to each student.
3. *An Instant Help Tool:* The virtual chat support is made to accomplish a fantastic job of giving prompt replies to any student's question. Assignment submission, email, text message responses, and feedback are all tasks that students can automate. The chatbot option helps students complete their work more quickly by suggesting online study materials. By using the assistance tool, they can also enroll and get information on applying to colleges. In addition, with online applications for colleges now being the most popular, the number of applications has substantially increased, making monitoring more challenging. An AI chatbot can substantially assist in this situation by sorting online applications and relieving some administrative staff's workload.
4. *Acts Like a Learning Medium:* Chatbots have improved student experiences and made learning more enjoyable in educational applications. Students understand all the complex ideas, and the online learning environment makes it simple to track students' progress—many students like being free to learn whenever they choose by sending periodic messages to a chatbot. Teachers can record responses and conversations with chatbots to assess student performance. Another benefit of virtual assistance in the learning environment is that it offers learning modules, tests, and quizzes like a classroom while collecting and reporting these exams to the instructors.
5. *An Intelligent Feedback Mechanism:* Any learning process can be improved with feedback. Conversational forms and automatic responses can make the entire feedback procedure fascinating. To improve the learning experience for students, questionnaires and information on lecture quality can be collected conversationally. Teachers can use a mobile app with a chatbot feature to highlight important aspects and provide feedback for students' assignments in one place. The online discussion forum can also be utilized to assess teachers' performance.
6. *Better Support for Students:* Every student sometimes searches for supplementary online courses better to comprehend the concepts from the textbook or lecture. Here, a chatbot for education helps students with information for an assignment or recommends reading material based on their chosen subject. As a result, students learn more, and teachers have less work to do, so they may devote more time to teach students who learn slowly.
7. *Quality Education in the Future:* By providing students with the necessary information, AI chatbots make learning more exciting and alleviate their concerns about various subjects. On the other hand, it also lightens the load on

teachers and enhances the rapport between them and their students. The main benefit is that students must use these digital platforms in regular training to prepare for the future. As we all know, automation and technological advancements will be significant. In order to teach people how to attain their results faster, a chatbot is a suitable addition.
8. *Assessment and Evaluation:* Artificial intelligence and machine learning allow automatic evaluation and scoring of student responses. Based on discoveries from an AI chatbot, teachers can use technology to fill in the scorecards for their students.
9. *Proactive Assistance:* Chatbots can be correctly programmed to answer questions from students before they ask them. An improved student experience might result from proactive measures like helping with payments, adding a new module to the program, or meeting a deadline.
10. *Virtual Personal Tutoring:* AI chatbots can pay close attention to each student's unique learning habits. They may carefully monitor how students study and consume the material that will help them succeed in their chosen fields. Since not all students comprehend information and learn similarly, schools can provide tailored learning experiences. By ensuring that students gain the most knowledge possible outside of the classroom, chatbots may tailor the learning plan to each student's needs.
11. *Administrative Companion:* Chatbots can perform as administrative assistants. Chatbots are more convenient for getting information than going to the office and waiting for responses. The AI chatbot can provide access to a wealth of information, including tuition fees, course descriptions, scholarships, campus maps, school events, and much more.

10.11 How AI Chatbots Are Changing Mobile Learning

The way consumers use their mobile devices and the way businesses communicate with their customers are both being transformed by chatbots. Mobile user experiences are becoming more social and personalized than ever. These chatbots are therefore altering mobile learning.

Learning via mobile devices like tablets and smartphones is called mobile learning. According to eLearning Industry, 47% of companies use mobile devices in their training programs. Mobile learning is much more informal and social than traditional classroom-style learning, and chatbots improve this mode of learning's capacity to meet each learner's unique needs, enhancing the educational experience. Here are a few particular examples (Marc. 2020) of how chatbots are strategically improving mobile learning:

- Chatbots guide learners in virtual mobile learning environments. They offer feedback to students that aid them in overcoming roadblocks in their learning process and enables them to pick up new abilities more rapidly. They interact

with people as a teacher would, instructing them as they go along in the learning process.
- "Bots reinforce (the) learning experience by imparting relevant information at certain intervals, in response to various triggers," stated a contributor to eLearning Industry. This improves mobile learning and encourages learning throughout the educational process.
- Chatbots expand the possibilities for colleagues to engage with one another over mobile devices, enhancing the social, collaborative, and productive nature of mobile learning.
- Learners can receive reminders from chatbots to use their mobile devices to participate in training. The rate of employee participation in training may rise as a result.
- Mobile learners' performance and progress are monitored via chatbots.

10.12 How Universities Are Using Education Chatbots to Enhance the System

How universities incorporate chatbots into their educational systems (Aivo 2019) to enhance student learning and support.

Rapid Gains from Universities Implementing Chatbots in Education
Let us quickly run through the most frequently cited advantages of implementing chatbots on campus (Aivo 2020) before we move on to the more advanced applications of chatbots in higher education.

- *Speed up your responses:* Try implementing a chatbot to handle routine inquiries to satisfy today's millennials' inpatient needs.
- *Give nonstop service:* Applying a chatbot to your recruitment and student support processes allows you to respond to inquiries and concerns whenever they arise. By doing so, you can enhance their experiences and maintain their interest.
- *Spend less:* A chatbot can juggle several inquiries without lowering the standard of service it provides to any of them. You can save money on human help desk staff by using a bot to communicate with prospective employees and students around the clock.

Advanced Applications of Chatbots in Higher Education
Chatbots offer a unique opportunity for educational institutions to (Aivo 2020):

- *Assist Students in Making Wise Decisions:* Choosing a suitable professional path is a common source of anxiety for today's students. They want to ensure that the classes they sign up for are a good fit for them regarding their career goals, financial situation, and areas of academic interest. Then, they may have to make a second choice if their top choices for institutions also provide the necessary courses. Colleges and universities can use chatbots to reach out to and interact with prospective students who are a good fit for their programs. Chatbots powered by AI can guide students to the appropriate resources, such as web pages or explanation videos about the material they are studying. A well-designed chatbot's conversational flow can help direct students toward their interests. Having more students sign up for classes and apply to a university could be a positive outcome.

- *Lessen the Effort Required for Registration:* Education enrollment processes can be simplified by using chatbots. Chatbots can aid students with problems like registering for sites, logging in, solving problems, and answering questions. They are an excellent resource for learning more about the school, its services, financial aid opportunities, and enrolling in classes. The most frequently asked questions from the incoming class can be answered by deploying bots each year. So doing this will help the incoming class settle in quickly and easily.
- *Offer Omnichannel Support:* Young adults today have little patience for lengthy wait times. They want answers to their concerns immediately. Implementing automated student support services is crucial if you want to live up to the expectations of these young learners. Chatbots powered by artificial intelligence make it simple to automate routine conversations and offer instant help whenever needed. In educational settings, these bots might provide a different method of interaction between students. They can handle common student inquiries and report more complicated issues to the proper departments. The more it talks to people, the more it learns, so it can eventually deal with more complicated questions and scenarios. A pioneer in this field is Siglo 21 University (Aivo 2021). Using Aivo's AgentBot, they can deliver first-rate support to all their 52,000+ students, raising the benchmark in the industry. Every day, their bot responds to hundreds of student questions on everything from administrative to scholastic matters. Student satisfaction is tracked regularly by analyzing data from chats between students and the university's chatbot. This aids them in making sure their students have access to quick solutions without having to track down a human. The most significant benefit of integrating a chatbot into your educational institution is the ability to provide students with assistance across many channels. One of the most widely utilized means of communication among students is Facebook Messenger, which you may link your bot with. They will be able to get prompt aid with the communication app they are already familiar with.
- *Enrich the Learning Environment:* Using AI-powered chatbots alters how students take in and process information. AI and ML allow colleges to create individualized classroom experiences for each student. Educators may more readily reach their students, instruct and coach them, answer student questions on the fly, and speed up their learning with the help of chatbots. As a bonus, they provide feedback in a participatory and exciting manner. Intelligent tutoring systems can be developed to improve education by evaluating how pupils react. With constant and recurrent testing, chatbots can determine each student's current level of comprehension and tailor their presentation of subsequent chapters accordingly.
- *Share Relevant, Personalized Content:* You may tailor your message to each student with the help of a chatbot explicitly designed for use in the classroom. You

may keep students up-to-date on campus happenings, internship opportunities, and other news that might pique their interest. Your bot can be linked to external web services that provide information such as student balances, due dates, test scores, courses taken/not taken, etc. A more effective strategy to engage students is to provide them with tailored content. The prestige and respectability of your institution will rise as a result.
- *Compile Information About Students:* Also, universities can utilize bots to gather information about their students' preferences and usage of web platforms and services. It might assist you in figuring out what they liked and what you can do to improve their experiences. For instance, if many students have asked for more information on a particular subject, you could create a new page to accommodate their needs. Additionally, if students have trouble navigating your website, you can utilize that information to make it easier to discover the needed content.

10.13 Institutions that Deployed Educational Chatbots

Some institutions deployed education chatbots (Engati Team 2022).

- *University of Rochester:* The university aimed to provide professors and students quick access to OBGYN and mental health resources. Using a sophisticated chatbot was their method of choice for achieving this. Their bot encourages students and teachers to care for their bodies and minds by providing workout routines and meditation instructions. The platform was so user-friendly that they could create a nearly human-sounding bot in 14 days.
- *Podar Education Network:* The parent outreach efforts of Podar Education Network required a scalable infrastructure. They hoped they might increase their efficiency by streamlining their sales process, managing their consistently high volume of inquiries, and syncing their engagement software with their lead management system. Their bot can handle 79% of customer questions, passing on just the most challenging ones to human operators. Podar was able to reduce resolution time by 89% and increase MQL conversion by 31% as a result of this.
- *The UK Cabinet Office:* The UK Cabinet wished to launch a campaign targeting students, particularly those from underrepresented groups, to pique their interest in STEM fields. The "Just like me" campaign aimed to encourage children from traditionally under-represented groups to enter the Young Scientists competition and pursue careers in science, technology, engineering, and mathematics. It initiated the "Young Scientist Competition" with the Ministry of Innovation, Business, and Sustainability. To spread the news among students, they created an AI-powered chatbot. In order to increase exposure for the Young Scientists competition, the bot tells the stories of former winners and encourages current competitors to share information about the projects previous winners have completed on social media. With the bot's assistance, students could compose posts for social media and select appropriate hashtags. The UK Cabinet Office saw an increase in user engagement of 43.5 percent after using this chatbot.

- *Qassim University:* Qassim University in Qassim, Saudi Arabia, was founded as one of the world's earliest modern universities. The company was exploring online and social media strategies for interacting with and helping its students and potential customers. Faster responses to questions about enrollment, financial aid, campus life, faculty, and more were a priority for the university. Qassim University created a chatbot to answer these questions quickly and efficiently. The institution can now respond to 30 times as many inquiries thanks to the bot's deployment on Twitter, Telegram, WhatsApp, and the university's website. The university's response time has improved by 88%, and the bot can now handle 90% of incoming inquiries without routing them to a human representative. They provided in-depth help whenever necessary.

10.14 How Can Education Apps Benefit from Chatbots?

Artificial intelligence (AI) chatbots have been a significant factor in the rise of mobile app development across several sectors. The education sector is no exception to the rule, with technological advancements moving the sector forward alongside all others. Currently, tablets and mobile gadgets play a significant role in children's education.

Adding a personal touch is vital to keeping users interested. The level of customization provided by chatbots is unparalleled—this aids eLearning service providers and teachers in accomplishing their pedagogical aims.

The educational industry may greatly benefit from collaboration and engaging in meaningful dialogue with students. Artificial intelligence (AI) chatbots have substantially influenced the eLearning sector since their beginnings.

Conversational AI has ushered in a new era of education. New technologies provide more sophisticated educational opportunities.

The Benefits of Using Chatbots in Educational Mobile Applications The following are the various benefits of using chatbots in mobile educational applications (Rajput 2019):

- The availability of immediate support is guaranteed.
- Novel ways of learning.
- Improve your chances of connecting with more students.
- Efficiently gather feedback.
- The learning environment can be tailored to the individual instructor's needs.
- Locating weak spots in student's knowledge and skills.
- Monitor the needs of the students.
- Changing the face of education.
- 24/7/365 lessons availability.
- The pace of instruction can be adapted to each student's skills.

How Do Students Gain from the Integration of Technology into the Classroom? There is a higher chance of distractions when children have access to technology. It has been shown that incorporating chatbots into educational settings can benefit students. Not all students are children, but they should all be interested in the interaction process. This method must be well-researched in order to be efficient.

When technology use is guided, it can improve students' ability to learn. Students will be more engaged in their studies if they find them engaging. However, the educational process should be organized so students can easily absorb the course materials.

Lessons can get monotonous when written out. The capabilities of the chatbots span from texting to real-time file and video sharing to video conferencing. These features add excitement to the study experience.

Consequently, they prefer active participation to passive reading regarding education. Numerous prestigious online universities and colleges worldwide have already adopted this method. Research is being conducted to improve chatbots' capacity for education.

In What Ways May Chatbots Help Today's Educators? In many nations, the education system has restricted access to resources due to a lack of money, time, or both. Educators and academics have realized the value of chatbots incorporating artificial intelligence.

As shown below, the bots can help in four main ways (Rajput 2019) in offline and online settings:

- Curriculum, due dates, plans, and lesson-related questions are all areas where chatbots can be helpful.
- Bots can be used to assign grades in the classroom, making data analysis much more efficient.
- Bots allow educators to keep up with the latest grading theory and practice developments.
- Concepts can be interpreted in whatever way is most comfortable for the student.

Thanks to advances in artificial intelligence and machine learning, chatbots can now understand the context inside a dialogue. The students receive the individualized attention they need to learn effectively. They can give an interesting, unique, and conversational response.

Support for eLearning. The eLearning market has expanded at an astounding rate in recent years. Education is now accessible to more individuals because of the convenience of online courses. Everything from learning how to build websites and promote them to learning how to knit and build furniture may be done in the virtual realm.

However, no physical classrooms are necessary for web-based learning as everything occurs online. The inability to make adjustments based on individual preferences can be a hindrance. Chatbots, however, can help alleviate this issue to a great degree.

10.14 How Can Education Apps Benefit from Chatbots?

Traditional online courses have consisted of recorded lectures shared among students through the Internet. According to recent research, only 7% of people who start an online course finish it. The primary cause of this disheartening statistic is the lack of feedback and support the students receive. This problem can be solved by chatbots, which would improve the efficiency of education overall. With these bots playing the part of instructors, class time is transformed into an exciting and dynamic learning environment.

Managing Administration in Education. The educational circuit must include more than just the teaching and learning process. The administrative capacities of the organizations that adopt and use chatbots also improve.

For instance, these are some applications of bots (Rajput 2019):

- The course scheduling process.
- Accepting tuition payments.
- Help students fill out their applications.
- Address frequently posed questions.
- Appointments, phone calls, and other forms of human interaction can be planned.

Bots have lightning-fast response times and are always at your disposal. Furthermore, bots can be deployed across numerous channels. Therefore, they are among the top helpers in the educational sector regarding administrative work.

Chatbot: An Intelligent Tutoring System. Incorporating AI into chatbots allows for a more personalized classroom experience. You can think of chatbots as a kind of intelligent tutoring system. The system analyzes students' responses, yielding information on the student's comprehension of the material.

Eventually, AI can take a lecture and generate a string of messages. The bot acts as a substitute teacher by engaging in one-on-one conversations with the pupils via their devices. After determining each student's ability to take in information, the bot tailors its courses to their specific needs. Based on these assessments, the next section of the lesson is given.

The chatbot will show the students different content, such as text, graphics, video, or a combination. In order to demonstrate their comprehension of the material, students may submit written responses to questions posed by their instructors. Botsify makes use of this process to its advantage. It is an adequate improvement to the interface and performance.

When a new technology becomes available, the youth often rush to try it out. As current market trends show, people increasingly favor multipurpose communication and social interaction platforms over specialized apps. More effective student engagement is possible with the help of bots.

App developers are working with schools to create AI-driven chatbots with specific pedagogical goals. Tools like these have the potential to pique the interest of students, especially young ones.

These bots can be deployed to every communication medium with only a click. The students will eventually have a unified platform to share information and gain knowledge. They will not have to sign up for or manage several email or web-based accounts. After selecting a platform, they can start communicating with the bot directly. It simply takes a second or two, yet it maximizes your time.

A platform with the desired functionality built into the apps can be available in departments and classrooms. Bots can also increase communication and interaction between faculty and alums networks. Furthermore, students can always know when assignments are due, what is happening in the classroom, and any other relevant information.

Smarter Feedback With Chatbots. The increased opportunity for collecting user feedback is among the many advantages of incorporating chatbots into educational apps. Educators and students need to be able to have two-way talks in real time for traditional one-way web-based communication to be productive.

Both teachers and students need to be able to reflect on their experiences for the process to be mutually beneficial. Educators can track student progress in online lessons and highlight areas where pupils fall behind. Therefore, they made an extra effort to improve their performance.

Hubert, an AI-powered chatbot, has already created a name for himself in the educational scenario. Chatbots provide a medium for instructors and students to communicate on course materials, tests, and grades. Educators can learn where a student is struggling.

This app uses student interaction and the generation of course-related questions to inform and refine its design. Furthermore, the procedure can be improved with the input of the students.

Chatbots for Teaching Languages. Conversational interfaces like chatbots may help spread language education in established institutions. You are probably familiar with Duolingo, one of the most downloaded language learning apps.

A bot is used in Duolingo's mobile app. The students can also have real-time conversations with a cast of fictional characters developed by Duolingo. The method can help them improve their language skills.

Creating these chatbots is to make them seem as natural as possible in conversation. It has been shown that chatbots are more versatile and adaptable than more conventional language-learning programs.

The pupils' reactions and demonstrations of varying responses are based on the answers they provide. The two languages have a dialogue that sounds very close to each other.

More than that, there is no correct way for students to respond to inquiries. When the student gets stuck, the bot offers solutions to help them continue the dialogue.

Completing Repetitive Tasks. Certain activities are required of both the educators and the learners. Chatbots with specialized functionality can help handle routine, time-consuming activities.

Teachers' schedules must be simplified to allow the bots to handle these responsibilities. Many education professionals are adopting chatbots as virtual helpers in the classroom.

These bots are used to respond to commonly asked questions or those that are pretty similar. Typically, students have the same questions after each class, especially about the lecture. This can be related to the lessons, modules, syllabus, or homework.

10.14 How Can Education Apps Benefit from Chatbots?

The bots can keep tabs on how far the student has come and offer specific suggestions based on their findings. Consequently, lecturers will not have to field the same questions repeatedly.

Provision of Instant Assistance. One of the most challenging components of teaching is providing individual attention to students. For instance, if a teacher has a class of 50 students, speaking to everyone by name will take a lot of time. To help in a similar situation, chatbots are available.

Chatbots can supplement or aid teachers in giving students one-on-one support. These bots can provide immediate support to the students as well. They can ask questions, get responses, and read the Frequently Asked Questions (FAQ) page to resolve any confusion. Teachers' workload is lightened, and students' learning is facilitated. The teachers will help when they see that human interaction is required.

Creating mobile apps has been greatly aided by machine learning and artificial intelligence. When a chatbot is incorporated into a learning app, it reduces the human intervention required. Some degree of automation is achieved. One sector where these innovations have had the most impact is education.

Essay Scoring. Teachers utilize multiple-choice questions on exams as a way to streamline the assessment process. However, evaluating such essay-style responses is quite challenging. On the other hand, essay questions are the most effective way to get a more in-depth understanding of a student's knowledge. Their ability to think critically and methodically is put to the test.

Automated essay grading is now possible with AI-enhanced chatbots. After scoring the essays, teachers can compare the results to a standard to determine how well their students are doing.

In order to more accurately gauge each student's progress, chatbots will be built into these systems. The machine learning algorithms can fairly grade the pupils' work on specific subjects.

However, research and development into this technology are still in the early phases. There is potential for using essay-grading apps once they incorporate chatbots with similar capabilities.

Spaced Interval Learning. There are now chatbot-enabled educational apps that can monitor student progress. The students in a spaced interval learning class must review previously learned material before moving on to more advanced material. As a result, they are less likely to forget what they have already learned.

Before they forget it, the app prompts them to review previous lessons. This improves the students' abilities and aids in their retention of the acquired knowledge.

Integrating Chatbots in Education: How to Optimize the Benefits? The educational realm benefits significantly from the accessibility provided by chatbots. These resources can be incorporated into your app for training staff and managing the organization.

In order to enlarge your perspective (Rajput 2019), consider the following.

University Bot. Students typically find the search for universities to be a time-consuming procedure. A university bot can help streamline the procedure. Students can locate universities that meet their specific needs using these automated systems.

The purpose of creating these chatbots is to improve the efficiency of the search procedure. That way, when they apply for admission, they can choose wisely. In addition, many apps have cutting-edge capabilities like voice search. Because of this, they are perfect for helping students find suitable courses for them.

Chatbots for Business Courses Online. Chatbots can significantly help those who manage eLearning systems when teaching students online. These apps are available to international students enrolling in their chosen courses. They will be able to communicate with a sizable number of learners.

The sophisticated chatbots include functions including lead data storage, information dissemination, and client engagement through support desks.

Chatbots for Educating. You probably already know that chatbots are being utilized in classrooms worldwide. However, chatbots driven by artificial intelligence open up the possibility of utilizing NLP (Natural Language Processing) in various contexts.

Chatbots are available at all hours to make education more convenient for students. These smart teaching solutions transform traditional lecture formats into more conversational ones. In addition, chatbots have been created to respond to a wide range of questions from students.

How Education Apps Can Benefit from Chatbots From chatbots, educational apps can gain the following benefits (Rajput 2019):

- Their availability in messaging apps facilitates the use of chatbots. Institutions can use chatbots by making them available to students on messaging platforms like WhatsApp and Facebook Messenger.
- A chatbot's development procedure is simple and cheap. More potential customers can be reached when a business has a mobile app or website with a chat support option.
- Natural language processing (NLP) underpins the majority of bots. As a result, consumer satisfaction rises, and loyalty increases.

10.15 Future of AI Chatbots in the Education Industry

All students are unique, with varying strengths and weaknesses. Every student is given the same instruction in a traditional classroom. However, each learner has a unique combination of absorbing capacity and comprehension ability. For this reason, many students will not gain from treating them similarly in the classroom.

Now is an excellent time for your institution to experiment with artificial intelligence chatbots. Chatbots powered by artificial intelligence will soon play an integral role in the classroom, opening up a world of possibilities for students.

Conversational AI chatbots are allowing educators to provide students with tailored education. Furthermore, chatbots can swiftly assist students by fixing this issue, personalizing each student's interactions, and offering each student the most significant learning experience possible (Sinha 2022).

- A chatbot powered by AI can respond to each student by looking at their grades and profiles. With individualized instruction from a chatbot, students are more likely to retain what they learn.
- Artificial intelligence-powered chatbots are created in such a way that they can understand the purpose of any engagement with students.
- An AI chatbot solution is highly suited to enhance students' overall learning processes by tailoring it to their unique needs and academic histories.

The teachers may utilize a chatbot as their assistance. Chatbots, which use artificial intelligence, can assist teachers in completing their tasks without making them feel pressured or worn out. The good news is that AI chatbots can effectively carry out those repetitive duties. Use AI chatbots if you want the productivity of your institutional employees to rise.

10.16 Conclusion

Due to chatbots powered by artificial intelligence, many more shifts are expected to occur in the educational sector in the coming years. Bots have greatly aided educational institutions, including increased sales, new student inquiries, and the smooth running of classes. Technology has shifted the dynamics of competitiveness, and chatbots will continue to help raise instructors' games. The student's education will evolve and become more individualized as a result. In particular, chatbot features can be combined with other technologies to achieve even better outcomes. Educational institutions work with established app development firms to incorporate unique chatbots into their mobile applications. In order to strengthen your educational institution, you should get in touch with chatbots.

References

Aivo. (2019). *Chatbots also participate in education.* Aivo. https://www.aivo.co/blog/chatbots-also-participate-education

Aivo. (2020). *How Universities are using education chatbots to enhance the system.* Aivo. https://www.aivo.co/blog/how-universities-are-using-education-chatbots-to-enhance-the-system#:~:text=Universities can leverage chatbots to attract and engage students who,them make the right decisions.

Aivo. (2021). *Siglo 21 raises its standards for student support with AgentBot.* Aivo. https://www.aivo.co/customers/siglo-21

BotPenguin. (2023). *Why is education industry opting for AI Chatbots?* BotPenguin. https://botpenguin.com/why-chatbots-is-opted-in-education-industry/

Casey, B. (2016). *Can AI fix education ? We asked Bill Gates/How personalized learning is changing schools.* The Verge. https://www.theverge.com/2016/4/25/11492102/bill-gates-interview-education-software-artificial-intelligence

CB Insights Research. (2021). *Lessons From The Failed Chatbot Revolution – And 7 Industries Where The Tech Is Making A Comeback*. https://www.cbinsights.com/research/report/most-successful-chatbots/

ChatCompose. (2022). *How to use chatbots for education and learning*. ChatCompose. https://www.chatcompose.com/chatbot-learning.html

Das, P. (2021). *How do Chatbots transform the traditional education process?* LinkedIn. https://www.linkedin.com/pulse/how-do-chatbots-transform-traditional-education-process-poulami-das/?trk=public_profile_article_view

Docken, C. (2023). *Top 4 Best Chatbots for Higher Education 2023*. O8.Agency. https://www.o8.agency/blog/best-chatbots-higher-education

Engati Team. (2022). *Can education chatbots replace teachers?* Engati. https://www.engati.com/blog/chatbot-applications-in-education

Gill, M. (2019). *5 ways artificial intelligence and chatbots are changing education*. Towards Data Science Monica. https://towardsdatascience.com/5-ways-artificial-intelligence-and-chatbots-are-changing-education-9e7d9425421d

Khan, A. (2020). *8 benefits of chatbots in education industry*. Botsify. https://botsify.com/blog/education-industry-chatbot/#:~:text=Artificially intelligent chatbots do not,the administrative staff as well.

Marc. (2020). *Chatbots in education – benefits, use cases and tips*. Onlim.

Rajput, M. (2019). *How education apps can benefit from chatbots*. Datafloq. https://datafloq.com/read/educational-apps-benefit-chatbots/

Sinha, S. (2022). *The future of AI chatbots in the educational sector*. Ameyo. https://www.ameyo.com/blog/what-does-the-future-hold-for-ai-chatbots-in-education/

Verma, M. (2021). *Why is education industry opting for AI chatbots?* Chatbots Life Sign. https://chatbotslife.com/why-is-education-industry-opting-for-ai-chatbots-93f800bd8b46

Chapter 11
AI-Assisted Remote Proctored Examinations

11.1 What Is Remote Proctoring?

"Remote proctoring" refers to scalably authenticating, approving, and controlling online examinations. It is a method that guarantees the highest level of security while allowing organizations to conduct assessments at any time, from any location.

Exams can be taken from the comfort of one's home, eliminating applicants' need to travel to a central location.

For a standard exam, an invigilator must be present at the testing facility to verify the identities of those taking the test. One invigilator is needed for every 30–40 exam takers. However, you would require more than 25 invigilators to manage the testing procedure for 1000 or more students.

Online proctoring can be done using the candidate's webcam and an Internet connection. Not only can it record video of an entire exam, but it can also record screenshots of the computer's desktop, logs of online chats, and even still photographs from the camera's frame.

Different kinds of proctoring (see Fig. 11.1) include the following (Takyar 2022):

- *Video Proctoring:* Video proctoring is a service that helps students take tests with high stakes while keeping a close eye on them via live video. A candidate's video activity during the exam is recorded, and the assessment controller analyzes their conduct to determine whether or not the candidate engaged in any form of cheating or unfair tactics.
- *Image Proctoring:* Using image proctoring in areas with poor Internet connection is appropriate. For instance, every 30 or 45 s, the system would take a photo of the candidate while they answer questions on the exam. Educational institutes can use the photographs to verify that a legitimate student took the online exam and rule out any possibility of cheating. The goal of this variety of proctoring is to randomly re-verify distant candidates many times. The cost of image proctoring is significantly lower than the quality of video streaming.

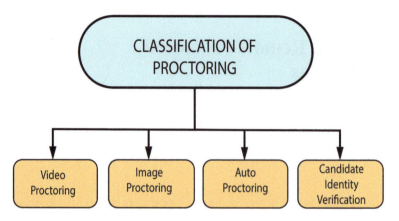

Fig. 11.1 Different kinds of proctoring

- *Auto Proctoring:* To automate the process of monitoring and analyzing distant applicants, "auto proctoring" might be used. It monitors live-streaming activities from candidates in different regions for online testing. Images and videos are analyzed to determine if a candidate has cheated on an exam by, for example, utilizing a mobile phone, having someone else take the test for them, or consulting a reference book.
- *Candidate Identity Verification:* This proctoring form checks students' identification before they begin their online exam. The camera will record the candidate as they provide their identification document and exam ticket. The proctor checks the candidate's identification card and grants or denies access based on the information provided.

One of the most effective uses of a webcam and screen-sharing software for proctoring is automated proctoring. In place of a human proctor, this system uses algorithms to detect potentially fraudulent actions.

ML allows remote proctoring systems to learn, adapt, and become increasingly intelligent. However, the goal of incorporating AI into proctoring is not to do away with human monitors altogether but to improve proctoring accuracy by assisting human monitors in picking up on subtle cues like low sound levels, whispers, reflections, shadows, etc.

11.2 Online Proctoring System (OPS): An Overview

The use of remote proctors is not a novel concept in education. Most, if not all, adaptive and competitive tests like the GRE, GMAT, and CAT require a proctor. Despite the pandemic, several schools continued to use proctoring systems for online classes. Virtual tools (tab switching, time stamps, audio levels, etc.) are used to evaluate students taking tests in online proctoring. To maintain honesty, many

11.2 Online Proctoring System (OPS): An Overview

Table 11.1 Characteristics of online proctoring system

S.no.	Features	Description	Newer technologies
1.	Authentication	Candidates' and proctors' identities are checked as part of the authentication process in proctoring software	A proctoring system uses one-time passwords (OTPs) and/or facial recognition technology for user authentication
2.	Browsing tolerance	Software that acts as a proctor limits how much time can be spent using various systems and services (such as other tabs of browsers, other face detection during live proctoring, etc.)	Methods such as log tracking and analysis, face detection, object detection, etc., are used to accomplish this
3.	Remote authorizing and control	It allows the proctor to manage the proctoring system (e.g., by remotely beginning or ending an exam for a specific student)	Most of this is accomplished by employing tiered security models and granting users administrative privileges
4.	Report generation	The focus here is on the student's report and exam activity log	Technologies like Python, ASP.net, and other open-source programming languages are typically used for this

examinations are administered online or at designated off-site locations (Foster and Layman 2013).

Two primary components are essential to the online proctoring system: a webcam recording of the student's exam performance and a means by which the examiner or proctor can watch that recording. The examiner/proctor has the right to investigate any suspicious activity during the exam, including cheating. The second component, locking, makes it such that students cannot access any other pages in their current browser window. This is sometimes referred to as a browser or computer lockdown (Alessio et al. 2017). Here are some of the characteristics of proctored exams that have been tabulated in Table 11.1 based on research by Hussein et al. (Hussein et al. 2020):

It was determined that there are three distinct types of proctoring systems (Hussein et al. 2020). Proctoring systems are depicted in Fig. 11.2:

- *Live Proctoring*
  - Real-time proctoring system.
  - Human proctor is involved.
  - Suitable for theoretical exams and long exams which last for 2–3 h.
  - A human proctor can track eye movements, recognize the faces of students, and flag them if they are caught cheating or engaging in malpractice.
  - Requires proficiency in the use of technological enhancements.

- *Recorded Proctoring*
  - Videotaping the candidate during the examination and keeping a detailed journal is required.

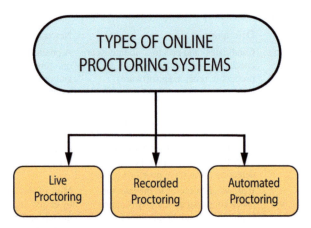

Fig. 11.2 Types of online proctoring systems

- The post-proctoring process includes recording and analyzing logs, data from the object and face detectors, and tracing students' eye movements.
- The involvement of humans is essential, but it takes a long time and costs much money.

- *Automated Proctoring*
    - Cost savings due to the absence of human proctors.
    - Greater complexity in design.
    - More advanced version in which humans do not proctor the entire time but instead evaluate.
    - System detects fraud and cheating via a variety of algorithms and technologies.

11.3 What Is AI Proctoring?

Artificial intelligence (AI) proctoring prevents students from cheating on online exams (Kathpalia 2021). AI proctoring closes security loopholes by using an adaptive set of anti-cheating measures. The cutting-edge AI algorithm at Mercer | Mettl has been trained on data from over 2.8 million proctored exams. Over 95% accuracy is achieved in identifying up to 18 dynamic deviations (Kathpalia 2021). The smart algorithm can alert the user in unusual situations, such as when a face or presence is not visible, a mobile phone is detected, an extra person is present, the user's gaze wanders, etc.

11.4 How Can AI Improve Remote Proctoring Services?

The following are the various remote proctoring services where AI can create an impact (Takyar 2022).

- *Improved accuracy:* AI acts as an additional set of eyes for human proctors, raising the alarm for any suspicious behavior it detects that humans would miss.
- *Additional scalability:* Increased efficiency in spotting suspicious conduct makes it possible for remote proctoring software to proctor online exams without compromising the extra security a human proctor provides.
- *Unmatched security:* The remote proctoring system can take prompt action against the applicant if it detects any inappropriate activity or use of unauthorized resources that a human proctor might overlook. This feature can instill even more trust when avoiding or correcting cheating would be ideal in high-stakes exams.
- *Mimic human behavior:* Artificial intelligence can assist humans in detecting abnormal behavior in real time. If the machine can eventually match human accuracy, human care for each applicant will no longer be necessary.
- *Creating a smarter AI system:* The success of an AI model depends on its precision. To achieve accuracy, the system needs hundreds of data points. This means that the more data your AI has to analyze, the smarter it will get.

11.5 How AI-Based Remote Proctoring Work?

The three main themes of AI-enabled remote proctoring are (Takyar 2022):

- Detect identity fraud
- Analyze cheating behavior
- Discover content theft

Throughout thousands of iterations, the AI-powered remote proctoring process builds, trains, and refines each and every event defined in the system. Identify fraud, content theft, and cheating can all be exhibited in a single incident.

If someone is observed glancing off-screen to the left, for instance, the observation can be treated as a discrete data point, and the relevant segment of the video can be identified as evidence of dishonest investigation tactics. Initiating the ongoing construction, training, and improvement process happens when the number of data points exhibiting the same behavior reaches the threshold.

Each of the millions of actions taken throughout the process is flagged for possible dishonesty. A session's integrity would be suspected if all the occurrences met the criteria.

Numerous forms of AI technology are already being employed to improve remote proctoring services and provide a more streamlined method of exam

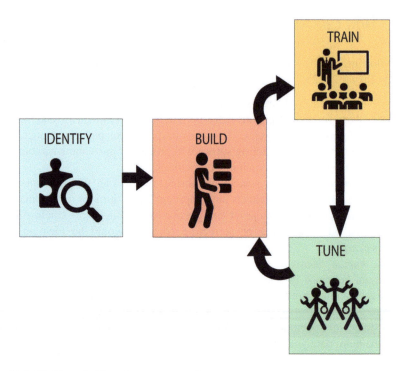

Fig. 11.3 Working of AI-based remote proctoring

administration for educational institutions. Figure 11.3 provides an overview of the working of AI-based remote proctoring.

11.6 How AI Prevents Cheating in Remote Proctoring Exams?

Every organization hopes for a cheating-free environment regarding online proctored exams, and AI can interpret human behavior precisely to give just that. Let us look at how AI makes online tests completely honest (MapleLMS 2021).

- *Live proctoring for maximum accuracy:* AI utilizes online camera proctoring to observe candidate behavior. It records every candidate's action, including eye tracking, voice and face recognition, multiple face logging, and more.
- *Optimum security:* If the AI-enabled system detects suspicious activity, the candidates will see a warning message on their screens. In addition, the human proctor is looking for suspicious behavior from the candidates.
- *Recording:* The sessions are recorded for future audits and reviewed afterward to ensure no violations were committed.

- *Reporting and analytics:* These AI-powered proctored testing environments collect exam data for more accurate reporting and analysis. This is useful for determining how well and how intuitively the application functions. Insights that can be put to use in the future to improve the user experience are gleaned through analytics.

11.7 AI-Assisted Proctoring Software for Monitoring Online Exams

This section details an AI-assisted proctoring software designed (Bartamani et al. 2021) to keep tabs on students taking tests online. Python software that can count the times a student speaks and identify when they are out of frame has been built. Furthermore, the time and date that these occurrences occurred can be noted. The analysis engine will use these factors to identify suspicious behavior or attempts at cheating. Figure 11.4 gives the block diagram of AI-assisted proctoring software.

- *Methodology:* The student's performance on the online exam is recorded in real time via video and audio using a camera and microphone. An AI-enhanced analytical engine is fed the live video and audio a microphone acquires. The analyti-

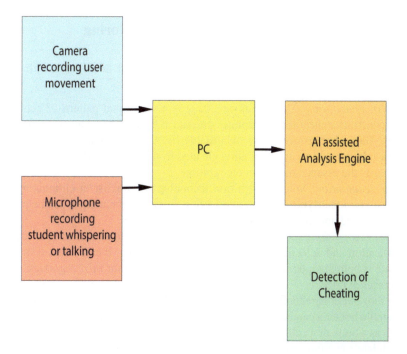

Fig. 11.4 Block diagram of AI-assisted proctoring software

cal engine is written in Python and uses machine learning to spot out-of-the-ordinary activity patterns. The python code is compiled using the Thonny IDE.
- *Data analysis:* Using the recorded audio and video feed, python software detects the following:
  - The timestamps and the number of times the student leaves the camera's view. When a human face is present, the occurrence is accepted as typical, but it is viewed as suspicious when one is absent. We employ the face recognition method known as the Haar Cascade classifier to achieve this goal.
  - The Google API for speech recognition is used to decipher spoken words.
  - With the help of the time stamp, we can also calculate how long the student spent outside of the camera's field of view.
  - The analysis engine is "trained" with data from students who take the exam honestly and those who cheat.
- *Results:* The Python, facial, and speech recognition programs accurately detect the number of times a student exits the camera's field of view and the words spoken by the student during the online exams. The system can also track when the student is no longer in view. Anomaly events must be detected using the data collected.

11.8 AI Technologies Used for Remote Proctoring

The following is a list of the various forms of artificial intelligence utilized in Remote Proctoring.

- *Pattern recognition:* There (Takyar 2022) is no universal pattern of behaviors that constitutes cheating. It examines the data at hand to detect any recurring patterns. Data patterns are easily identifiable by AI. Classifying data using prior knowledge or statistical information gleaned from patterns and/or their representations is the essence of pattern recognition.
- *Voice recognition:* Voice recognition technology can assist in eliminating dishonesty by identifying speech patterns in a noisy environment. It can help identify expected and unexpected noises during testing.
- *Facial recognition:* Facial recognition has several applications, such as identity verification and detecting new faces in a testing setting. It can detect if the candidate is being helped in any way during the online exam by recognizing multiple faces at once.
- *Eye movement detection:* Using artificial intelligence, eye movement detection can tell whether a candidate is staring at the screen or distracted by anything else, such as a book or a cell phone. Unfair practices can be uncovered by tracking the candidate's eye movements for telltale signs of misconduct.

- *Plane detection:* Through plane detection, remote proctoring software can learn the spatial definition of the candidate's actual testing environment. By incorporating object recognition, the system can learn more about the world around it.
- *Mouth detection:* Like eye detection, important facial points are utilized, and test-takers must maintain an upright posture. You can track the gap between the lips' pivot points in many frames. An infringement is recorded if the average distance between users' lip points is more significant than a threshold.

11.9 Challenges and Opportunities

While there may be several advantages to taking an online exam powered by artificial intelligence, doing so requires several factors to be in place first. Scaling this technology requires more individuals, even if many already have such a system at home.

Mohan of the Upgrade explains that "in a country like India, the looming challenges for students in remote areas with poor or no internet connectivity and limited infrastructure can restrict their access to this model" since a hiccup in the network could prevent multiple students from logging in at once and finishing the exam. As an additional technological hurdle, he says, "there could be insufficient bandwidth for the webcam application to perform efficiently" (Anu Thomas 2020).

"Even though innovations enable students to take virtual exams, significant difficulties remain before they can become popular in India," says Kumar, CEO of BasicFirst Learning. Many students cannot take online tests because they do not have access to reliable Internet at home or do not have the necessary equipment.

Further, Testbook co-founder Ashutosh Kumar notes, "while the rising trend of online proctoring has been seen in other nations, India still has a few difficulties to overcome before it can be made ubiquitous" (Anu Thomas 2020). Therefore, making the AI proctoring model more accessible can boost its overall efficacy and guarantee its full utilization at all academic levels.

Despite the obstacles, Doshi of GreyAtom sees a potential to leverage proctoring systems as a tool for more reliable test administration and personalizing the learning process.

Doshi believes this is an opportunity to build further examinations in which artificial intelligence (AI) evaluates students repeatedly, providing immediate feedback and a suggested improvement strategy. All sorts of personalization and prediction tests can be carried out if "the systems are intended to capture data from the beginning," she says.

She argues that proctoring exams can be utilized to identify a student's knowledge gaps and lead to more effective learning. This is just one aspect of the broader problem statement of continuously evaluating students.

She explains: "As a student takes additional tests, the system updates its model of the student's understanding and modifies the curriculum depending on the behavioral and cognitive signals. The more students use the system, the more hidden relationships between ideas are revealed. After these new associations are made, the ML algorithms revise the knowledge graph to reflect them, allowing for more accurate gap analysis, course recommendation, and improved student test scores" (Anu Thomas 2020).

11.10 Future of AI-Based Proctoring Systems

Over the past decade, educational institutions and corporate organizations have gradually embraced online proctoring software worldwide to conduct distance tests properly and ensure that the applicants gave the exam in a known setting. Remote proctoring solutions are in high demand because of the current COVID-19 pandemic. These platforms allow for the smooth administration of examinations while preventing exam cheating by candidates. The year 2020 will mark the introduction of remote proctoring (Nigam et al. 2021).

There are several advantages for an organization to use remote proctoring for an assessment rather than the old-fashioned paper and pen method. Arranging exam dates is far less of a hassle when you do not have to worry about reserving space at approved testing facilities. The examiner and examinee's communication ability is facilitated by fewer barriers and in less time. The examination results can be generated more quickly, sometimes even instantly. Because of the scalability of online testing, organizations can administer exams to many candidates without worrying about testing centers reaching capacity (Arora 2021).

A serious effort is needed to create proctoring technology to ensure that online examinations are on par with offline examinations in terms of quality (including the integrity of marks scored and the prevention of misconduct by applicants). Furthermore, the general public's attitude regarding online examinations must be altered, and the advantages of these examinations must be known. As mentioned above, current technologies must be used to solve problems when creating an AI-based proctoring system. While it is true that technological progress will help engineers build more reliable and secure systems in the future, there is still work to be done to ensure that today's tools can cope with future demands (Pimple 2021).

There must be a foolproof method for verifying the user's identification in any proctoring software. The proctoring software requires candidates to provide identification information or other forms of personal data, which are then checked. The security of online examinations is particularly vulnerable to impersonation, so several measures are taken to verify that the designated examiner is administering the test. Some systems have started using fingerprint scanners as biometric authentication (Nigam et al. 2021), commonplace on modern mobile devices and computers.

Regarding biometric authentication, iris scanning is one of the safest methods (Nigam et al. 2021). Even though this verification method is more widely available nowadays, it is still not a failsafe way to confirm a person's identification. However, machines with the hardware capabilities for the abovementioned procedure do not yet exist on the market; thus, candidates will have to shell out additional cash to acquire these components. Preventing people from using remote proctoring software because they do not have the proper hardware or software would be counterproductive to expanding its use worldwide. Consequently, when developing proctoring software, it is essential to incorporate the "necessary evil" of continuous human proctoring throughout the exam.

Biometrics are becoming increasingly popular; thus, mobile devices (phones, tablets, laptops) are outfitted with fingerprint and facial recognition scanners. If these gadgets were mass-produced, then everyone would use some form of biometric authentication. Multi-factor authentication is an excellent option if you are concerned about a test taker's identity being compromised. In any OPS, a password can serve as the initial module, while OTP-based verification, facial recognition, and fingerprint authentication can be utilized in the second stage. While several AIPS has employed iris tracking in addition to other methods, it should be kept in mind that doing so necessitates sophisticated technology that is not within the financial reach of the average person (Nigam et al. 2021).

Light Detection and Ranging (or LIDAR for short) is another technology making headlines. LIDAR is a type of remote sensing technology. LIDAR uses a pulsed laser to determine the varying distances of objects from a light source. These light bursts produce precise three-dimensional data of the object of interest and its immediate surroundings.

In addition to its long history of use in astronomy (e.g., the Phoenix Mars Lander used LIDAR technology to detect snowfall), LIDAR is finding promising new uses in fields as diverse as biology, meteorology, and autonomous cars. LIDAR was first launched in mobile phones and is now being implemented into self-driving cars to model the road better and detect adjacent obstructions.

LIDAR enhances the precision of distance measurements and facilitates augmented reality (AR) use. More precise location data is sent to apps for a more dependable augmented reality experience. LIDAR is a valuable technology that has yet to see mass manufacturing in mobile phones to make it more affordable, so while this is excellent news for AIPS, it comes at a hefty price.

We must find a way to unite the two worlds of online learning and testing. Several programs seek to study student behavior in online classes, collect students' unique behavioral features, and share this data with proctoring services for improved invigilation of online tests. In the future, much more similar software will be launched to help improve the many foundations of online education. The future is sludgy (Slusky 2020).

The revolutionary shift the pandemic has wrought will not ease in the following years. All this has done is further solidify the concept that online education is viable, highly efficient, and successful. There are many opportunities to acquire a degree from the convenience of home through distance learning. As a result, AIPS is not going away and will continue to advance.

The usage of OTP-based verification (Joshy et al. 2018), user interface configuration (Karim and Shukur 2016), and anti-plagiarism measures are also taken into account alongside the use of EEG devices (Norris 2019) (Dendir and Maxwell

2020). Prospective findings in identifying incidences of misconduct have been found in studies using these variables.

The cost of incorporating these strategies into a Proctoring System powered by AI may be prohibitive, but this may change as more and more technologies are combined.

11.11 Conclusion

AI-powered remote proctoring has the potential to revolutionize the education system and make the impossible feasible. Integrating AI into computer systems safeguards the integrity of the examination by discouraging the candidate from using unjustified practices during the assessment. Examinations at schools and universities are not postponed or canceled because of the COVID-19 pandemic because of AI-assisted Remote Proctoring. By incorporating AI technologies, schools, and teachers can speed up and improve the reliability of their online testing. Scalability, quick processes, high accuracy, and assessment integrity are only a few advantages AI and ML algorithms provide—a safe and inexpensive method of detecting and punishing exam takers who cheat on online tests. AI in remote proctoring allows for the safe administration of online tests to distant users. Online exam fraud can be detected and prevented with system algorithms. With artificial intelligence, remote proctoring makes it simple to administer examinations online while keeping them safe.

References

Alessio, H. M., Malay, N., Maurer, K., Bailer, A. J., & Rubin, B. (2017). Examining the Effect of Proctoring on Online Test Scores. *Online Learning, 21*(1), 1–16. https://doi.org/10.24059/olj.v21i1.885

Anu Thomas. (2020). *Opportunities & Challenges Of Conducting Exams Through AI-Based Proctoring In India.* Analytics India Magazine.

Arora, P. (2021). *Is Remote Proctoring The Future Of Academia?* ELearning Industry. https://elearningindustry.com/is-remote-proctoring-future-academia

Bartamani, N. N. H. A. Al, Hadhrami, N. H. J. Al, Al-Azri, S. Said, & Muralidhran, R. (2021). AI Assisted Proctoring of Online Exams. *The Industrial Revolution Four (IR4).*

Dendir, S., & Maxwell, R. S. (2020). Computers in Human Behavior Reports Cheating in online courses: Evidence from online proctoring. *Computers in Human Behavior Reports, 2*(July), 100033. https://doi.org/10.1016/j.chbr.2020.100033

Foster, D., & Layman, H. (2013). *Online Proctoring Systems Compared.* chrome-extension://efaidnbmnnnibpcajpcglclefindmkaj/https://caveon.com/wp-content/uploads/2013/03/Online-Proctoring-Systems-Compared-Mar-13-2013.pdf

Hussein, M. J., Yusuf, J., Deb, A. S., Fong, L., & Naidu, S. (2020). An Evaluation of Online Proctoring Tools. *Open Praxis, 12*(4), 509–525. https://doi.org/10.5944/openpraxis.12.4.1113

Joshy, N., Kumar, M. G., Mukhilan, P., Prasad, V. M., Ramasamy, T., & Harini, N. (2018). Multi-Factor Authentication Scheme for Online Eamination. *International Journal of Pure*

References

    and Applied Mathematics, *119*(15), 1705–1712. https://scholarworks.lib.csusb.edu/jitim/vol29/iss1/3

Karim, N. A., & Shukur, Z. (2016). Using Preferences as User Identification in the Online Examination. *International Journal on Advanced Science Engineering Information Technology*, *6*(6), 1026–1032.

Kathpalia, B. (2021). *How is AI – Based Virtual Proctoring Redefining Recruitment?* Blog.Mettl. Com. https://blog.mettl.com/ai-virtual-proctoring/

MapleLMS. (2021). *How AI Reduces Cheating In Remote Proctoring Exams.* www.maplelms.com. https://www.maplelms.com/blog/how-ai-reduces-cheating-in-remote-proctoring-exams/

Nigam, A., Pasricha, R., Singh, T., & Churi, P. (2021). A Systematic Review on AI-based Proctoring Systems: Past, Present and Future. *Education and Information Technologies*, *26*(September), 6421–6445. https://doi.org/10.1007/s10639-021-10597-x

Norris, M. (2019). University online cheating – how to mitigate the damage. *Research in Higher Education Journal*, *37*, 1–20.

Pimple, O. (2021). *Digital Education For All – Is Mobile Learning The Way Ahead?* The Media Bulletin. https://www.themediabulletin.com/guest-articles/digital-education-for-all-is-mobile-learning-the-way-ahead/

Slusky, L. (2020). Cybersecurity of Online Proctoring Systems Cybersecurity of Online Proctoring Systems. *Journal of International Technology and Information Management*, *29*(1), 56–83. https://scholarworks.lib.csusb.edu/jitim/vol29/iss1/3

Takyar, A. (2022). *Remote Proctoring using AI – Enabling Seamless Management of Online Examinations*. LeewayHertz. https://www.leewayhertz.com/remote-proctoring-using-ai/

Chapter 12
Ethics of Artificial Intelligence in Education

12.1 Ethics in AI

AI ethics aims to guide the creation and ethical application of AI technology. As AI becomes more embedded in everyday life, organizations are working to establish AI codes of ethics.

An AI code of ethics, also known as an AI value platform, is a policy declaration articulating AI's intended to function in human progress (Lawton and Wigmore 2021). The goal of creating a code of ethics for AI is to provide people with pointers to follow when they need to make a moral choice about employing AI.

The science fiction writer Isaac Asimov anticipated the problems posed by autonomous AI agents long before they were developed, and he wrote "The Three Laws of Robotics" to mitigate those threats. The first rule of Asimov's code of ethics is that robots must not intentionally hurt or allow harm to come to humans by failing to act. Following the first two rules, robots must take precautions for protection by the third rule. In the absence of explicit violations of the first law, robots are required by the second law to follow the instructions of their human masters (Lawton and Wigmore 2021).

Groups of professionals have responded to the rapid development of AI over the past 5–10 years by creating safeguards to defend against the risk that AI poses to humans. Max Tegmark, a cosmologist at MIT, Jaan Tallinn, co-founder of Skype, and Victoria Krakovna, a researcher at DeepMind, formed a nonprofit institute to study these issues. Asilomar AI Principles are a set of 23 standards developed by the institute in collaboration with AI researchers, developers, and academics from various fields (Lawton and Wigmore 2021).

The director of KPMG's Digital Lighthouse, Kelly Combs, has stated that "it is imperative to include clear guidelines on how the technology will be deployed and continuously monitored" must be included in any AI code of ethics (Lawton and Wigmore 2021). These regulations should call for safeguards to prevent algorithmic bias in machine learning, ongoing algorithmic and data drift monitoring, and identifying persons responsible for training algorithms and their data sources.

12.2 Ethical Implications of Artificial Intelligence

Responsibility is a source of debate when discussing deep learning and other forms of AI. The trainer in a conventional classroom setting is responsible for verifying the veracity of the training materials before they are distributed to students. If not, they are liable.

In contrast, with AI, the inventors of the algorithms do not also serve as the content providers (Hauptfleisch 2016). This creates difficulty in an accident, as machines cannot be held responsible like people.

Mustafa Suleyman, CEO of Google DeepMind, discussed the duty of designers and technologists to think critically when constructing such systems at the Disrupt London tech conference (Hauptfleisch 2016). He warned that developers could unwittingly embed their prejudices into the technologies they create.

As a test, Microsoft launched a chatbot on Twitter. The more people tweeted at it, the more it learned. The tweets moved from "people are cool" to "Hitler was right" in less than 24 h, demonstrating the influence our shortcomings may have on AI systems.

Data processing systems do not learn from the algorithms but rather from the data they process (Hauptfleisch 2016). Liability for algorithm developers would be unreasonable from a legal standpoint. In addition, this could be a severe issue in sectors where safety and compliance are paramount, such as a school setting.

In order to guarantee that the data being processed by AI systems is accurate and fair, it is up to the humans in charge of those systems. To the same extent that educators must provide students with reliable information.

There will be deep-seated changes in both the quality and price of education. There is no denying the efficacy of deep learning in online education. On the other hand, unintended repercussions may be challenging to anticipate and manage.

We must take chances for the future, just like our ancestors did, because of the exponentially increasing benefits of learning and information communication advances.

12.3 Ethical Issues of AI in Education

Let us have a deep dive into the ethical issues of AI in education.

The aims of education. Reiss and White (Reiss and White 2013) argued that education's overarching goal should be to foster human flourishing, but, in a larger sense, the nonhuman environment's flourishing. This expansion is crucial because it comes when the human race becomes increasingly aware of its devastating effects

12.3 Ethical Issues of AI in Education

on the planet through deforestation, climate change, and species extinction. Using AI as a learning tool highlights the importance of reevaluating education's core goals.

The goal of education might be more broadly conceived as contributing to the flourishing of each student (Reiss 2017). Although it is not incompatible with helping students gain strong knowledge (F.D.Young 2008)—the kind of knowledge that students would not learn without schools—establishing that human flourishing is the aim of education is not the same. The claim that education should promote human flourishing begins with the idea that there are two parts to this goal: preparing students to live flourishing lives for themselves and assisting others to live flourishing lives.

Schools should provide students more freedom to choose activities that interest them to facilitate their maturation into self-reliant adults (Reiss 2021). In particular, one may argue that education's primary purpose is to ready students for a life of self-directed, whole-hearted, and fruitful participation in meaningful relationships, activities, and experiences. To achieve this goal, it is necessary to introduce students to many paths they can choose, with the understanding that students will have varying degrees of competence in making such "choices." Teachers, like parents, are likely to have a more substantial role in guiding young children. Both schools and parents have a responsibility to help their children develop the skills they will need to make decisions on their own.

In his Nicomachean Ethics and Politics, Aristotle emphasizes that humans should (can) enjoy thriving lives; this is one of the earliest ethical ideas (Reiss 2021). There are various conceptions of what makes a life triumphant. Maximizing positive emotions while reducing negative ones is the goal of a Benthamite hedonist. From a more mundane point of view, it could be linked to financial success, public acclaim, material possessions, or the gratification of one's most profound, fundamental need. Each of these explanations has its flaws. One issue with achieving one desire is that it can lead to unhealthy living, such as a person devoting their entire life to keeping their bedroom neat (Reiss 2021).

The concept of Bildungsroman expands our understanding of success in school. This German term describes the stages of development during which a person comes into their own as an individual while also becoming a contributing part of society. This idea is exemplified by the vast body of literature known as Bildungsroman (Reiss 2021) (often translated as "coming-of-age" novels), in which a protagonist undergoes a moral and psychological transformation from childhood to adulthood (examples include Candide, The Red, and the Black, Jane Eyre, Great Expectations, Sons and Lovers, A Portrait of the Artist as a Young Man, and The Magic Mountain).

This has implications for a future where artificial intelligence plays a more significant role in education because, while it is true that all teachers should reflect on their goals, this is especially important when the teacher in question lacks self-awareness and the ability for reflexivity and questioning, as is the case when AI provides the teaching. There is also a risk that AI education systems may prioritize a restricted conception of education, where knowledge acquisition or a narrow set of skills will become dominant due to the historical focus on disciplines like mathematics in computer-based learning. Creating effective AI packages for teaching literature may be more challenging than teaching physics without assuming a Dead Poets Society perspective. The overarching goal of our pedagogy is to help students develop into engaged, well-informed citizens. This involves nudging people toward civic engagement on freedom, individual autonomy, equitable regard, and cooperation at the state, national, and international levels out of a concern for the common good. Moreover, young people need to know what these attitudes require, such as an awareness of the complexities of democracy, the range of perspectives on it, and how it might be applied to their social context (Reiss 2017).

12.3.1 Possible Impacts of AI on the Working Conditions of Educators

Students are not the only ones whose lives will be altered by the rise of AI in the classroom. The ramifications for (human) educators are impossible to foresee. Every educator would welcome the possibility that AI might lead to more motivated students so that they could devote less time and energy to classroom management difficulties and more to enabling learning. However, the privacy problems and growing surveillance culture may also apply to educators. Once upon a time, a teacher's classroom was their haven. Teachers may discover they are under as much scrutiny as their students as data on student performance and achievement grow (Reiss 2021). Teaching may become considerably more stressful than it is, even if AI has little or no effect on the number of needed teachers.

It would appear that a teaching assistant's job is more precarious than that of a teacher. The shocking conclusion, well supported by statistical analysis, reached by Blatchford et al. (Blatchford et al. 2012) in their landmark study evaluating a significant expansion of teaching assistants in classrooms in England—an expansion costing about £1 billion—was that students who had the most help from teaching assistants performed much worse academically than their peers who had gotten less assistance. Subsequent research has shown that this result can be turned around if teaching assistants provide adequate resources and instruction (Webster et al. 2013). However, the case for a significant number of teaching assistants in a post-AI world seems weaker than the case for a high number of teachers in the future.

12.3.2 Special Educational Needs

Students with special educational needs (SEN)—a catch-all category that includes attention deficit hyperactivity disorder (ADHD), autism spectrum disorder (ASD), dyslexia (LD), dyscalculia (DY), and specific language impairment (SLI), as well as less well-defined categories like moderate learning difficulties (MLD) and learning disabilities (LD)—should benefit significantly from the potential of AI to tailor the educational offer more precisely to a student's needs and wishes (Astle et al. 2018). In a standard classroom of, say, 25 students, students with special needs are statistically guaranteed to have a smaller proportion of the material covered in any given lesson be directly applicable to them than students without special needs. Naturally, this is true for students labeled as gifted and talented (G&T) and those who find learning (in general or for a specific subject) much tougher than most, taking substantially longer to progress.

However, to be clear, while some students in school may need a binary decision of whether they are SEN or not or if they are G&T, these are not dichotomous variables; instead, they fall on continua. AI has many benefits, one of which is that it does not have to resort to oversimplified categorizations that are sometimes necessary for traditional teaching methods (funding decisions and allocation of specialist staff).

The number of students with SEN is hard to pin down. Definitions have shifted, but in England, the average is still around 15%. Even with this rudimentary categorization, it is evident that roughly one-fifth to one-sixth of students fall into the SEN or G&T categories. The percentage of students who are G&T is usually substantially more petite, with estimates ranging from 2% to 5%. However, there are still many other students who, in the eyes of any parent, have special needs while not falling into formal categories (Reiss 2021).

It is not hard to picture a future when AI aids in this kind of education but does not entirely replace human instructors. Indeed, it appears likely that AI will be of particular use when it supplements human teachers by offering access to topics (even whole disciplines) that individual teachers cannot, so expanding the educational offer.

12.3.3 Student Tracking

In the West, we often find ourselves shaking our heads at how the combination of biometrics and AI in some nations leads to the ever-stricter tracking of people. Betty Li, at age 22, is a student at a school in northwest China. She must pass through scanners to enter her dorm, and facial recognition cameras above the blackboards in class monitor her and her classmates' participation (Xie 2019). Cameras of this type are being utilized in some Chinese secondary schools to track and record the emotional states of their students. Although such information is not being used now, this may change as technology improves.

According to Sandra Leaton Gray's writing (Gray 2019), she has nightmares about how artificial intelligence and biometrics will merge in the classroom. She argues that publishers already know how long students spend on each page and which pages they skip because of the widespread use of digital textbooks in schools. As she continues:

In the future, companies may even be able to observe students' faces as they read the material or link their responses to online questions throughout the course to their final GCSE or A-Level scores, mainly if the same parent company developed the test. While this is not happening, it is theoretically feasible. (Gray 2019)

In 2019, Leaton Gray (Gray 2019) raised valid concerns about integrating AI and biometrics. Technology studies frequently repeat the cliche that technologies are neutral, at best, and often downright harmful, depending on their application. This could improve education, but imagining the nightmarish effects of widespread monitoring in the panopticon style is simple.

12.4 The Ethical Framework for AI in Education

In the summer of 2018, Sir Anthony Seldon, Priya Lakhani OBE, and Professor Rose Luckin proposed the Institute for Ethical AI in Education. Their goal was to create an ethical framework to ensure all students could reap the most significant possible benefits from using AI in the classroom while being shielded from potential dangers.

After extensive stakeholder engagement, the Institute is prepared to provide The Ethical Framework for AI In Education (The Institute for Ethical AI in Education 2020). The Framework is based on an agreed-upon ideal of ethical AI in education and will ensure that all students can reap the most significant possible benefits from AI in the classroom while being safeguarded from its potential dangers. Those responsible for purchasing and implementing AI-related educational resources must find a helpful framework.

Leaders and practitioners in educational settings are critical to maximizing the benefits of AI for students while mitigating any associated hazards. To better incentivize providers to develop AI ethically and with learners' best interests in mind, decision-makers can use the Framework throughout the procurement phase to help guarantee that only ethically created resources are used and purchased.

The AI Learning Framework gives educators the tools to steer AI development, acquisition, and deployment for students' benefit. However, it is not their job to ensure that students get the most out of AI in the classroom. Those responsible for creating AI materials must guarantee that their creations adhere to pedagogically sound standards and do not unfairly target any one demographic of students.

The Framework provides a reliable technique for shielding students from potentially harmful artificial intelligence (AI) resources (The Institute for Ethical AI in Education 2020). The Framework integrates the ethical expectations of individuals creating and developing AI systems, eliminating the need for a separate framework. Several places in the Framework suggest that decision-makers request pertinent information during procurement to ensure that AI resources are created ethically. The Institute expects that procurement decisions will be quickly affected if organizations involved in designing, developing, and providing AI resources cannot provide the information the Framework requires.

Designers are also tasked with upholding local data protection rules and standards, such as the Information Commissioner's Office's Age Appropriate Design Code (or "Children's Code"). In addition, The Institute recommends that by September 2021, all providers of AI goods and services used in schools comply with the standards in The Ethical Framework for AI in Education (The Institute for Ethical AI in Education 2020). These groups are urged to consider the data procurers will require and take preventative measures to guarantee they have all the data they need to show that their resources were developed with ethics in mind.

The Institute for Ethical AI in Education believes educational reforms are necessary to ensure that all students receive the most advantage from artificial intelligence (AI) in the classroom (The Institute for Ethical AI in Education 2020). Artificial intelligence (AI) can potentially solve many systemic issues plaguing education today, from a thin curriculum to ingrained social immobility. With the help of AI, nations may be able to abandon their antiquated evaluation methods, paving the way for universal access to low-cost, high-quality lifelong education.

While it is outside the purview of the Institute to propose a design for how these reforms could be supported using AI, it is evident that not all students will benefit from the reforms if the digital divide is not overcome promptly and decisively.

The effects of digital exclusion were made starkly apparent during the day schools were closed because of COVID-19. The worst effects were seen by students who lacked proper access to technology and/or the Internet. Many of the most impoverished children and teenagers' severe academic decline was preventable. If the Institute's findings are considered, it is less likely that the same mistakes will be made again.

The epidemic could end up being a game-changer in the history of education in the long run. Assuming that all people have access to the required hardware, infrastructure, and connectivity, societies can hope that AI's ethical and purposeful use can help them overcome massive educational disparities and unleash the full potential of all students.

The Institute for Ethical AI in Education strongly recommends that all governments implement policies to ensure all students have access to a device and Internet connection (The Institute for Ethical AI in Education 2020). Only then will students everywhere reap the full benefits of AI in education.

12.5 Investigating the Moral Implications of AI for K-12 Classrooms

Due to COVID-19, online learning has become more commonplace in K-12 classrooms in recent months. Everything from checking your email to using a search engine now uses artificial intelligence. It also exists in the classroom, for example, through personalized learning or assessment systems. However, what about the moral and ethical repercussions of this?

Two researchers from Michigan State University investigated the potential benefits and drawbacks of using artificial intelligence in elementary and secondary schools. Their findings are presented below.

Lead author of the paper published in AI and Ethics and doctoral candidate in the College of Education's Curriculum, Instruction, and Teacher Education (CITE) program, Selin Akgun, elaborated on the benefits of AI in the classroom: "Artificial intelligence can help students get quick and helpful feedback and can decrease workload for teachers, among other affordances." Some educators promote student-to-student dialogue through social media, while others supplement lesson delivery with online platforms in hybrid or multi-level settings. While numerous potential benefits exist, we also wanted to address potential drawbacks.

To help educators make the most of AI in the classroom, Akgun and Christine Greenhow have outlined four key areas, as shown in Fig. 12.1, to explore (Akgun 2021).

1. *Privacy.* Users of many AI systems are asked to agree to the system's usage and access to personal data in ways they might not fully comprehend. Think about the "Terms and Conditions" you are asked to agree to before downloading any new software. In some cases, users may click "Accept" without fully understanding the implications of doing so. On the other hand, individuals can learn about the more nuanced ways the software can use their data, such as by understanding their location, provided they read and comprehend it. Further, others say that parents and children are being "forced" to share data if platforms are mandated as part of the curriculum.
2. *Surveillance.* A user's actions can be monitored by AI algorithms, leading to a tailored experience. Some examples of such systems exist for analyzing student performance and determining where improvement is needed in the classroom. Monitoring and tracking students' online chats and behaviors also may limit student participation and make them feel unsafe taking ownership of their ideas.
3. *Autonomy.* The reliance on AI systems on algorithms such as estimating a student's test score might make it hard for students and educators to feel they have

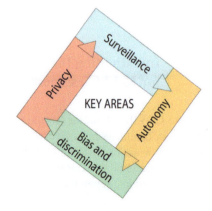

Fig. 12.1 Key areas to explore when using AI in the classroom

control over their work. Experts say this phenomenon "raises problems about fairness and self-freedom."
4. *Bias and discrimination.* According to academics, every time an algorithm is developed, it is accompanied by data representing society's historical and systemic biases, which ultimately morphed into algorithmic biases. One way in which these can manifest in AI is through the translation of words and phrases based on gender ("She is a nurse," but "he is a doctor"), for example. Different AI-based platforms exhibit varying degrees of gender and racial bias, even though these prejudices are unintentionally built into the underlying algorithm.

12.6 Artificial Intelligence in Higher Education: Ethical Questions

Concerns about ethics typically center on the potential impact of AI systems on various demographics, as well as on educational ideals and how such values might be affected by the technology (Zeide 2019).

- *The Black Box.* Understanding what is happening within AI systems is challenging due to the high degree of complexity in which they operate. The premise is that computers can perform tasks beyond human thought's capabilities. For this reason, simplifications are generated when we attempt to explain the underlying mechanisms at play.
- *Invisible Infrastructure.* By deciding what information to include in admissions, financial aid, and student information systems, these AI technologies set the ground rules for what matters in the higher education sector. Because of this, the supporting structures will be hidden from view. The people responsible for building the infrastructure do not take this into account explicitly. A prime instance is when instructional software mandates concrete goals for users' progress. Indeed, that is a central tenet of any sound educational or institutional plan. However, many teachers fail to recognize that implementing new technologies is similar to mandating a new set of standards regarding student performance.
- *Authority Shifts.* Most of the time, a private company is responsible for gathering and presenting the data. Therefore, the business is responsible for making many decisions that will have far-reaching and subtle effects on the fundamental qualities of various systems. These private corporations may have less of an incentive to be transparent with the people who matter most to schools, the kids. The shift in power and the resulting changes in motivation necessitate careful consideration before implementing these technologies.
- *Narrowly Defined Goals.* The data-driven applications that are now available tend to support particular aims. In other words, these systems cannot function unless they explicitly define what constitutes an optimal outcome. One example is getting a well-rounded education instead of focusing on a particular area. There will be less room for improvisation than how people currently engage in

classes and college campuses. More abstract educational aims, such as developing citizens capable of self-governance or encouraging creativity, may be pushed aside to optimize learning outcomes. The latter are things that, strictly speaking, could be represented in data, albeit through extremely imprecise approximations. Which means they might not be tracked or given any importance.

- *Data-Dependent Assessment.* The data-driven evaluation also has some similar issues. Data collection tools focusing primarily on online interactions may miss subtleties that human educators can pick up. Let us pretend a student gives the wrong response to a question. The machine will record one wrong answer. However, if the teacher knows the student is sick with a cold, she may overlook the mistake.
- *Divergent Interests.* The interests of universities and tech companies and those of universities and their students may not always align. This might lead to hasty product launches or an overemphasis on scaling at the expense of ensuring that the highest-quality platforms are being used and that their effectiveness is being measured in meaningful ways. Not all tech creators have this issue, but it is essential to remember that some do. Those working in information technology are motivated to create systems that utilize ever-increasing amounts of data to produce what they believe to be ever-more accurate outcomes. Demonstrating the value of their systems in this way is a key objective.
- Differences in priorities across schools and students are more pronounced and less noticeable. It is acceptable if the school takes action to fix the problem or prevent it from happening. On the other hand, it may not always be in the best interest of the institution's administration to do so. Predictive analytics and early warning systems to identify and help at-risk students are commonly cited as a technique to increase student retention rates.
- A few years ago, the president of Mount St. Mary's University in Maryland was widely known to have used a predictive analytics test to identify at-risk students. The plan was to push them out the door before the university had to turn in its enrollment data to the federal government, boosting its retention rates and academic reputation in the process. The president claims his idea will benefit both the school and the students by reducing money on tuition. There is no denying that this questions the very nature of the educational and institutional endeavor.

12.7 Elements to Consider and Questions to Ask

To achieve the best and most equitable AI tool implementation, several factors (as shown in Fig. 12.2) must be taken into account (Zeide 2019):

- *Procurement.* To fulfill contractual responsibilities to deliver student data, it is essential to consider the technologies and companies most relevant to your spe-

12.7 Elements to Consider and Questions to Ask

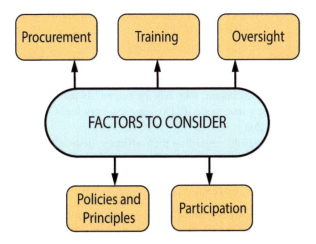

Fig. 12.2 Factors to be considered to achieve the best and most equitable AI tool implementation

cific student body. When choosing a company to work with, be sure they have a good track record of responding to customer concerns.
- *Training.* The personnel responsible for implementing and using these tools must be trained and shown their potential and limitations.
- *Oversight.* Establish a system to evaluate the tools' efficacy regularly, focusing on whether they benefit specific student subsets or produce inflated results. This is challenging but crucial, as these tools rapidly become obsolete.
- *Policies and Principles.* Plan how your organization will adopt analytics-driven tools and develop guiding principles for how these will be implemented.
- *Participation.* Collect feedback from students and teachers about the problems they are experiencing and the improvements they would like to make. The messiness and potential for controversy associated with this stage prevent many people from taking it, despite its benefit in the long run.

The Educational Technology Leadership Committee at the University of California created some of the most robust policies and ideas in this area in 2015 (Phillips and Williamson 2019). The committee listed and explained the six guiding principles: ownership, ethical use, transparency, freedom of expression, protection, and access/control. The committee says security providers should benefit from learning more about data privacy policies in the following areas: data ownership, usage rights, opt-in, interoperable data, data without fees, transparency, service provider security, and campus security (University of California: Learning Data Privacy Principles and Recommended Practices 2016).

Finally, six crucial issues should be asked for a successful AI application within higher education (Zeide 2019):

- For what purposes does the information exist? If you are implementing the systems correctly, you cannot simply look at a red, green, or yellow light to determine whether or not students are succeeding.
- Which choices are we missing out on? This involves not only categorization and visualization but also computational choices.
- When it comes to the content, who has the reigns? Is the fault with your system or with the company that made it? Do your teachers feel OK with that? How at ease are you with that?
- How do we verify results regarding their efficacy, distribution, and positive and negative effects?
- What gets lost with datafication?
- Whose or what needs do we put first?

While these questions will not provide any magic solutions, they will provide a framework for thinking about the less evident characteristics of these systems.

12.8 Recommendations to Enhance AI Implementation in Education

Here are some recommendations (Jackson et al. 2021) based on research on various parties' roles and potential contributions to policymaking. These recommendations urge various actors to increase the use of AI in schools in order to boost equality and learning results. The AI integration with various parties is shown in Fig. 12.3.

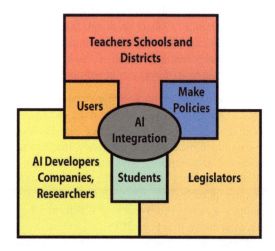

Fig. 12.3 AI integration with various stakeholders

12.8.1 Legislators

A scalable policy could be encouraged by establishing municipal, district, or state procedures to safeguard consumers from unfair trade practices. Companies and consumers who use AI technology may be subject to these procedures mandated by regulatory bodies.

12.8.1.1 Recommendations

Legislators are encouraged to:

- In order to reasonably safeguard consumers from exploitative business activities, legislation must be enacted.
- To ensure the safety of both companies and customers, legislation must be passed to establish a regulatory agency.

12.8.2 AI Developers, Companies, and Researchers

Companies working in artificial intelligence (AI) would do well to employ a diverse staff of developers and seek feedback from diverse auditors. As the AI product development process progresses, the end-users, such as school administrators, classroom teachers, students, and parents, will be educated on the potential benefits of AI in educational settings.

The Edtech Equity Project uses a certification mechanism to push for structural reforms inside an AI system. This methodology is used by several artificial intelligence (AI) developers and projects, such as the Digital Promise Product Certification, in collaboration with The Edtech Equity Project. Regarding the end-users capacity to understand the system's output, AI systems that employ models like decision trees, support vector machines, and others are generally accepted as being interpretable.

Understanding how AI is trained would be facilitated using such systems and disclosing interpretability. Transparent testing procedures could stimulate research to create the AI system, keeping all parties informed [citation needed]. In addition, sharing the system's success in the classroom requires transparent reporting.

12.8.2.1 Recommendations

AI developers and companies are encouraged to:
- Hire an inclusive group of programmers, and gather input from diversity auditors (people who either identify with or have extensive experience working with the intended audience).

- The end-users (administrators, teachers, students, and parents) must be informed of the data's intended use.
- Learn the methodology used to train AI and indicate any relevant limitations about target demographics and application settings.
- To record and disseminate the underlying pedagogical strategy (to allow for appropriate classroom application and alignment).
- Conduct studies and disclose findings openly on the effectiveness of ecological efficacy.

These suggestions call for concrete actions to be taken by policymakers and planners so that the gap between AI experts and those working in the field of education can be bridged. The current state of affairs [citation needed] is characterized by walls separating theory from the application. Separating the various aspects of AI research into their departments will increase openness and diversity. Ensuring academics work in tandem with developers to provide guidance on research threads and disseminate knowledge to education practitioners is an excellent first step toward closing the chasm between the two. By doing so, researchers' results would be included in the product development process, ethical practices would be incorporated, and educators would be equipped with the knowledge and understanding necessary to make informed decisions about using artificial intelligence in the classroom.

12.8.2.2 Recommendations

AI researchers are encouraged to:

- Collaborate with those creating AI to provide input on various research strands.
  - Products and their uses must be assessed to see if they produce the desired results.
  - Ethical product development.
  - Effects of scale and reach.
- Share their findings by:
  - Networking with professionals in the field of education to disseminate cutting-edge methods and discoveries.
  - Collaborating with experts in research communication to create blogs, newsletters, and reports that everyone can read.

12.8.3 Districts, Schools, and Teachers

Without any other regulations, schools and districts are urged to enact and uphold rules that reasonably protect educators, students, and their families from predatory behaviors. This category may include but is not limited to Data Privacy and Use

12.8 Recommendations to Enhance AI Implementation in Education

Practices. It will be crucial for these policies to incorporate strategies for better educating and preparing educators to use the new technology. Practitioners like district/school officials and educators are urged to grasp appropriate use through continuing training sessions thoroughly.

Teachers will understand who, what, where, when, why, and how data is collected, kept, utilized, and shared, as well as how to evaluate technologies and their ability to promote equitable educational practices and effectively integrate them. Both students' and teachers' privacy and the intended use of the data must be protected; thus, policies should be as detailed as possible. Teachers and parents should be allowed to forego specific data uses outlined in the policy. In the case of an AI system designed to improve teacher-parent communication, for instance, the collected data cannot be utilized to assess the effectiveness of the educator in question.

12.8.3.1 Recommendations

Districts and schools are encouraged to:

- Educators, students, and their families need to be reasonably protected from predatory behaviors; therefore, policies should be developed and strictly enforced.
- Spending money on training should include ongoing professional development for educators to learn about AI systems, ethical considerations, risks, and potential rewards.

Administrators are the most effective source of assistance for educators. Instructors must be familiar with the best practices for integrating technology into the classroom. Now more than ever, teachers have access to classroom orchestration technologies powered by artificial intelligence, which can enhance students' opportunities for active learning. Students may be able to game these systems in some circumstances, as with the rudimentary models accessible in Autograder systems that conduct keyword searches in the background in the name of AI implementation [citation needed]. When all these considerations are considered, it becomes clear that AI is a potent weapon that must be used carefully. Educators and school leaders must work together for AI technology to be successfully implemented in classrooms. Educators and school leaders who employ AI in the classroom should be familiar with the best practices for using the tool. Facilitating this through training on technical developments and forming collaborations with administrators to promote equitable educational practices when employing AI in schools is a significant next step.

12.8.3.2 Recommendations

Teachers are encouraged to:

- Identify when and how to deploy artificial intelligence.
- Obtain and maintain current knowledge as technology evolves.

- Understand how to assess whether or not the implementation of technological solutions in the classroom leads to more fair outcomes for all students.
- Effectively and appropriately integrate it.
- Have the support of district officials and administrators.
- One must be aware of who is collecting, storing, using, and sharing data and the specifics of the data being collected.

12.9 Conclusion

Hold out against the mechanical hordes for the time being. Use caution and forethought when implementing AI projects, and remember that technology is not a silver bullet. Despite all the excitement, these AI technologies are still computers, despite what the media might have you believe. In some cases, they may even go wrong. All of these things have been made by humans. Business and government have a significant impact on shaping their morals. Rather than being objective, their information is shaped by precedents.

References

Akgun, S. (2021). *Exploring the ethics of artificial intelligence in K-12 education.* Michigan State University. https://education.msu.edu/news/2021/exploring-the-ethics-of-artificial-intelligence-in-k-12-education/

Astle, D. E., Bathelt, J., Team, T. C., & Holmes, J. (2018). Remapping the cognitive and neural profiles of children who struggle at school. *Developmental Science, 22*(September), 1–17. https://doi.org/10.1111/desc.12747

Blatchford, B. P., Russell, A., & Webster, R. (2012). *Reassessing the Impact of Teaching Assistants: How research challenges practice and policy.*

F.D.Young, M. (2008). *Bringing Knowledge Back in.* Routledge: Taylor & Francis Group.

Gray, S. L. (2019). *What keeps me awake at night? The convergence of AI and biometrics in education.* LinkedIn. https://www.scmp.com/news/china/politics/article/3027349/artificial-intelligence-watching-chinas-students-how-well-can

Hauptfleisch, K. (2016). *This Is How Artificial Intelligence Will Shape eLearning For Good.* Elearningindustry.Com.

Jackson, T., Pakhira, D., Narayanan, A. B. L., Ruiz, P., Fusco, J., Glazer, K., Eaglin, P., & Eguchi, A. (2021). School Policies for Integrating AI in Classroom Practices. *Digital Promise*, 1–11. https://doi.org/http://hdl.handle.net/20.500.12265/130

Lawton, G., & Wigmore, I. (2021). *AI ethics (AI code of ethics).* Techtarget.Com. https://www.techtarget.com/whatis/definition/AI-code-of-ethics

Phillips, J., & Williamson, J. (2019). *UC's Learning Data Privacy Principles Gaining National Attention.* UC IT Blog, University of California. https://er.educause.edu/articles/2019/8/artificial-intelligence-in-higher-education-applications-promise-and-perils-and-ethical-questions#fn11

Reiss, M. J. (2017). The curriculum arguments of Michael Young and John White. In *Sociology, Curriculum Studies and Professional Knowledge: New perspectives on the work of Michael Young* (pp. 121–131).

References

Reiss, M. J. (2021). The use of AI in education: Practicalities and ethical considerations. *London Review of Education, 19*(1), 1–14. https://doi.org/10.14324/LRE.19.1.05

Reiss, M. J., & White, J. (2013). *An Aims-based Curriculum The significance of human flourishing for schools.*

The Institute for Ethical AI in Education. (2020). *The Ethical Framework for AI in Education.*

University of California: Learning Data Privacy Principles and Recommended Practices, 10 (2016).

Webster, R., Blatchford, P., & Russell, A. (2013). Challenging and changing how schools use teaching assistants: findings from the Effective Deployment of Teaching Assistants project. *School Leadership & Management: Formerly School Organisation, 33*(1), 78–96. https://doi.org/10.1080/13632434.2012.724672

Xie, E. (2019). *Artificial intelligence is watching China's students but how well can it really see?* South China Morning Post. https://www.scmp.com/news/china/politics/article/3027349/artificial-intelligence-watching-chinas-students-how-well-can

Zeide, E. (2019). *Artificial Intelligence in Higher Education: Applications, Promise and Perils, and Ethical Questions.* Educase. https://er.educause.edu/articles/2019/8/artificial-intelligence-in-higher-education-applications-promise-and-perils-and-ethical-questions

Printed by Libri Plureos GmbH
in Hamburg, Germany